CROWN HEIGHTS

Brandeis Series in American Jewish History, Culture, and Life

Jonathan D. Sarna, Editor
Sylvia Barack Fishman, Associate Editor

Edward S. Shapiro
Crown Heights: Blacks, Jews, and the 1991 Brooklyn Riot

Kristen Fermaglich
American Dreams and Nazi Nightmares: Early Holocaust Consciousness, Jewish Social Scientists, and Liberal America, 1957–1965

Andrea Greenbaum, editor
Jews of South Florida

Sylvia Barack Fishman
Double or Nothing: Jewish Families and Mixed Marriage

George M. Goodwin and Ellen Smith, editors
The Jews of Rhode Island

Shulamit Reinharz and Mark A. Raider, editors
American Jewish Women and the Zionist Enterprise

Michael E. Staub, editor
The Jewish 1960s: An American Sourcebook

Judah M. Cohen
Through the Sands of Time: A History of the Jewish Community of St. Thomas, U.S. Virgin Islands

Naomi W. Cohen
The Americanization of Zionism, 1897–1948

Seth Farber
An American Orthodox Dreamer: Rabbi Joseph B. Soloveitchik and Boston's Maimonides School

Ava F. Kahn and Marc Dollinger, editors
California Jews

Amy L. Sales and Leonard Saxe
"How Goodly Are Thy Tents": Summer Camps as Jewish Socializing Experiences

Ori Z. Soltes
Fixing the World: Jewish American Painters in the Twentieth Century

Gary P. Zola, editor
The Dynamics of American Jewish History: Jacob Rader Marcus's Essays on American Jewry

David Zurawik
The Jews of Prime Time

Ranen Omer-Sherman
Diaspora and Zionism in American Jewish Literature: Lazarus, Syrkin, Reznikoff, and Roth

Ilana Abramovitch and Seán Galvin, editors
Jews of Brooklyn

Pamela S. Nadell and Jonathan D. Sarna, editors
Women and American Judaism: Historical Perspectives

CROWN HEIGHTS

BLACKS, JEWS, AND THE 1991 BROOKLYN RIOT

EDWARD S. SHAPIRO

Brandeis University Press
WALTHAM, MASSACHUSETTS

PUBLISHED BY
UNIVERSITY PRESS OF NEW ENGLAND
HANOVER AND LONDON

Brandeis University Press
Published by University Press of New England,
One Court Street, Lebanon, NH 03766
www.upne.com

Printed in the United States of America
5 4 3 2 1

Library of Congress Cataloging-in-Publication Data
Shapiro, Edward S.
Crown Heights : Blacks, Jews, and the 1991 Brooklyn riot / Edward S. Shapiro.
p. cm.—(Brandeis series in American Jewish history, culture, and life)
Includes bibliographical references and index.
ISBN-13: 978–1–58465–561–9 (cloth : alk. paper)
ISBN-10: 1–58465–561–5 (cloth : alk. paper)
1. Crown Heights (New York, N.Y.)—Race relations. 2. New York (N.Y.)—Race relations. 3. African Americans—New York (State)—New York—Relations with Jews. 4. Jews—New York (State)—New York. 5. Race riots—New York (State)—New York—History—20th century. I. Title. II. Series.
F128.68.C76S53 2006
305.8009747'23—dc22 2005032839

To the memory of

Thomas Shapiro

(1910–2003)

Yeoman Third Class, United States Navy

(July 19, 1944–February 28, 1946)

Contents

Acknowledgments

Ecclesiastes tells us, "And furthermore, my son, be admonished: of making many books there is no end; and much study is a weariness of the flesh" (12:12). How true, but the writing of a book also has its pleasures. One of these is the opportunity to acknowledge one's indebtedness to others. First and foremost, mine includes Professors Jonathan Sarna and Stephen Whitfield of Brandeis University and Phyllis Deutsch of University Press of New England for their confidence in this project. Edward Croman and Rabbis Joseph Spielman and Nissen Mangel of Crown Heights helped me understand the inner workings of the Lubavitch community. The conscientiousness of Rabbi David Kaye, my research assistant, shortened the time spent in research. I pray that this experience did not sour him on historians or dampen his love of history. Bruce Shoulson, an extraordinary lawyer, assisted me in fathoming some of the legal ramifications of the riot. On several occasions I sought to meet with former mayor David N. Dinkins to learn firsthand his interpretation of those hectic days in August 1991. He never responded to my entreaties. I was also rebuffed in my efforts to interview Norman Rosenbaum by his American consigliere.

Conversation with friends in West Orange, New Jersey, helped clarify my thinking on several points and continually impressed upon me the need to make the book accessible to lay readers as well as to fellow historians. This need was reinforced when I spoke about the riot under the auspices of the Jewish Historical Society of MetroWest and Congregation Ahawas Achim B'Nai Jacob and David of West Orange. I also thank the editors of *American Jewish History* and *Congress Monthly* for publishing some of my early musings on the riot.[1]

Several institutions were helpful in the writing of the book. The librarians at Seton Hall University in South Orange and the Seton Hall University Law School in Newark were invariably accommodating with my often overbearing requests. A grant from the Oxford Center for Hebrew and Jewish Studies enabled me to spend four months in England ensconced in a quite congenial academic environment. David Pollack and Michael S. Miller of the Jewish Community Relations Council of New York kindly allowed me to examine their agency's records on the riot and patiently answered my questions. Also gracious in opening their files to me were Professor Robert (Baruch) Bush, a member of the faculty of Hofstra University Law School and a legal representative of the Crown Heights Lubavitch community; Robert J. Miller, the attorney for the family of Anthony Graziosi; and Beth Gilinsky, the founder of the Jewish Action Alliance. The American Jewish Committee and the Anti-Defamation League permitted me to examine their libraries' sparse holdings on the riot. The files of the New York City chapter of the National Urban League, the preeminent black organization in the city, had nothing on the riot.

Daryl Shapiro, my favorite proofreader, carefully read the manuscript and offered many useful recommendations. It was her misfortune to have to live with the riot for so long. The suggestions of my son Marc, the Weinberg Professor of Jewish Studies at the University of Scranton, were also helpful. His wife, Lauren, and my other sons and their spouses—Alan and Maria, David and Sylvia, and Evan and Orly—have been a source of delight, not least in providing me with grandchildren, an endless source of pleasure during my dotage.

This book is dedicated to the memory of my father, who died during its writing. A member of what Tom Brokaw has called the "greatest generation," he was a patriot in the truest sense of the word. He was called to naval duty during World War II despite the fact that he was then thirty-four years old, married with one child, and working in a sensitive position in the federal government. Although he never quite understood my choice of a profession, he was invariably supportive. Devoted to family and country, he never complained or believed that the world owed him anything. He was an optimist about America; even during the collapse of the stock market in the early years of this century he continued to invest in growth stocks. He had a sunny disposition, and in his final days his only regret was that he would have liked to live to one hundred and then be shot by a jealous husband. We miss him dearly.

Note

1. "Interpretations of the Crown Heights Riot," *American Jewish History* 90 (June 2002): 97–122; "History, Memory, and Crown Heights," *Congress Monthly* 69 (March–April 2002): 14–17.

Introduction

The Crown Heights riot of August 19–22, 1991, was the most serious anti-Semitic incident in American history. For nearly three days, bands of young blacks roamed through this Brooklyn neighborhood, home to the Lubavitch sect of Hasidic Jews, assaulting Jews and damaging property. The police and civilian authorities seemed paralyzed in the face of this lawlessness. For Jews, the riot seemed to refute the claims of historians and social scientists that anti-Semitism had been relegated to the fringes of American life and that Jews need no longer be concerned with anti-Semitism. Orthodox Jews in general and the Orthodox Hasidic Jews of Crown Heights in particular were skeptical regarding these reports. Many Lubavitchers were survivors of the Holocaust or the children and grandchildren of survivors. Their attitude toward the non-Jewish world was shaped more by these horrific recollections of victimization and by anecdotal evidence of contemporary anti-Semitism than by the empirical conclusions of supposedly dispassionate social scientists. Memory, the prominent Jewish historian Yosef Hayim Yerushalmi noted, "is always problematic, usually deceptive, sometimes treacherous . . . [and] among the most fragile and capricious of our faculties."[1]

Orthodox Judaism encouraged an insularity from and a distrust of the non-Jewish world. For Orthodox Jews, the most fundamental division in society was not between whites and blacks, rich and poor, children and adults, or men and women, but between Jews and Gentiles. Their religion was predicated on maintaining impermeable barriers between Jews and non-Jews. The riot confirmed what this community had always believed: that the non-Jewish world was not a friendly place and that anti-Semitism in America had not diminished, but remained latent and only required a catalyst to bring it to the surface.

American Jews who were not Orthodox also took seriously the threat of anti-Semitism. History had made them sensitive to any manifestation thereof; indeed, fighting anti-Semitism was a principal component of their identity as Jews. This sensitivity persisted even though American history had been free of the pogroms and government-sanctioned social and economic restrictions on Jews that had marked their history in Europe and the Arab lands—and even though by the mid-twentieth century such Jews as Rabbi Joshua Loth Liebman and Dr. Joyce Brothers had become what Stephen Whitfield of Brandeis University called American "wisdom figures." There have been anti-Semitic American politicians, but not one ever successfully ran for office on a platform of anti-Semitism. One of the arguments of Will Herberg's 1955 *Protestant-Catholic-Jew,* the most popular book on American religious sociology published during the 1950s, was that Judaism had achieved parity with Protestantism and Catholicism as one of the three great religions of American democracy. Other bits of evidence, including the popularity of books, movies, and television shows with Jewish themes and recognizably Jewish characters, such as *Exodus, Marjorie Morningstar,* and *Seinfeld,* indicated that Herberg had not exaggerated the coming of age of American Judaism and of America's Jews.

Public opinion polls taken in the 1980s and 1990s, however, revealed that nearly 90 percent of American Jews believed American anti-Semitism was still something to be concerned with, and only one Jew in twenty regarded anti-Semitism as no longer a problem in America. These fears existed at a time when eleven Jews were in the United States Senate and two were on the United States Supreme Court. The presidents of Harvard, Princeton, and Yale were Jews; the chairman of the Federal Reserve System was a Jew; and a Jew was nominated by a major political party in 2000 as its vice-presidential nominee. The economic and social position of America's Jews had never been better, and it appeared that they had achieved their major objective: legitimacy and freedom as Americans. Yet incidents during these decades, several of which involved blacks, reinforced long-standing anxieties regarding the presence, albeit latent, of widespread anti-Semitism. These anxieties are an example of what social scientists call "cognitive dissonance"—the conflict between reality and the perceptions of reality.

The Crown Heights riot was more significant to Jews for what it supposedly indicated about the extent of anti-Semitism in America generally, and in central Brooklyn in particular, than for what had actually occurred to the residents of Crown Heights during those four days in August 1991. The loss of life and damage to property resulting from the riot was negligible compared to what had happened in Newark, Detroit, Los Angeles, and other American cities during the riots of the 1960s. Only seven businesses were looted in the Crown Heights riot, and of these, three were owned by Korean-Americans, one by an Arab-American, and three by Jews.[2] Property damage came to a little over a million dollars. Two Jews died as a result of the riot, one by suicide. By contrast, dozens of blacks died in Newark, Detroit, and Los Angeles, and the loss of property in these cities was in the hundreds of millions of dollars. But Jews did not compare the devastation of August 1991 to other American riots. This was the first anti-Semitic riot in American history, and they feared that worse would follow.

The riot was also politically disorienting to Jews; it challenged their widespread assumption that Jews and blacks, the two classic victimized groups, were natural allies. Traditionally, blacks and Jews had been the two demographic groups most loyal to the Democratic Party; their representatives in Congress had voted similarly; and leaders of the two groups had cooperated on a variety of matters. But during the 1980s and 1990s there was a series of issues—racial quotas in employment and university admissions, the political ambitions of Jesse Jackson, and the politics of the Middle East—that seemed to presage the dissolution of the fabled black-Jewish coalition. The tendency of Jews to romanticize their affinity toward black Americans overlooked the social and economic differences between Jews and blacks. It also ignored the fact that there were Jews who—particularly those who because of place of business or residence came into daily contact with blacks—were not sympathetic to blacks. Public opinion surveys indicated that Orthodox Jews were particularly skeptical regarding the conventional liberal outlook of the Jewish establishment. Their skepticism would deepen as a result of the riot.[3]

The riot heightened the pessimism of Jews toward issues of race and community relations. In his dissertation on the riot, Henry Goldschmidt emphasized the difficulty that blacks and Jews of post-riot Crown Heights experienced in living together as neighbors and in sharing the streets.[4] Yet the recent history of Crown Heights refutes such gloom. Although the attitudes of the residents toward one another did not fundamentally change, there were no additional serious incidents. The lesson here is that ethnic, religious, and racial groups do not have to be imbued with the virtues of tolerance and understanding to live in peace.

The politics of the Crown Heights riot reminds one of the distinction the eminent historian Richard Hofstadter made between interest politics and status politics. By interest politics he meant such things as taxes, land policy, government regulation of business, banking legislation, and tariffs, concerns that directly affected the voters' economic and social interests. Status politics, by contrast, involved "lifestyle" issues such as the regulation of the consumption of liquor and gambling, the proscription of languages other than English in certain settings, and the restriction of various activities on the Sabbath. These issues largely entailed the distribution and recognition of prestige among the country's many ethnic, religious, social, and geographic groups. Status issues, as Hofstadter noted, frequently came to a head over symbolic matters. The political furor of Jews resulting from the Crown Heights riot was in part a case of status politics in action. Jews feared that they had been displaced in the city's pecking order by blacks and that the city's leadership was either unwilling or unable to make the symbolic gestures that would comfort them.

Missing from the complaints of Jews regarding Mayor David N. Dinkins's handling of the riot were specific recommendations to improve the performance of the police, to enhance black-Jewish relations, and to do something to improve the social and economic conditions in Crown Heights. Rather, their attention focused on such symbolic issues as the mayor's failure to show up at Yankel Rosenbaum's funeral procession, the mayor's refusal to use the word "pogrom" when talking about the riot, and the city's dilatory offer of a reward for information leading to the arrest of those responsible for the murder of Rosenbaum. The mayor was understandably mystified by the hostility of Jews to him (especially the handbills accusing him of murder). Dinkins had always been sensitive to Jewish concerns; he numbered Jews among his closest advisers, and took pride in his civility. He did not deserve such treatment. But Dinkins erred in not fully recognizing the symbolic importance his actions (or lack of actions) would have on Jews. In this regard, he was tone-deaf. People crave symbolic action from their political leaders, and Dinkins failed to provide it. Jews in Crown Heights and in other parts of the city wrongly concluded that they did not have a friend in city hall. Dinkins's lethargic approach to governance compounded his political difficulties. "Whether responding to public fears about crime or grappling with homelessness, he has often stewed but declined to act," Todd S. Purdum of the *New York Times* noted. His style consisted of "excellence at reaching out, difficulty in reaching conclusions and taking decisive action."[5]

In his book *Antisemitism: A Reference Handbook,* Jerome A. Chanes noted that it was impossible for Jews to "discount the effects of societal traumas they have experienced, such as the impact . . . of the 1991 riots in the Crown Heights neighborhood of Brooklyn." The riot, he wrote, was an example of the relationship of intergroup tensions to anti-Semitism "that requires significant study."[6] This volume, the first scholarly book on the Crown Heights riot, is a modest contribution to the study called for by Chanes. It lays out the social framework for the riot; traces its course from August 19 through August 22, 1991; examines its impact; chronicles the post-riot healing process; discusses the various interpretations of the riot; shows how the riot was used by blacks and Jews for their political agendas; relates the various legal proceedings resulting from the riot; discusses the image of the riot in popular culture; and surveys how the riot became a political football that contributed to the defeat of the only black mayor in New York City's history in his bid for reelection. Throughout, the emphasis of my book is on the riot as a "public" event. I seek to show how the riot was perceived by the public and how its aftermath was played out in public venues such as voting booths and judicial proceedings.

I do not attempt to answer some of the more speculative questions involving the riot such as why it happened and why it occurred in August 1991 and not earlier or later. A 1984 Carnegie Corporation report described Crown Heights as "awash in a sea of ethnocentrism, prejudice, and violent conflict." If so, why did it take seven more years for the riot to erupt? The social and economic circumstances of blacks and Jews in Crown Heights in 1991 were not significantly different from those noted in the Carnegie report. There were many explanations for the riot, but none are convincing, particularly those that emphasize the economic conditions and the thwarted ambitions of those blacks who were caught up in the riot. The rioters were largely teenagers or in their early twenties; it is unlikely they were responding at such an early age to economic frustrations.

The chapter "Conflicting Narratives" discusses the most important interpretations of the riot. The argument of some observers that the riot was in essence a racial confrontation between whites and blacks distracts attention from the riot's most singular characteristic. It was the only riot in American history in which the violence was directed at Jews. But blaming the riot on endemic anti-Semitism among blacks is not persuasive. Granted, public opinion surveys indicated that anti-Semitism was more widespread among American blacks than whites during the 1990s. But this generalization does not explain why the Crown Heights riot occurred when and where it did, and why other riots motivated by black anti-Semitism did not occur. Explanations attributing the 1991 riot to the spread of black nationalistic ideologies are also unconvincing. Such ideologies had been around for decades without causing riotous attacks on Jews. Harold Cruse's book *The Crisis of the Negro Intellectual*, for example, blamed Jews for the failure of black nationalism, but it was published more than two decades before the riot, and it was not mentioned by any of the participants.

Why did additional riots *not* break out in Crown Heights after August 1991 if the Carnegie report's conclusions on conditions in the neighborhood were accurate? More effective policing can explain why such riots would not escalate; it does not explain why they would not begin in the first place. Also, why were there not riots in other parts of the city where Jews and blacks lived in close proximity (particularly in the Williamsburg neighborhood of Brooklyn where a large group of Hasidic Jews of the Satmar sect lived alongside a majority population of blacks and Hispanics)? Finally, why is the Crown Heights riot the only anti-Semitic riot in American history? There have been other anti-Semitic incidents in American history—most notably the Leo Frank case—but none of these ever escalated into a full-scale riot.

This book makes no pretense at having uncovered the "causes" of the Crown Heights riot, although it does discuss the factors that made the riot possible. From the perspective of the twenty-first century, the riot appears to be an aberration, and its ultimate causes are shrouded in mystery. But the various meanings the riot had for contemporaries are clear. It brought to the surface the prickly relationship between the Jewish establishment (headquartered in Manhattan) and Jews living in the outer boroughs; the relationship between black urban politicians and their Jewish constituents; the extent of black anti-Semitism; the state of black-Jewish relations; the condition of urban liberalism; and the continuing viability of the black-Jewish political entente. These issues were of more concern to Jews than to blacks, and it was only natural that Jews would be far more interested in the ramifications of the Crown Heights riot than blacks. Thus I cite Jewish newspapers and magazines and secondary sources written by Jews more frequently than I do black newspapers and magazines and secondary sources written by blacks.

Despite what was said in the immediate aftermath of the riot, it was hardly a watershed for Jews, blacks, New York City, or Crown Heights. Although zealots on both sides sought to inflame relations between blacks and Jews, the relationship between the two groups did not fundamentally change after the riot. Jews continued to be far more supportive of black concerns than were other whites. Jews did not flee from Crown Heights after August 1991. In fact, the Lubavitch population of Crown Heights increased after the riot, the area in which they reside has expanded, and property values in the area have risen dramatically. The riot also did not cause the Lubavitch community to modify any of its fundamental tenets or practices. The death of their leader, Rabbi Menachem Mendel Schneerson, in 1994 was a far weightier matter for his followers than the riot.

The only area in which the riot might have had a significant impact concerned the police. The riot led the police department to reevaluate its policies and tactics; in terms of both personnel and equipment it became better prepared to deal with civil disturbances. This reevaluation might have been a factor in the department's laudatory response to the events of September 11, 2001.

The riot acted as a searchlight illuminating the tensions present in the city, particularly as the riot occurred in the media center of the country if not of the world. In addition to the rifts between blacks and Jews and between the liberal Jewish establishment in Manhattan and Jews in the outer boroughs (many of whom were Orthodox), there was the competition between the black political establishment and radical and nationalist black politicians on the make; the pressures facing the city's first black mayor in convincing his white constituents that he would rule fairly; and the strains between native blacks and blacks from the West Indies. The riot was a test case in the escalation of these strains and in the breakdown of the controls that normally governed daily behavior in the city.

No question was more frequently asked in the aftermath of the riot than, Who caused it? The most popular explanation was that outside agitators were responsible. The deus ex machina of the outside agitators enabled the blacks of Crown Heights to absolve themselves of responsibility for the riot, and it confirmed the belief of Crown Heights Jews that there was nothing essentially wrong in their relations with their black neighbors. In either case, fundamental changes in race relations were not called for. The "outside agitators" explanation illustrated how popular memory can conflict with historical complexity. If an appreciation of the complexity of the Crown Heights riot renders additional riots less likely, then this book will have served its purpose.

Notes

1. Yosef Hayim Yerushalmi, *Zakhor: Jewish History and Jewish Memory* (Seattle: University of Washington Press, 1982), 5.
2. Andy Logan, "High Winds in Brooklyn," *New Yorker* 68 (December 28, 1992): 84.
3. For black-Jewish relations, see Murray Friedman, *What Went Wrong? The Creation and Collapse of the Black-Jewish Alliance* (New York: Free Press, 1995), and Hasia R. Diner, *The Jews of the United States, 1654–2000* (Berkeley and Los Angeles: University of California Press, 2004), 265–76, 334–41.
4. Henry Goldschmidt, "Peoples Apart: Race, Religion, and Other Jewish Differences in Crown Heights" (Ph.D. diss., University of California at Santa Cruz, 2000), 345.
5. Todd S. Purdum, "Buttoned Up," *New York Times Magazine*, September 1, 1993, 44–52.
6. Jerome A. Chanes, *Antisemitism: A Reference Handbook* (Santa Barbara, Calif.: ABC-CLIO, 2004), 19.

CROWN HEIGHTS

1

TWO DEATHS IN BROOKLYN

The United States has been remarkably free from major anti-Semitic incidents and state-sanctioned anti-Semitism. True, there had been isolated incidents of anti-Semitic violence in America; anti-Semitic literature had freely circulated in all sectors of the country; and country clubs, resorts, and posh neighborhoods had excluded Jews. But never in American history had there been a riot directed at Jews, and by the late twentieth century Jews lived without fear of anti-Semitic violence. Informed Jews and Gentiles alike viewed anti-Semitism in America as a marginal phenomenon, found only among the psychologically maladjusted and educationally deprived. For Jews, this sense of security and belief that America was truly different would be challenged—and for some, would be shattered—in August 1991, when there erupted the only anti-Semitic riot in American history.

On the afternoon of Monday, August 19, 1991, Rabbi Menachem Mendel Schneerson, the spiritual leader of the worldwide Lubavitch Hasidic movement (headquartered in the Crown Heights section of Brooklyn), visited the Old Montefiore Cemetery in Queens. A police car with two officers from the 71st Precinct accompanied his automobile. The New York City police had been providing such protection to Schneerson for about a decade even though, in contrast to the protection the police provided other prominent religious figures such as the pope when he visited New York, Schneerson was not a visitor but a resident of the city. This protection resulted from the political influence of the Lubavitch community, which argued that Schneerson was a worldwide political figure and that threats had been made against his life by rival Hasidic elements in Brooklyn.

There were two purposes for these frequent trips to the cemetery, the only occasions when Schneerson left the cozy confines of Crown Heights. The first was to pay respect at the graves of his wife, Hayya Mushka, and his predecessor and father-in-law, Joseph Isaac Schneerson, whom he deeply revered for his spirituality and wisdom. The other purpose of these visits was to read to the latter the hundreds of letters "the rebbe" had received from Lubavitchers and others asking for his blessing and advice on a host of religious and secular matters.[1]

Visiting the graves of righteous and scholarly rabbis is an ancient Jewish tradition, and particularly common among the mystically inclined Hasidim who believe that their "rebbes" were transcendent and immortal spiritual figures. The practice of visiting graves stemmed in part from Jewish beliefs in the immortality of the soul and the efficacy of prayer. Through intense prayer, it was believed, the pious could connect with the souls of the departed who remained spiritually alive. During these visits to the cemetery, which generally lasted several hours, Schneerson sought inspiration and guidance from the previous rebbe.

On its return to Crown Heights, the procession was joined by a third car, a 1984 Mercury Grand Marquis station wagon containing four young members of the Lubavitch community, who had arrived earlier at the cemetery to make preparations for Schneerson's arrival. The station wagon traveled behind Schneerson's car to provide security against an accident to the rear of Schneerson's automobile. The procession arrived in Crown Heights at dusk. Traveling west on President Street, it reached Utica Avenue at approximately 8:20 P.M. Gavin Cato, the seven-year-old son of Guyanese immigrants, was on the sidewalk near his apartment house at 1677 President Street, a few feet from the northwest intersection of President and Utica. He was repairing the chain of his bicycle. His seven-year-old cousin Angela was playing nearby. The police car and Schneerson's automobile crossed Utica on a green light and proceeded along President Street at a normal speed. Until this point there had been nothing to distinguish this journey of Schneerson from the hundreds of other occasions he had traveled to Queens.[2]

The details of what happened next remain unclear. The third car had fallen behind the other two cars and, not wishing to lose contact with the middle car containing Schneerson, either crossed Utica on a yellow light, according to the car's occupants and some witnesses, or ran a red light, according to other witnesses and Peter Petrosino. Yosef Lifsh, the driver of the station wagon, claimed that he thought he had the right-of-way as he was an integral part of a procession led by a police car with its rooflight flashing. While crossing the intersection, the front of the station wagon collided with the right rear section of Petrosino's 1981 Chevrolet Malibu, moving north on Utica. Lifsh said he had tried to apply the brakes after the collision, but either they failed or by mistake he pressed the gas pedal instead. The station wagon veered out of control and traveled approximately seventy-five feet onto the sidewalk on President Street. There it knocked over a six-hundred-pound stone pillar from a building and struck both Gavin and Angela Cato, pinning them beneath the car on the sidewalk alongside the wall of the apartment building adjacent to their apartment house.[3]

The speed of the Grand Marquis as it crossed the intersection is also in dispute, but most reports agreed that it exceeded the speed limit of thirty miles per hour. Spectators gave widely disparate estimates ranging from twenty-five miles to sixty-five miles per hour. Richard Hermance, an accident reconstruction expert hired by the attorney for Lifsh, estimated that it was traveling at no more than thirty to thirty-five miles per hour when it hit the Chevrolet. Dr. James Pugh, a metallurgist and professor of biomechanics, was hired by the office of the Kings County (Brooklyn) District Attorney to reconstruct the accident. He calculated the speed at between forty-five to fifty miles per hour.[4]

A crowd of several hundred immediately gathered at the scene of the accident, and the police soon arrived moments after an ambulance from Hatzolah, a volunteer Jewish ambulance service, appeared. The time was approximately 8:23 P.M. By then the mood of the crowd was very hostile, and the police feared for the safety of the four Lubavitchers. One was led to safety by an unidentified black man, while two police officers attempted to protect the other three occupants. "When we arrived," one of the Hatzolah attendants told the *Jewish Week,* "three or four black people were trying to get him [i.e., Lifsh] out and were beating him. He was in the station wagon—halfway in—and he was bleeding from the face and head."[5]

The police told the driver of the Hatzolah ambulance to get them out of the area as soon as possible. The Cato children, the Hatzolah driver was informed, would be cared for by a city Emergency Medical Services ambulance that had just arrived. The three Lubavitchers were taken to Methodist Hospital in the Park Slope section of Brooklyn. There the twenty-two-year-old Lifsh was given a breath-alcohol test by the police seventy minutes after the accident. The test results were negative. Lifsh also received eighteen stitches in his head and face. Meanwhile, the EMS ambulance transporting Gavin Cato arrived at Kings County Hospital Center, a mile from the scene of the accident, at 8:32 P.M. He was pronounced dead shortly after arriving at the hospital. The medical examiner's report said that the cause of death was blunt force injuries to the head, body, and extremities. Back at the accident scene, another Hatzolah vehicle had arrived at the scene of the accident. While located in neighborhoods with sizable Jewish populations, the Hatzolah ambulances serviced Jews and non-Jews alike, and an emergency medical technician from the second Hatzolah ambulance immediately began assisting Angela Cato. A second EMS ambulance then appeared and took her also to Kings County, where she was treated for multiple fractures of her right leg.[6]

The first two cars of the Schneerson procession had proceeded on their way, their occupants oblivious to the fact that they had been involved in an incident that would trigger the most lethal anti-Semitic event in American history, influence the politics of the city and state of New York for a decade, cause a crisis in black-Jewish relations, and precipitate three days of rioting and New York City's most important riot since the 1970s. The state report on the riot called it "the most extensive racial unrest in New York City in over twenty years."[7]

The automobile accident occurred at a tense time between blacks and Jews. A few weeks earlier a quarrel had erupted over remarks by Professor Leonard Jeffries, the chairman of the black studies department of the City College of New York, accusing Jews of responsibility for the demeaning imagery of blacks in Hollywood movies. While Jews criticized Jeffries and demanded that he be disciplined by City College, black militants sprang to his defense. Exacerbating the situation in Crown Heights on the night of August 19 was the presence of hundreds of young people at a B.B. King concert at Wingate High School, about a mile south of the accident. As they left the concert, they were harangued by speakers regarding the death of Gavin Cato and other nefarious deeds of the Hasidim. Speakers were also encouraging the growing crowd at the scene of the accident to resort to violence. Charles Price was one of the speakers. "We can't take this anymore," he said. "The Jews get everything they want. They're killing our children. We get no justice, we get no respect."[8] Another speaker proclaimed, "Let's go to Kingston Avenue and get the Jews" (Kingston Avenue was the major Lubavitch shopping thoroughfare.)[9] Agitated by the speakers, young blacks broke up into bands and went on a rampage in the neighborhood, assaulting and robbing Jews and throwing stones, bottles, and debris at police cars, automobiles, houses, and bystanders.[10]

The circumstances of the accident had brought to the surface and crystallized long-simmering and distorted attitudes among blacks regarding the Lubavitch community. In their eyes, the police escort for Rabbi Schneerson illustrated the favoritism shown to the Lubavitchers by the political authorities. Lifsh's disregard for the traffic light demonstrated the arrogant disdain of the Lubavitchers for laws and regulations that did not directly benefit them. That the Hatzolah ambulance had transported Lifsh and the two other Lubavitchers to the hospital rather than aiding the Cato children indicated the Lubavitch lack of interest in—and even contempt for—the lives of non-Jews. Colin A. Moore, the Cato family attorney, claimed that the mob that rampaged through Crown Heights was "justifiably angry because Lifsh left the children to die."[11] These attitudes toward the Lubavitchers had been nurtured by a history of victimization, racial violence, double standards, and powerlessness that made it difficult for blacks to perceive the accident simply as a mishap. Rather, the accident was viewed as part of a racist pattern all too familiar to blacks, with Gavin Cato becoming the latest symbol of the black condition in white America.[12]

Over the next several days rumors circulated that Lifsh's car had deliberately run down Gavin and Angela, that Lifsh had been drinking and did not have a valid driver's license, that he had been talking on a cellular phone at the time of the crash, that Gavin had died because the Hatzolah ambulance refused to assist him or to transport him to the hospital, that Lifsh's blood-alcohol tests were altered with the connivance of the police and the office of the Brooklyn District Attorney, that the police beat Carmel Cato when he attempted to rescue his son from beneath the station wagon, and that the police had prevented bystanders from lifting the car off of Gavin's shattered body. None of these were correct, but all fueled the growing fury in Crown Heights.[13]

THE MURDER OF YANKEL ROSENBAUM

The most serious incident in the immediate aftermath of the accident occurred at approximately 11:20 P.M. in Crown Heights, three hours after the accident involving Lifsh and Cato. Its victim was twenty-nine-year-old Yankel Rosenbaum. Rosenbaum, a non-Lubavitch Orthodox Jew, was an aspiring academician from Melbourne, Australia. He was in New York doing research on pre–World War II Jewish life in East Europe in the archives of YIVO (Institute for Jewish Research), the major repository of source material for the study of East European Jewry, for his doctoral dissertation in history at the University of Melbourne. He was scheduled to return to Australia the following week. Shortly after 11:00 P.M. on August 19, Rosenbaum was walking north on Brooklyn Avenue to his lodgings after visiting relatives in another section of Brooklyn. He was unaware of what had been taking place during the past two and a half hours in Crown Heights. When he reached President Street, the six-foot-four Rosenbaum saw a group of anywhere from a dozen to twenty young blacks running toward him and shouting, according to several witnesses, "kill the Jew," "there's a Jew," "let's get the Jew," or words to that effect. Although not a Lubavitcher, Rosenbaum was readily identifiable as an Orthodox Jew by his beard, his dark suit, and the fringes hanging out from his ritual undergarment. Rosenbaum retreated to the southeast corner of President Street and Brooklyn Avenue in front of Saint Mark's School where he was surrounded. The blacks proceeded to beat him, and he suffered a fractured skull. Although most of the gang probably intended merely to rough up Rosenbaum, one of its members had other plans. He stabbed Rosenbaum several times with a folding-knife. Some blacks would later make the improbable claim that Rosenbaum had provoked the assault by taunting members of the gang, who were peacefully protesting the behavior of the police following the death of Gavin Cato.[14]

The first two police officers to arrive at the scene of the attack on Rosenbaum saw a group of at least ten black males beating him. The police sounded an alarm, and the group quickly dispersed. The officers radioed for assistance and purportedly mentioned that one of the attackers was wearing a red shirt and a baseball cap. Less than a minute later other officers arrived, including Mark Hoppe. Officer Hoppe soon apprehended sixteen-year-old Lemrick Nelson, Jr., a student at Paul Robeson High School, where he was enrolled in a program for children with learning and behavioral problems. Nelson was discovered hiding behind a bush in the yard of a house at the corner of Brooklyn Avenue and Union Street, one block north of President Street. He was wearing a red shirt and baseball cap and had a bloody knife with the word "killer" on the handle in his right pants pocket. In the same pants pocket were three one-dollar bills stained with blood; Nelson's pants and knife also contained bloodstains. These bloodstains were consistent with Rosenbaum's blood type but not with Nelson's. The stains also contained enzymes found in only 1 percent of the population. Rosenbaum belonged to this 1 percent.[15]

Nelson and four other suspects in the attack were taken by the police to Rosenbaum to be identified. Rosenbaum was only able to identify Nelson, and he said that Nelson had stabbed him. Accounts varied as to what Rosenbaum uttered next. According to one police officer, Rosenbaum looked at Nelson and exclaimed, "Why did you do that to me, you in the red shirt. You are tougher with your friends. Now you ain't tough without your friends." Rosenbaum also spat a wad of blood at Nelson and cursed him. Nelson was then transported to the 71st Precinct in Crown Heights where he was advised of his rights. There he confessed to the police that he had been a little high from drinking beer and had indeed stabbed Rosenbaum. Neither the police or any of the bystanders, however, saw any indication that Nelson was intoxicated. Unfortunately the police did not take notes or make a tape recording during the interview with Nelson, and he refused to sign a statement that he had stabbed Rosenbaum and that he understood his *Miranda* rights. At 3:40 A.M. on Tuesday morning, Nelson was moved to another police precinct. By then news had spread of Nelson's arrest, and Jews and blacks had gathered outside this precinct. Nelson saw them when he left the building and, perhaps for the first time, realized the gravity of his situation. "How much trouble am I in and what's going to happen to me?" he asked a detective.[16]

Meanwhile an ambulance had transported Rosenbaum to Kings County Hospital, where he arrived at 11:36 P.M. While being placed into the ambulance, Rosenbaum had called out, "Cowards! Cowards!" to a friend, referring to his attackers. "It was twenty-to-one! Unfair! Unfair!" Mayor David N. Dinkins and Police Commissioner Lee P. Brown visited Rosenbaum in the hospital a little after midnight. "I held his hand," Dinkins would say later in an angry response to comments that he had been indifferent to Rosenbaum's condition. "He held mine. He looked up into my eyes. I looked into his. We talked to one another."[17] The mayor and police commissioner were reassured by the hospital staff that Rosenbaum would recover from his wounds. Instead, he died at approximately 2:25 the next morning, a victim, his eulogist said, of the violence of New York's streets. "Yankel came here to study the European Holocaust," Rabbi Shmuel Butman, a spokesman for the Crown Heights Jewish community, said. "Little did he know he could not survive his own Holocaust."[18]

Mike McAlary, a reporter for the *New York Post,* discovered that Nelson had a history of anti-Semitism. He had a grudge against the Jewish landlord of the apartment building on Linden Boulevard in the East Flatbush neighborhood of Brooklyn, where he lived with his father. The landlord had complained to the father about the noise coming from the apartment, and the father, a strict disciplinarian, in turn, chastised his son. Lemrick responded by carving a Star of David and his nickname, OJ, in the lobby of the apartment building. On the evening of August 19, Nelson was in Crown Heights visiting his girlfriend. After spending a couple of hours with her drinking beer, he left and encountered the mob confronting Rosenbaum. It is not clear what led Nelson to join it. He did not know anyone in the mob, and he had never had any contact with Rosenbaum. McAlary speculated that Nelson, in a moment of hate, saw his landlord in the figure of Yankel Rosenbaum and took his revenge. "It shows," he wrote, what can happen "when a kid tries to lay his own problems on an entire race [*sic*] of people."[19]

But Nelson's attack on Rosenbaum may not have been entirely fortuitous. The prosecution in the second federal trial in 2003 introduced a fuzzy videotape that allegedly showed that Nelson, before visiting his girlfriend, had been part of the crowd at Utica Avenue and President Street that Charles Price and other speakers had incited into a frenzy of anti-Semitism. It is possible that Nelson was then convinced that the Cato children had been purposely run down, that the Hatzolah ambulance had ignored them, and that revenge was required. It is also possible, as the defense argued in the 2003 trial, that the person identified by the prosecution as Nelson in the videotape was someone else and that Nelson was never in the crowd that Price harangued.[20]

A week later a grand jury answered the question Nelson had posed to the detective. It indicted Nelson on two counts of murder in the second degree and one count of criminal possession of a knife. The indictment charged that Nelson, "acting in concert with others," intentionally caused the death of Rosenbaum.[21] The police and the Brooklyn district attorney's office believed the conviction of Nelson would be a slam dunk. They had a confession, the murder weapon, the stained pants and dollar bills, and a positive identification by Rosenbaum. What more did they need? They would soon find out.

Charles Price, who helped rile up the crowd that gathered after the Cato accident, would also be indicted for the murder of Rosenbaum. The Lubavitch community was dismayed that these were the only two indictments arising from the Rosenbaum case. The police were never able to identify conclusively any of the others who took part in the attack, and they were never certain that Rosenbaum's estimate of the number of people who attacked him was correct. It was often difficult in cases of this kind to find suspects to indict. In the August 1989 murder of Yusuf K. Hawkins, a sixteen-year-old black attacked by a mob of approximately thirty whites in the Bensonhurst section of Brooklyn, only one of the assailants was found guilty. "I think we have a great deal of difficulty showing shared intent beyond a reasonable doubt" in such situations, Brooklyn District Attorney Charles J. Hynes said.[22]

THE SILENCE OF THE REBBE

One of the more troubling and enigmatic aspects of the death of Gavin Cato was the failure of Rabbi Schneerson to express his personal condolences and to offer an apology to the Cato family. "As Racial Storm Rages, Hasidic Leader is Aloof," a headline read in the *New York Times* one week after the accident.[23] Gavin Cato was killed, after all, by an automobile accompanying Schneerson returning from the cemetery, and some statement of remorse from him seemed appropriate. While Jews, both Lubavitch and non-Lubavitch, visited the Cato family and issued statements expressing regret for their loss, no official statements or calls for public prayer ever emanated from Lubavitch headquarters at 770 Eastern Parkway.

Instead, when referring to the accident and the riot, Schneerson spoke cryptically to his followers. "It's not in the nature of Jewish people to have war," he said shortly after the riot broke out. Did this mean that it was in the nature of black people to have war? Did this bromide suggest what should be the proper behavior of the Lubavitch community during the crisis? Should Lubavitchers seek to console the Cato family?[24] On Sunday, August 25, 1991, Schneerson did speak on the need for every individual to make his surroundings a place of peace, tranquillity and holiness. While his disciples interpreted this as an allusion to the previous week's events, its meaning to outsiders was obscure. Lubavitch rabbi Yehuda Krinsky justified Schneerson's seeming aloofness.

"The Rebbe is an international figure," he said. "If there is an incident in Washington, D.C., should the President get involved with white and black leaders to settle the insurrection?"[25]

For many the answer was an unequivocal yes. Alan Helmreich and Paul Marcus, two psychiatrists, speculated that a "symbolic act" by Schneerson immediately after the accident "might have greatly diffused the situation and prevented the violence that followed." Why, they asked, was "the moral, psychological, and political response of the Hasidic leadership" so muted? Schneerson's behavior befuddled those outside the Lubavitch community.[26] Kenneth S. Stern, a researcher for the American Jewish Committee, noted that the allegorical manner in which Schneerson spoke about the Crown Heights crisis was no different than how he spoke about other topics. Still, his concern was not conveyed in a way that blacks and other outsiders could appreciate. "Without an intercommunity translation to explain that the Rebbe spoke out in the same way he always addresses important concerns," Stern noted, "how could black residents of Crown Heights not believe the Rebbe was indifferent?"[27] If Schneerson had been younger and more alert, observers speculated, perhaps he would have acted differently.

Schneerson's performance deeply disappointed Christian ministers in Crown Heights and Jews who had urged him to become personally involved. His refusal to do so did not go unnoticed. Albert Vorspan, an official with the Union of American Hebrew Congregations (Reform) and a frequent commentator on social reform matters, claimed that Schneerson had "failed utterly to heal the rift" between Jews and blacks following the death of Gavin Cato. "If the Rebbe had shown at least as much zeal in this local crisis as he spent in seeking to change Israel's Law of Return," Vorspan contended, "he could have moved mountains—reaching out to his neighbors, visiting the family of the dead Black boy, teaching his own community to understand the heart of the stranger and teaching the Black community something about Jewish compassion."[28] The Jewish left-wing activist and writer Michael Lerner also condemned the Lubavitch leader. "Had Schneerson been the kind of morally sensitive leader that the Jewish people need," Lerner said, "he would long ago have created within the Lubavitch community a dynamic of caring about others, including non-Jews, that would have led them to immediately declare a day of mourning for the Black children that had been run over by the Rebbe's caravan." [29]

For the Lubavitchers and most other observers, the accident at President and Utica was an accident, tragic but still an accident for which Lifsh apologized. Claims that it was something other than an accident were redolent of the medieval "blood libel," the Lubavitchers believed, as was the slander that Hatzolah had refused to treat Gavin Cato. "Traffic Accidents Are Not Racial," read one homemade sign waved by a Hasid during a demonstration captured on the television news.

The Lubavitchers constantly described Lifsh as a courageous figure. They claimed that he was not speeding, that he attempted to cross Utica Avenue while the light was yellow, and that he intentionally steered his automobile away from a group of adults on the sidewalk in front of the Cato apartment. While Gavin and Angela Cato were unfortunately struck, Lifsh's quick-witted response undoubtedly averted even greater carnage. This interpretation contradicted Lifsh's own claim that he had lost control of his car when it collided with Petrosino's automobile. The Lubavitch also alleged that Lifsh was in the process of aiding Gavin Cato when he was attacked and beaten by blacks. The state report on the Crown Heights riot denies this.[30] Finally the Lubavitch asserted that Lifsh had been commended by the city's fire department for rescuing two black children from a burning building. Investigators, however, could find no record of this, and it is highly unlikely that it ever happened.[31]

EULOGIES FOR CATO

At a memorial service for Gavin Cato on Sunday, August 25, at First Baptist Church in Crown Heights, Mayor Dinkins pleaded with the audience not to transform Gavin Cato's death into a racial issue and not to forget the death of Yankel Rosenbaum. Dinkins was on friendly grounds at First Baptist. Its largely middle-class membership was headed by the Reverend Clarence Norman, Sr., a powerful figure within the city's black social and political establishment. His son, Clarence Norman, Jr., represented Crown Heights in the New York State Assembly and was the chairman of the Brooklyn Democratic Party. The Reverend Norman and his son were close allies of the mayor. "We have invited the mayor here this morning mainly to let him know that we support him, that he is among friends," he told his congregants.[32] A few days earlier, Dinkins had received a different reception when he visited the Cato home and urged an end to violence. Upon leaving, he was met with a barrage of bottles, rocks, and cries of "traitor" and "the mayor's not safe" by a crowd that had gathered outside the Cato home.[33]

Dinkins's soothing words did not disappoint the congregants at First Baptist. He warned against "irresponsible leaders from outside the community" who sought to exacerbate rather than to placate tempers. While Dinkins never identified these "leaders," few in the congregation doubted that he was referring to people such as the Reverend Al Sharpton, who had incited the black residents of Crown Heights during the preceding week. Dinkins put the deaths of Cato and Rosenbaum into perspective. "Two tragedies—one a tragedy because it *was* an accident, the other a tragedy because it was *not*," he told the packed pews. "Two precious lives lost, senseless, for no reason. And yet, brothers and sisters, in the tragic deaths of these two young people, also lie the seeds of our redemption. We have an opportunity now to right old wrongs—to heal old wounds—and to make our city a better, more just place." The deaths of Cato and Rosenbaum, the mayor hoped, could be "catalysts for meaningful changes that will prevent other deaths." In concluding, he pledged to rid the city of "the scourge of racial hatred and violence," and to address the causes of the longstanding tensions between blacks and Jews in Crown Heights.[34]

While well-meaning, the mayor's words were also inconsistent. On the one hand, he said the deaths of Cato and Rosenbaum were "senseless." On the other hand, he claimed that "meaningful changes" could prevent future loss of life. If the latter was true, then the deaths of Cato and Rosenbaum could be explained by social conditions, in particular the tensions between blacks and Jews, and thus were not as senseless as his remarks seemed to indicate. Dinkins was thus guilty of precisely the same thing he warned against: elevating two senseless occurrences—the accident that killed Cato and the attack that killed Rosenbaum—into events of social significance. This striving for political correctness came at the expense of logical consistency and threatened to exacerbate rather than calm the anxieties that permeated Crown Heights.

Dinkins's speech at First Baptist reflected the deep social and ideological rift within the black community. The mayor represented the city's black economic, social, and political establishment, which identified with the classic integrationist goals of the civil rights movement of the 1950s and 1960s. Opposed to Dinkins was a collection of blacks preaching a pastiche of black solidarity, black nationalism, back-to-Africa, economic radicalism, and racial exclusiveness. These blacks had never embraced Dinkins's moderate policies or low-keyed style. Al Sharpton had previously denounced Dinkins as an "Uncle Tom" and "that nigger whore turning tricks in City Hall"; attorney Alton H. Maddox, Jr., had called him "an Ed Koch in blackface"; and C. Vernon Mason had accused him of wearing "too many yarmulkes."[35] Even such an erstwhile black establishment figure as Calvin Butts, pastor of Harlem's Abyssinian Baptist Church, said that Dinkins no longer enjoyed "the respect or support of the grass roots in terms of the African-American community." More troubling than Butts's attack on Dinkins was his claim that Dinkins's black political enemies spoke for the grass roots of the city's black population. If this claim were true, then the possibility of transcending the racial differences exhibited in Crown Heights was problematic.[36]

The events in Crown Heights provided Dinkins's enemies with an opportunity to challenge the black establishment. This challenge was manifested at Gavin Cato's funeral at Saint Anthony's Baptist Church in Crown Heights in the morning of August 26, which the journalist and historian Jim Sleeper called "a carnival of hatred so obscene that his bewildered, grieving parents were all but forgotten."[37] Dinkins attended the funeral, sitting quietly through much of the proceedings. He did read a brief statement, pleading for peace and faith in the sanctity of human life, that was well received by the congregation.

But the day at Saint Anthony's Church belonged to Sharpton and other black radicals who had attached themselves to the Cato family and who opposed the mayor's message of peace and racial reconciliation. "Gavin and his family, like myself, are immigrants to this country, the land of the free and the home of the brave," Colin Moore told the congregation, "but what we discover is that justice is, not just sometimes, but often, white, blind and deaf." Sharpton's eulogy received most of the attention in the press. Gavin Cato, he said, was not simply the victim of an automobile accident. "The world will tell us he was killed by accident. Yes, it was a social accident. It's an accident for one group of people to be treated better than another group of people. It's an accident to allow a minority to impose their will on a majority. It's an accident to allow an apartheid ambulance service in the middle of Crown Heights. It's an accident to think we will keep crying and never stand up and call for justice."

From Sharpton's perspective, the death of Gavin Cato was akin to murder, and he grouped Cato with other black victims such as the Scottsboro boys. This meant that Yosef Lifsh and the other occupants of the station wagon were cruel murderers. The black community, Sharpton declared, "will not allow any compromise or sellouts or anything less than the prosecution of the murderers of this young man." "Have we lost all of our shame," Sharpton continued, "that even children are not above some crumbs from the table of people who have nothing but wickedness and hate in their hearts?" Sharpton's targets were not simply the Lubavitchers, however, but *all* the Jews of New York City. He claimed they did not want peace and quiet but the continuance of the unequal social relations between blacks and Jews, particularly in Crown Heights. Sharpton then attempted to comfort the Cato family. "Don't worry. . . . I prayed and called heaven this morning. The boy is all right. He's in the hands of an eternal God. In fact, they told me he was in the playroom. They introduced him to four little girls who got killed in Birmingham one morning. Yusuf Hawkins and Michael Griffith—they'll babysit him. Don't worry. They'll bring him over and introduce him to his uncle, Brother Malcolm."[38]

At no time did Sharpton or the other speakers at the funeral service refer to Yankel Rosenbaum as this would have deflected attention from the "murder" of Gavin Cato. Sharpton, in fact, seemed to exonerate the young black rioters, including the killers of Rosenbaum. "We must not reprimand our children for outrage when it is the outrage that was put in them by an oppressive system," he said. "The Bible says that a man sows, that shall he also reap. Well, who sowed violence?" This implied that the Lubavitch, who had arrived in the United States largely after World War II, and Rosenbaum, a temporary visitor from Australia, were getting their just deserts because they were part of the violent and oppressive system that had afflicted blacks since slavery. Sharpton's eulogy concluded with a bow to the claims of Afrocentric enthusiasts. "We are the royal family on the planet. We're the original man. We gazed into the stars and wrote astrology. We had a conversation and that became philosophy. We are the ones who created mathematics. We're not anybody to be left to die waiting on an ambulance. We are the alpha and omega of creation itself."[39]

Few blacks condemned Sharpton's eulogy. Whites, however, and Jews in particular, considered his words frightening. "It was simply another statement of the . . . poison of anti-Semitism and Afrocentrism, pitched to the righteous cadences of classic civil rights oratory," said Philip Gourevitch, a writer for the *Forward,* a weekly Jewish paper. It was "a standard-issue compression of lies, bigotry, and nationalist swagger." Sharpton's eulogy for Gavin Cato evoked memories of his involvement in the Tawana Brawley hoax and other racially charged incidents in the state and city during the previous decade and a half. An article in the August 28, 1991, issue of the *New York Post* on Sharpton was accompanied by the headline "Here We Go Again."[40] Jim Sleeper, writing in the left-wing Jewish magazine *Tikkun,* warned progressive blacks that if they did not repudiate Sharpton they would destroy any hope for a transracial political coalition on the Left. "The time for squirming and temporizing has ended."[41]

The Reverend Herbert D. Daughtry, Sr., pastor of the House of the Lord Pentecostal Church in Brooklyn, also spoke at the Cato funeral. He agreed with Sharpton that the killing of Gavin Cato was not simply an accident but akin to murder. He compared the Lubavitchers with the Ku Klux Klan, and he predicted that if the supposed preferential treatment accorded them by the police and politicians continued it would result in "the fire next time." If Lifsh was not arrested, Daughtry exclaimed, "it will be one more example of the Hasidic community getting away with murder."[42] Daughtry also predicted that black violence against Hasidic Jews would spread from Crown Heights to Williamsburg, a neighborhood in Brooklyn with a large number of Satmar Hasidim.[43]

Daughtry was well known for making anti-Semitic comments and threats. In 1978, newspapers reported him telling a crowd of blacks protesting the beating of Victor Rhodes, a sixteen-year-old black attacked by Hasidim who believed he had assaulted an elderly Hasid, "We'll get the Jews and the people in the long black coats." The Hasidim, he said, were "terrorists" and "oppressors." Daughtry denied ever uttering such words. Rather, he claimed, he merely said, "when men meet men, we will see then what the people in the long black coats will do." This was hardly a "defensive" statement, as he claimed, particularly in view of the tense relations between Jews and blacks in Brooklyn at that time. Also adding fuel to the fire was his claim that the Lubavitchers "symbolized" the "oppression" of blacks, and his threat that if any Lubavitchers touched black kids, "we will tear this community up."[44] Statements of this ilk continued after the Crown Heights riot. In 1993, on the eve of the release of the New York state report on the riot, Daughtry declared that Lubavitchers had difficulty "adjusting within a pluralistic society," had problems "living with other peoples" not of their peculiar persuasion, and were prone to violence. They were a savage, violent, corrupt, selfish, moneygrubbing, manipulative, and racist people, Daughtry avowed, and the "scourge" of Crown Heights.[45]

Sonny Carson, a former gang member, street hustler, drug peddler, and kidnapper turned black militant and anti-Semite, went even further in his attitude toward the Hasidim. Carson denied that he was prejudiced against Jews. He simply hated all white people, he said. The motivation of the rioters in Crown Heights was clear to him. They merely sought "the liberation of the community held hostage by a minority who have permission from the city authorities to do what they do with arrogance."[46] At the Cato funeral, Carson expressed pride in the behavior of young blacks in Crown Heights during the previous week—including, evidently, the murder of Yankel Rosenbaum. Carson then entered a surrealistic world of his own, comparing the death of Cato to that of the victims in Milwaukee of the cannibal Jeffrey Dahmer. Whites have taken to eating blacks, Carson told the mourners.[47]

THE CHALLENGE TO THE BLACK ESTABLISHMENT

The Reverend Norman and his son and other establishment black leaders recognized the threat presented by the radicals. A couple of the radicals were running in the September 12, 1991, Democratic primary for city council, and their candidacies were feared by the black political establishment. Congressman Charles Rangel of Harlem contributed three thousand dollars (the maximum allowed under the law) to longtime Jewish councilman Stanley E. Michels running in upper Manhattan, who was being challenged by C. Vernon Mason. Mason was notorious for having represented Tawana Brawley and for supporting Leonard Jeffries. Michels swamped Mason, winning 50 percent of the vote to Mason's 21 percent.[48]

In a predominantly working-class West Indian immigrant community in East Flatbush, the leading candidate was incumbent Susan D. Alter, the wife of a prominent Orthodox rabbi. She had supported Dinkins in his 1989 race for mayor. Seven black candidates opposed her, including Guyana-born Colin Moore. Moore had been the attorney for the woman who sparked the controversial boycott against a Korean grocery store in Flatbush a year earlier. During the campaign, Moore attacked Alter for closing her office on Saturday, the Jewish sabbath. He claimed that this indicated her inability to represent the black residents of the

45th District. The Brooklyn Democratic Party did not throw its weight behind any of Alter's opponents, and she was easily reelected with 38 percent of the vote. Moore received 22 percent.[49]

According to Peter F. Vallone, the speaker of the New York City Council and its most influential member, the most significant result of the 1991 election was the defeat of Mason and Moore, "two racial inflamers."[50] Vallone could also have included the victory of Mary Pinkett in Crown Heights. Pinkett, a moderate black who had cordial relations with the Lubavitch community, defeated Pete Williams, a radical professor at Medgar Evers College who had expressed sympathy for the rioters.

The call by radicals such as Moore that Lifsh should be brought up on criminal charges was part of the political theater that almost immediately attached itself to the Crown Heights story. The radicals were helped in their demand by the fact that the lawyer for Lifsh and the Lubavitch community was Barry Slotnick. Several years earlier, Slotnick had represented Bernhard Goetz, who had shot four young blacks in a New York subway whom he believed were muggers. The New York *Amsterdam News* called the hiring of Slotnick "an act of provocation."[51] Actors in this racial drama sought to raise the status of Gavin Cato from an unfortunate victim of an automobile accident to a martyr in the unending war of blacks against racism, social and economic injustice, and the political and legal favoritism shown to the Hasidim. After the funeral service, mourners walked the five miles from Saint Anthony's to the Cypress Hills Cemetery in Brooklyn to the accompaniment of shouts of "no justice, no peace." Some of the same people had chanted "No arrest, no rest!" during the riot.[52]

The ten African Americans, five Latinos, and eight Caucasians who composed the grand jury looking into the accident, however, were more impressed by the official police report and the investigation of the accident by the Brooklyn District Attorney's Office than by slogans. The grand jury heard evidence for two weeks from more than thirty persons, including eyewitnesses, police officers, Lifsh, and the two accident reconstruction experts. After deliberating for an hour on September 5, 1991, the jurors refused to indict Lifsh either for criminally negligent homicide or assault in the third degree.[53] (Ironically, that same afternoon a car hit a black youth about twenty feet from where Gavin Cato had been struck. In this case however, the driver was black, the victim was not seriously injured, and there was no rioting.) New York courts had traditionally ruled that the standard of negligence in a criminal case must be greater than in a civil negligence case, and, as Richard Uviller, a professor at the Columbia University School of Law, noted, grand juries were "reluctant to impute criminal negligence to what began as a traffic accident."[54] Jewish spokesmen even questioned why a grand jury had been impaneled in the first place. Grand juries had not investigated recent automobile accidents where the drivers were black and the victims were Jews.

A fatal traffic crash was certainly a tragedy, but its gravity did not make it a crime, nor had the courts of New York City traditionally viewed it as such. Generally in cases of vehicular death the driver of the automobile would be punished by having his driver's license suspended for negligent driving. Only in rare cases, such as in the case of drunken driving, would the accident rise to the level of criminal conduct. "Merely going through the red light is not sufficient to constitute a crime of criminally negligent homicide," said defense attorney Marvyn Kornberg. "Sure, it's negligent . . . but you have to have more than one traffic infraction to support that criminality. . . . It's certainly civilly wrong, and you could be held accountable in a civil suit, but it doesn't necessarily rise to a violation of a criminal wrong."[55] For Lifsh to have been indicted, there would had to have been evidence of two violations, for example, driving while intoxicated *and* at an excessive speed. No such evidence was presented. In fact, he never even received a ticket for running a red light because the police were not sure that any traffic infraction had even occurred. Furthermore, the standard of guilt is higher in a criminal case than in a civil one. Criminality requires proof beyond any reasonable doubt. Such proof was lacking in the Lifsh case where even the eyewitnesses and experts could not agree on whether he had run a red or yellow light or on the speed of the Mercury station wagon as it attempted to cross Utica Avenue.

While the grand jury was deliberating, Brooklyn District Attorney Hynes took the unusual step of appearing on WLIB, a black-owned radio station in New York catering to the city's black population, to explain the circumstances of the case. He noted that tests showed no alcohol in Lifsh's system, that an automobile accident resulting in death is not necessarily a crime, and that running a red light in a motorcade might not be gross negligence. Hynes cited twenty-two similar cases, most of which involved black and Hispanic drivers, in which there had been no indictments.[56]

There had been two hundred and two fatalities resulting from automobile accidents in Brooklyn in 1990. Only twelve had resulted in indictments and, as Hynes pointed out, none of these were similar to the accident involving Lifsh and Cato.[57] This, the *New York Times* argued, was a sensible policy. It made no more sense to indict Lifsh, the paper editorialized, than it would to file criminal charges "against someone who starts a fatal fire by forgetfully leaving an iron on. . . . Accidents are tragic and painful. But to equate them with criminal behavior makes little practical or humane sense." This reasonableness, of course, did not preclude the Cato family from suing Lifsh in a civil court. The grand jury's decision, the *Times* said, was a victory for "the rule of law."[58] Except for the fact that a grand jury rarely investigated accidents such as the one involving Lifsh, he was treated the same as several black drivers who had fatally injured Hasidim and not been indicted. In an accident that occurred on October 24, 1989, for instance, a five-year-old Hasidic boy was killed by a van driven by a black man with a suspended sentence and without insurance. No criminal charges were filed in this case either.[59]

Members of the Cato family refused to cooperate with the grand jury in its investigation and were angered by its decision. Some court observers conjectured that the Cato family attorney, Colin Moore, had advised them not to cooperate with the grand jury because he anticipated that Lifsh would not be indicted, and he wanted the family to be able to claim later that the grand jury's proceedings had been prejudiced because they had not participated in them. By contrast, the Jews of Crown Heights welcomed the grand jury's decision. According to Rabbi Shmuel Butman, September 5 was "a happy day for all human beings regardless of race, color, or creed."[60] Others were not so confident. The major concern was whether the grand jury's actions would inflame blacks. "The wounds our city has suffered will not be healed with anger," Mayor Dinkins warned. "And most importantly of all, the problems in Crown Heights will not be solved with anger."[61] In a statement accompanying the grand jury's finding, Hynes pleaded to the residents of Brooklyn "to refrain from senseless violence. We as a society have a continuing obligation and moral responsibility to protect the civil rights of all and to work to preserve harmony and to enhance unity."[62] But for some blacks, Hynes and the grand jury were not part of the solution but part of the problem. "We expected less than justice coming from a tainted prosecutor," Sharpton said. "We're going to hit the street."[63]

Moore accused Hynes of being a pawn of the Hasidim and part of a conspiracy to cover up the truth about the death of Gavin Cato. He should have disqualified himself, Moore said, and then Governor Mario M. Cuomo should have appointed a special prosecutor who could convene a second grand jury to hear the testimony of the Cato family. Hynes was partial to the Hasidim, Moore charged, offering in support the fact that Hynes had established a Jewish Advisory Council and had been on a trip to Israel paid for by a Jewish organization when the Cato accident occurred.[64] Moore did not mention that Hynes had also established nine other advisory councils (including an African American one); that Hynes had attended the dedication of the Reverend Martin Luther King, Jr., Museum in Memphis in 1991 as the guest of a black civil rights group; and that Robert Johnson, the black Bronx District Attorney, had accompanied Hynes on the trip to Israel. Hynes's office had vigorously prosecuted civil rights cases in which blacks were victims, and he had good relations with mainstream black leaders. Responding to Moore's accusations, Hynes accused him of being a "faker," noted that he had been involved in the infamous Tawana Brawley hoax, and had suppressed a key piece of evidence in what came to be known as the Korean grocery boycott.[65]

The attacks of radical blacks on Hynes intensified after the grand jury's decision. On September 7, Sharpton led a march of more than one hundred blacks through the quiet private beach community at Breezy Point in the Rockaway section of Queens, where Hynes had a summer home. Sharpton said it was shameful for the district attorney to live in "an apartheid village." The demonstrators shouted, "Hynes, Hynes, have you heard? This is not Johannesburg!" In fact, Breezy Point was ethnically and racially integrated.[66] Ironically, four weeks later Sharpton's office in mid-Manhattan was picketed by members of the militant Jewish Defense Organization. They demanded that the landlord evict Sharpton because of his racism and anti-Semitism. "The management can't do that," Sharpton exclaimed. "The PLO has offices here, and they also can't be evicted."[67]

New York's radical black press joined the attack on Hynes. The headline of an editorial in the weekly Brooklyn paper *City Sun* denouncing the grand jury's decision of September 5 read "Crown Heights: No Justice, No Peace!"—implicitly threatening more violence resulting from what the weekly called "the most contemptible and contemptuous miscarriage of justice" since the New York State attorney general had refused to bring indictments in the Brawley case. According to the *City Sun*, the refusal to indict Lifsh laid bare the racism permeating the criminal justice system in New York. The message sent by the grand jury and

District Attorney Hynes was clear: "the lives of people of color have no value." Hynes, the paper concluded, was presiding over a "two-tiered criminal-justice system that continues to usurp their rights, their dignity and their humanity." [68]

THE FLIGHT OF LIFSH

During the grand jury proceedings, Lifsh was in seclusion in an unidentified location in Crown Heights. Immediately after the jury announced its decision, he returned to his home in Israel. For Sharpton, Daughtry, and others of this ilk, Lifsh had literally gotten away with murder, and they called for his extradition.[69] The failure to indict Lifsh, they argued, resulted not from the requirements of the law but from racism and the political power of the Hasidim. On September 17, the day before Yom Kippur, Sharpton and Alton Maddox flew to Israel in order to serve Lifsh with formal notice that he was about to be sued in a wrongful-death civil lawsuit brought by the Cato family. According to New York law, in order for a New York court to render a binding and enforceable judgment against Lifsh, he had to be served with a summons personally and be given notice of the lawsuit. The summons conveyed by Sharpton and Maddox requested Lifsh's presence in New York three days after Yom Kippur to provide a deposition.[70] When their plane landed in Israel, several of the passengers recognized Sharpton and yelled at him to "Go to hell." Sharpton responded, "I already am in hell."[71]

While unable to locate Lifsh during their three hours in Israel, Sharpton and Maddox were noticed by the Israeli media, which had been alerted to their arrival. Sharpton told an Israeli audience that, in view of the imminence of the Jewish Day of Atonement, Israel should hand over Lifsh. This would help Israel repent for her sins, particularly the sin of having military and commercial relations with the government of South Africa. (A dozen black African nations were also guilty of this sin.) Sharpton and Maddox failed to convince the Israeli authorities. "It seems that the Israeli government has erected a wall of silence to protect Yosef Lifsh," Maddox said after arriving in the country. "Officials here have refused to cooperate at all with our efforts to locate and serve them, even through they are aware of our arrival and purpose here." Sharpton and Maddox then boarded a plane for the United States.[72] Few people were impressed by what appeared to be a publicity stunt. "If Sharpton was serious about serving this man with papers," Lifsh's lawyer said, "he would send someone anonymous to serve him quietly and discreetly." Even then it was doubtful that Lifsh could have been extradited legally to the United States.[73]

A few weeks after returning to the United States, Sharpton, Maddox, and Moore announced they were filing a $575 million lawsuit on behalf of the families of Gavin and Angela Cato against Rabbi Schneerson, Lifsh, Yehuda Zirkind (the owner of the Mercury station wagon), Hatzolah, Charles Hynes, and the police department. Sharpton made the announcement of the lawsuit on the steps of the Lubavitch headquarters at 770 Eastern Parkway in Crown Heights. When no one opened the door so that Sharpton could serve Rabbi Schneerson personally with the papers, he stuffed them in the handle of the front door and left. Lubavitch leadership was contemptuous of what they perceived as another publicity stunt. "The documents could have been served to our attorney," Rabbi Shmuel Butman said. "To do it in this fashion is an additional demonstration of insensitivity, hatred, harassment, racism and terrorism."[74] For his part, Hynes said he would seek financial sanctions against Moore for filing a frivolous lawsuit and would donate any money awarded him to charity. Sharpton, Maddox, and Moore refrained from proceeding with the $575 million lawsuit.[75]

Other lawsuits arising from the riot had better prospects for success. One of these was a $35 million malpractice suit filed by the family of Yankel Rosenbaum against the city's Health and Hospital Corporation, the agency that controlled Kings County Hospital. The suit, David Edelman, the lawyer for the Rosenbaum family, announced, was for "wrongful death and causing pain and suffering as a result of negligence." The city initially denied culpability for Rosenbaum's death. "It appears based on my preliminary discussions that the trauma center protocol for this type of injury was followed in the treatment of Mr. Rosenbaum," Dr. Benjamin K. Chu, the HHC's senior vice president for medical affairs said. Other city and state officials, however, disagreed.[76]

INVESTIGATING KINGS COUNTY HOSPITAL

Governor Cuomo requested the state's health department to look into the circumstances surrounding the death of Rosenbaum, and the department, in turn, appointed a team of doctors to conduct an inquiry.[77]

Their Statement of Deficiencies was issued on September 23, 1991. The Statement of Deficiencies agreed with the internal investigation by Kings County Hospital that improper medical care and not the severity of Rosenbaum's wounds were responsible for his death. "The patient was not provided care that meets generally acceptable standards of professional practice," the state report stated. This conclusion was precisely what the Rosenbaum family was looking for. "There was a serious failure of the hospital and its personnel to take care of this young man," David Edelman said. "We say he was killed twice, in the streets of Eastern Parkway and [in] the hospital."[78]

Part of the problem at Kings County stemmed from the unwillingness of graduates of American medical schools to work in the city's hospitals. "They are short of American graduates," one official at Kings County said regarding its emergency unit. "Once you start getting thirsty for staff, then you get desperate, and lower quality people cover the emergency room."[79] Dr. Pamela Damian, the forty-year-old surgical resident in charge of the trauma center at Kings County on the night of August 19, appeared to be a prime example of the staffing problems afflicting Kings County.

Dr. Damian's academic credentials were weak. She had attended several undergraduate colleges in Texas before going to medical school at the Universidad Autónomo of Juárez in Mexico. It took her five years rather than the customary four to complete her medical studies. After graduation in 1981, she enrolled in a pathology residency program at Presbyterian Hospital in Denver but dropped out after several months. Three years later Damian received a license to practice medicine in Colorado. She then relocated to New York and enrolled in a residency program in surgery at the hospital of the State University of New York at Stony Brook. She was at Stony Brook for five years, but left voluntarily after she was not promoted to fourth-year status. Damian then spent a year at Nassau County Medical Center doing a residency in surgery before being let go for not making satisfactory progress. According to officials at Nassau County, Damian's failure to secure a license to practice medicine in the state, even though she had been a resident doctor in New York for nearly seven years, was a factor in her dismissal. A few days after her dismissal and seven weeks before the Crown Heights explosion she was hired by Kings County. In her previous positions Damian had been closely supervised by senior doctors; at Kings County, however, she had broad authority to determine medical procedures for critically ill patients.[80]

The state's Statement of Deficiencies sharply criticized the procedures followed by the residents in the Kings County trauma center unit and the failure of the hospital to supervise the residents adequately. When Rosenbaum arrived at Kings County at 11:45 P.M., his blood pressure and respiration were stable, his pulse rate was high but not critical, and the attending physicians were confident he would recover. The wounds to Rosenbaum, one doctor said, were merely "peripheral lung injuries." However, Damian and her assistant, Sanjay Kantu, a second-year resident, did not detect one of the three stab wounds in his chest until 12:30 A.M. Damian and Kantu also failed to monitor his vital signs and did not read his chest X-ray until more than a full hour after his admittance. The undiscovered wound caused Rosenbaum's chest cavity to fill with blood, resulting in the collapse of his left lung.[81]

By 1:45 A.M., Rosenbaum's condition had become grave. His blood pressure had dropped, the pupils of his eyes were dilated, and he was unconscious. He was rushed into an operating room where doctors opened up his chest to stop the bleeding. By then it was too late. Rosenbaum went into cardiac arrest and was pronounced dead at 2:25 A.M. Hemorrhaging was given as the cause of death.[82] Jewish law requires burial as soon as possible. A funeral service for Rosenbaum took place in Crown Heights on the morning of August 21, and his body was then flown immediately to Australia for burial. The funeral for Gavin Cato was attended by the city's leading political figures. None were present at the service for Rosenbaum, an omission that did not go unnoticed by the city's Jewish press.[83]

The care provided Rosenbaum by Kings County was grist for the mill of black militants such as Moore and Sharpton. They claimed that because the death of Rosenbaum was due directly to the negligence of the staff at Kings County, Lemrick Nelson could not be guilty of his murder. The militants also noted that it took the death of a white man to throw a spotlight on the long-standing problems at the emergency unit at Kings County, the city's busiest, which served mainly a black and Hispanic population. "Mr. Rosenbaum died of the same terrible standard of care that has been killing black and Hispanic patients here for years," the *City Sun* quoted Dr. Kildare I. Clarke, the black assistant medical director of emergency services at Kings County. According to Clarke, the care provided by the emergency unit at Kings County resembled "a colonial plantation run by absentee landlords."[84]

The problems at Kings County had been chronic and pervasive. A recent investigation by the federal government had listed so many deficiencies at the hospital, including poor emergency care, that the government had threatened to close it down. A state report issued in January 1991 had also severely criticized the hospital's emergency care unit. Why, black militants asked, had public officials not been equally concerned when blacks and Hispanics were the victims of improper medical care? The answer seemed obvious: institutional racism.[85]

The state's report, an internal investigation by Kings County itself, and calls for an investigation of Kings County by Brooklyn District Attorney Hynes and Norman Rosenbaum, the brother of Yankel, led Mayor Dinkins to order James Dumpson, the chairman of the Health and Hospitals Corporation, to undertake "a thorough, top-to-bottom review" of the emergency room procedures at Kings County. Dinkins also called for a city review of the credentials of the more than eight thousand residents and staff doctors in the city's hospital system. Stanley H. Lowell, a New York lawyer prominent in liberal politics and Jewish affairs, was selected to be the special counsel to the investigation. His appointment was a wise choice.

Lowell had been a deputy mayor during the administration of New York City Mayor Robert Wagner and chairman of the city's commission on human rights from 1960 to 1965. He was also an important member of the city's Jewish establishment. Lowell had been a former chairman of the National Conference on Soviet Jewry and was currently vice chairman of the Jewish Community Relations Council, the official voice of New York's Jews on matters of community relations. He was specifically charged with discovering whether there had been adequate oversight on emergency room policies at Kings County, whether changes proposed in the state's Statement of Deficiencies had been implemented, and whether Rosenbaum's death resulted from criminal negligence. The mayor gave Lowell thirty days to submit his report.[86]

"What occurred with respect to Yankel Rosenbaum should not have happened," the mayor said when he announced the city investigation of Kings County. "You don't need to be a trained physician or a medical person to see that. And I want to get to the bottom of it." At the same time, the office of the Brooklyn District Attorney launched its own criminal investigation of the medical treatment received by Rosenbaum. The mayor recognized that Rosenbaum's treatment at Kings County had the potential of becoming a political bombshell that could affect his reelection prospects in 1993. It was not coincidental that one of the leading critics of the mayor and of Kings County was City Council President Andrew J. Stein, an expected rival to Dinkins in the 1993 Democratic primary.[87]

Stanley Lowell's dispassionate report (fifty-three pages, double-spaced) was released on November 1, 1991, several days after the mayor's announced deadline. The report was prepared by Lowell and his staff of four lawyers. This occupational slanting explains why the report resembles a legal document and, in contrast to the state report, why it does not discuss the specifics of the medical treatment received by Rosenbaum. Instead, the report focused on more general concerns such as deficiencies in the hospital's administrative structure, quality assurance program, admission procedures, monitoring of residents, and record keeping, and on its ambiguous relationship with the State University of New York Health Science Center at Brooklyn ("Downstate"). As befitting Lowell's liberal credentials, his report's last sentence drew attention to "the effect that the absence of a national health policy has on the delivery of health and hospital care in the City of New York."

Despite this obiter dictum, the Lowell report reinforced the conclusions of the investigations by the state, the Brooklyn district attorney's office, and Kings County itself that Rosenbaum had been the victim of grossly inadequate medical care and that the culture of the hospital was, in certain crucial respects, dysfunctional. The Lowell report claimed that the emergency room at Kings County was a microcosm of the "administrative disorganization," "lack of accountability," and "departmental fragmentation" that characterized the hospital at large.[88] The report provided additional fodder for the Rosenbaum family's suit against the Health and Hospitals Corporation.

NORMAN ROSENBAUM'S CAMPAIGN

Bringing to justice those responsible for his brother's death became a personal crusade for Norman Rosenbaum, who was four years older than his brother. "I am here for the long haul. I'm not going away," he told a reporter for the *Jewish Week* of New York in 1992. Despite a flourishing legal practice in Melbourne, a teaching position at the University of Melbourne's law school, and a wife and children, Rosenbaum visited New York City nearly seventy times during the next decade, staying for weeks on end while representing the Rosenbaum family at political events and legal proceedings and consulting with the detectives and lawyers he had hired to look into the circumstances of Yankel's death. Newspapers soon referred to these activities as "Norman's Conquest." Four things in particular angered Rosenbaum: the failure of the New York City police to arrest more than two persons for the death of his brother; the quality of care Yankel received at Kings County; the refusal by some New York political figures to acknowledge fully the anti-Semitic dimensions of his brother's death; and the contrast between the police's seemingly lethargic investigation into Yankel's murder and their more vigorous pursuit of the culprits in other highly charged racial incidents where the victims were blacks.[89]

Others shared Rosenbaum's anger at the failure to apprehend more than two persons for the killing of his brother. "When Yusuf Hawkins was murdered," Rabbi Shmuel Butman noted, "six people were arrested. When Yankel Rosenbaum was murdered—amidst shouts of 'Kill the Jew'—only two arrests were made. The rest of those involved are free. A blatant case of double standard with all the trimmings."[90]

Unfamiliar with the sociology and history of New York City, American Jews, or black-Jewish relations, Norman Rosenbaum interpreted his brother's death through the lens of that with which he was most familiar: anti-Semitism and the Holocaust. The murder, he claimed, was "totally avoidable." If so, then who was responsible for not preventing this "totally avoidable" event? Rosenbaum did not have to look very far. The city's government, he explained, starting at the top with the mayor and his police commissioner, was rife with anti-Semites and with persons unwilling to stand up to anti-Semites. Also complicit were Jews who failed to recognize this political reality.

Rosenbaum soon became a popular figure within right-wing Orthodox circles. His florid rhetoric—"Jewish blood is not cheap"—confirmed their conspiratorial fantasies regarding blacks, city politics, and mainstream Jewish organizations. According to Dov Hikind, the state assemblyman from Boro Park, the principal lesson to be learned from Rosenbaum's death was the need for Jews to follow the example of Rabbi Meir Kahane. Kahane, the founder of the Jewish Defense League, had been expelled from the Israeli Knesset for advocating racism and the expulsion of Arabs from Israel. He was murdered in 1990 in New York City by an Arab. "Kahane, of blessed memory," Hikind told a rally of Jews outside Gracie Mansion, the official home of New York's mayors, "taught Jews to fight back."[91]

Norman Rosenbaum was also popular among the state's Republican politicians, particularly Governor George Pataki, Senator Alfonse M. D'Amato, and Rudolph W. Giuliani, who succeeded Dinkins as the city's mayor in 1994. They saw in Rosenbaum an instrument to help defeat the Democrat Dinkins and to weaken the loyalty of Jews to the Democratic Party. Almost immediately after his brother's death, Rosenbaum voiced suspicion of a "cover-up" by the Dinkins administration and the city police of the circumstances surrounding Yankel's murder. The Dinkins administration, he said, had provided the Rosenbaum family only "rhetoric, lies, disinformation." He called for a federal investigation into the case and for the prosecution of Dinkins and Police Commissioner Lee Brown for dereliction of duty in protecting the civil rights of his brother.[92]

While Rosenbaum continually emphasized the anti-Semitic motivation of his brother's killers (calling the act "beyond belief"), at times he seemed to deny that anti-Semitism was important at all. At a public event in Crown Heights on August 19, 1996, marking the fifth anniversary of his brother's death, Rosenbaum said, "The people that murdered my brother are criminals. Firstly and foremostly and only are they criminals, and criminals do not have the capacity to differentiate between race, creed or color."[93] According to Rosenbaum, however, the fact that Yankel Rosenbaum's death was a criminal rather than an anti-Semitic act did not diminish the culpability of the Dinkins administration and the New York police. Their most important responsibility had been to protect the safety and security of the city's residents, and they had failed to do this in Crown Heights on the night of August 19, 1991, and during the next two days.

Despite Dinkins's reminder that Gavin Cato had died as the result of an accident while Yankel Rosenbaum had died as the result of a murder, newspaper reports and the comments of politicians tended to see them as equally tragic events. Living in two very different communities and dying in dissimilar ways, the seven-year-old Cato and the twenty-nine-year-old Rosenbaum would be forever joined together in death as symbolic victims. If the Cato fatality symbolized for blacks the political favoritism shown to whites and the indifference of whites to black suffering, the murder of Rosenbaum symbolized to Jews the rampant anti-Semitism of the Gentile world, particularly within the black community. And while black spokesmen conflated the two deaths and claimed they were merely different sides of the same coin of racism, Jews insisted that the differences between the killing of Cato and Rosenbaum were far more important than any similarities.

The death of Cato need not have led to an anti-Semitic riot. Cato was not the first, nor would he be the last black child killed by a car driven by a Jew in Brooklyn or elsewhere. But none of these other incidents had resulted in anti-Semitic rioting. The diliatory response of public officials, most notably the mayor, to the rioting in Crown Heights was due in part to the fact that it was totally unanticipated. Nowhere in the extensive literature on black-Jewish relations prior to August 1991 was there any indication that a major anti-Semitic riot could occur in New York City, a city that contained more Jews than any other city in the world and where they had extensive political clout. Nor was it inevitable that the name of Yankel Rosenbaum would come to be remembered when the names of other Jews slain by blacks motivated in part by anti-Semitism had long been forgotten. The emotions resulting from the deaths of Cato and Rosenbaum were a product of the three days of rioting that followed.

Notes

1. Rabbi Schneerson discontinued these trips to the cemetery after suffering a stroke in March 1992.
2. *New York Post*, September 5, 1991.
3. In his autobiography, Al Sharpton claimed that all three cars in the motorcade ran a red light. The Reverend Al Sharpton and Anthony Walton, *Go and Tell Pharaoh: The Autobiography of the Reverend Al Sharpton* (New York: Doubleday, 1996), 194.
4. Richard H. Girgenti, *A Report to the Governor on the Disturbances in Crown Heights*, vol. 1, *An Assessment of the City's Preparedness and Response to Civil Disorder* (Albany, N.Y.: New York State Division of Criminal Justice Services, 1993), 55–56 (hereafter cited as Girgenti Report, vol. 1); *New York Post*, September 6, 1991; *Crown Heights: A Strategy for the Future: A Report of the Crown Heights Coalition in Cooperation with Borough President Howard Golden* (Brooklyn, N.Y.: Crown Heights Coalition, 1992), 1–2; Patricia Hurtado, "Was Car Accident a Crime?" *Newsday*, August 22, 1991; District Attorney of Kings County News Release, "Grand Jury Returns No True Bill in Death by Auto Investigation," September 5, 1991, Robert A. Bush Papers, Brooklyn, New York.
5. Stewart Ain, "Paramedic From Jewish Service Aided Black Child," *Jewish Week*, August 30–September 5, 1991; *Jewish Press*, August 30, 1991. It was not

accidental that the Crown Heights riot began on a hot summer evening. "Most ghetto riots have erupted during the warmer months, when a large proportion of persons in densely populated ghetto neighborhoods go outside to escape the stifling heat, and during evening hours, when pedestrian traffic on the streets is high." "Occurrence of precipitants near major intersections and heavy foot traffic often seemed to be a contributing factor." Joe R. Feagin and Harlan Hahn, *Ghetto Revolts: The Politics of Violence in American Cities* (New York: Macmillan, 1973), 160–61.

6. Girgenti Report, 1:56–57.
7. Girgenti Report, 1:9.
8. Henry Goldschmidt, "Peoples Apart: Race, Religion and Other Jewish Differences in Crown Heights" (Ph.D. diss., University of California at Santa Cruz, 2000), 71.
9. Richard H. Girgenti, *A Report to the Governor on the Disturbances in Crown Heights*, vol. 2, *A Review of the Circumstances Surrounding the Death of Yankel Rosenbaum and the Resulting Prosecution* (Albany, N.Y.: New York State Division of Criminal Justices Services, 1993), 28 (hereafter cited as Girgenti Report, vol. 2).
10. Guy Trebay, "Mean Streets: Death and Hatred at the Corner of Utica and President," *Village Voice* 36 (September 3, 1991), 32–33. For a minute-by-minute narrative of the first night of the riot, see Girgenti Report, 1:57–66.
11. Jim Sleeper, "Demagoguery in America: Wrong Turns in the Politics of Race," *Tikkun* 6 (November–December, 1991): 46. For a view of the accident from a radical black perspective, see Vinette K. Pryce, "Many Blacks, No Jews Arrested in Crown Heights," *New York Amsterdam News*, August 24, 1991.
12. Goldschmidt, "Peoples Apart," 66. The New York *Amsterdam News* of September 7, 1991, listed the fifteen homicides in Brooklyn from August 14 to September 3. Fourteen of the victims were shot to death. The fifteenth occurred when "a senseless vehicular homicide took the life of 7-year-old Gavin Cato."
13. Girgenti Report, 1:56–57; Russell Ben-Ali, "Grandma: Boy Played With Jews," *Newsday*, August 21, 1991; Karen Phillips et al., "Sharpton Sparks New Crown Heights Furor," *New York Post*, August 28, 1991.
14. Goldschmidt, "Peoples Apart," 229; C. Carey Howard, "News Commentary: Crown Heights Double Standard," *City Sun*, September 4–10, 1996.
15. Nelson's I.Q. of 84 was on the low/normal scale of intelligence. According to the clinical psychologist who tested him, Nelson tended to lose control, lose judgment, and "become more impulsive, rely upon less information, and act before thinking." An administrator in the city's special education program testified that Nelson had an "attitude problem" and was very disruptive in class. He resisted directions, walked out of class without permission, and verbally abused teachers. Nelson, the administrator said, had the

intelligence of a twelve-year-old child and had difficulty processing information. Girgenti Report, 2:45.

16. Girgenti Report, 2:29–31, 71; George P. Fletcher, *With Justice for Some: Victims' Rights in Criminal Trials* (Reading, Mass.: Addison-Wesley, 1995), 88–89.
17. Michael H. Cottman and Jennifer Preston, "Dinkins Walks Through Racial Fire," *Newsday,* August 22, 1991.
18. Mitch Gelman, "Rabbi: Victim No Match for Hateful City," *Newsday,* August 22, 1991.
19. Mike McAlary, "Portrait of Teen in Hasid's Killing," *New York Post,* September 11, 1991.
20. Adam Dickter, "Nelson Trial Focuses on Intent," *Jewish Week,* May 2, 2003; Dickter, "Denials Debated in Nelson Case," *Jewish Week,* May 9, 2003.
21. Patricia Hurtado, "Teen Named in Jew's Slaying," *Newsday,* August 28, 1991; Fletcher, *With Justice for Some,* 91.
22. Alison Mitchell, "Prosecutor Cites Problems in Crown Heights Inquiry," *New York Times,* April 15, 1992.
23. David Gonzalez, "As Racial Storm Rages, Hasidic Leader Is Aloof," *New York Times,* August 26, 1991.
24. Trebay, "Mean Streets," 41; Jonathan Mark, "Crown Heights: 'Great Test' for Messianists," *Jewish Week,* August 30–September 6, 1991. For an example of Schneerson's obscure way of talking about the events in Crown Heights, see the interview with him and Roy Innis in the *Jewish Press,* October 11, 1991.
25. Gonzalez, "As Racial Storm Rages."
26. Alan Helmreich and Paul Marcus, eds., *Blacks and Jews on the Couch: Psychoanalytic Reflections on Black-Jewish Conflict* (Westport, Conn.: Praeger, 1998), 3–4.
27. Kenneth S. Stern, *Crown Heights: A Case Study in Anti-Semitism and Community Relations* (New York: American Jewish Committee, 1991), 15; Jonathan Rieder, "The Tribes of Brooklyn: Race, Class, and Ethnicity in the Crown Heights Riots," in *The Tribal Basis of American Life: Racial, Religious, and Ethnic Groups in Conflict,* ed. Murray Friedman and Nancy Isserman (Westport, Conn.: Praeger, 1998), 77.
28. *Amsterdam News,* December 7, 1991.
29. Michael Lerner and Cornel West, *Jews and Blacks: Let the Healing Begin* (New York: Grosset/Putnam, 1995), 182.
30. Goldschmidt, "Peoples Apart," 68.
31. Peg Tyre and Patricia Hurtado, "Hasidic Driver 'Remorseful,'" *Newsday,* August 27, 1991. The Jewish press contained many references to Lifsh's supposed rescue of the two black children. See, for example, *Jewish Press,* August 30, 1991; Debra Nussbaum Cohen and Jackie Rothenberg, "Fatal Brooklyn Traffic Accident Sparks Widespread Racial Violence," Jewish Telegraphic Agency, *Daily News Bulletin,* August 21, 1991.

32. Jennifer Preston, "Heal Wounds," *Newsday,* August 26, 1991.
33. Rieder, "Tribes of Brooklyn," 67–68.
34. Preston, "Heal Wounds."
35. Benjamin Ginsberg, *The Fatal Embrace: Jews and the State* (Chicago: University of Chicago Press, 1993), 170–74; Jay Nordlinger, "Power Dem: The Strange Rise of a Hatemonger," *National Review* 52 (March 20, 2000), 35; Stern, *Crown Heights,* 4; Tamar Jacoby, "Garvey's Ghosts," *New Republic* 203 (July 21, 1990), 18–19; Peter Noel and Rick Hornung, "Toilet Diplomacy: The Dinkins-Sharpton Connection, From Bensonhurst to Crown Heights," *Village Voice* 36 (October 8, 1991), 11–17; Philip Gourevitch, "Rev. Sharpton Warning Jews of Blacks' Ire," *Forward,* October 4, 1991.
36. Andy Logan, "Around City Hall," *New Yorker* 67 (September 23, 1991), 108.
37. Sleeper, "Demagoguery in America," 46.
38. Four black girls were killed in Birmingham, Alabama, in 1964 when their church was dynamited during the height of the civil rights movement. Yusuf Hawkins and Michael Griffith were recent victims of racial violence in New York City. Hawkins was killed in Bensonhurst in Brooklyn and Griffith in Howard Beach in Queens. "Brother Malcolm" refers to Malcolm X, who was murdered by Black Muslims in 1965.
39. The text of Sharpton's eulogy, "Gavin's Death Must Spark a Beginning," appeared in the *City Sun,* August 28–September 3, 1991.
40. Philip Gourevitch, "The Crown Heights Riots and Its Aftermath," *Commentary* 95 (January 1993), 31. See also Stern, *Crown Heights,* 17.
41. Sleeper, "Demagoguery in America," 92.
42. *City Sun,* August 28–September 3, 1991; Herbert D. Daughtry, Sr., *No Monopoly on Suffering: Blacks and Jews in Crown Heights (and Elsewhere)* (Trenton, N.J.: Africa World Press, 1997), 183–84.
43. Logan, "Around City Hall," 107; Peter Moses, "Tension Mounts in Williamsburg After Threats," *New York Post,* August 28, 1991.
44. Dorothy Rabinowitz, "Blacks, Jews, and New York Politics," *Commentary* 66 (November 1978), 45–46; Daughtry, *No Monopoly on Suffering,* 38, 61–62, 95, 110, 142.
45. *New York Post,* July 20, 1993 (the title of this editorial is "Mongering Hate"); Tara Shioya, "He's Got It Wrong, Expert Says," *Newsday,* July 19, 1993.
46. Merle English, "United Front in Crown Heights," *Newsday,* August 22, 1991.
47. Basha Majerczyk, "Jews All Over the World Shaken by Crown Heights Anti-Semitic Explosion," *Algemeiner Journal,* August 30, 1991.
48. Ginsberg, *Fatal Embrace,* 170–74.
49. Alessandra Stanley, "A Combustible Contest in a Smoldering Brooklyn," *New York Times,* September 5, 1991; Sam Roberts, "Council's New Era Takes Shape in New York Vote," *New York Times,* September 13, 1991.
50. Roberts, "Council's New Era."

51. *Amsterdam News,* August 31, 1991 (the editorial is titled "No Justice, No Peace and the Business of Denouncing"). This same editorial predicted that the situation in Crown Heights would not be resolved peacefully so long as Slotnick continued to make charges "reminiscent of the late Senator Joseph McCarthy."
52. Felicia R. Lee, "Bitterness Pervades Funeral for Crown Heights Boy, 7," *New York Times,* August 27, 1991; Vinette K. Pryce, "Crisis in the Heights," *New York Amsterdam News,* August 31, 1991; Jill Brooke, "Stations Omit Incendiary Quotes," *New York Post,* August 28, 1991.
53. Goldschmidt, "Peoples Apart," 72.
54. James Barron, "Examining Legal Issues in Crash," *New York Times,* August 23, 1991.
55. Hurtado, "Was Car Accident a Crime?" For a contrary view by a legal scholar that Lifsh was criminally negligent and should have been indicted, see Fletcher, *With Justice for Some,* 86.
56. Stern, *Crown Heights,* 5.
57. Abraham Fuchsberg, "Crown Heights," *Jewish Press,* September 20, 1991.
58. *New York Times,* August 29, 1991, and September 7, 1991.
59. Patricia Hurtado, "Few Drivers Face Charges in Deaths," *Newsday,* August 27, 1991.
60. Basha Majerczyk, "Grand Jury Clears Chasidic Driver," *Algemeiner Journal,* September 13, 1991.
61. Merle English et al., "Driver Is Cleared," *Newsday,* September 6, 1991.
62. District Attorney of Kings County News Release, "Statement of Kings County District Attorney Charles J. Hynes Announcing No True Bill in Gavin Cato Auto Death Investigation," September 5, 1991, Bush Papers.
63. English et al., "Driver Is Cleared."
64. Charles M. Sennott et al., "In Gavin Death: Hasidic Driver Cleared," *Daily News,* September 6, 1991; Colin A. Moore, "Unequal Justice Under the Law: Charles Hynes and the Hasidim," *City Sun,* December 16–22, 1992; Vinette K. Pryce, "Black Community Speaks Out on WLIB Over Grand Jury Decision," *Amsterdam News,* September 14, 1991.
65. Karen Phillips, "Grand Jury Probably Won't Call Driver Who Struck Kid: Slotnick," *New York Post,* August 29, 1991; Patricia Hurtado, "Hynes Calls Bias Charges Bizarre," *Newsday,* August 26, 1991; Karen Phillips, et al., "Sharpton Sparks New Crown Heights Furor," *New York Post,* August 28, 1991; Todd S. Purdum, "Prosecutor in a Mine Field Known as Crown Heights," *New York Times,* August 28, 1991; Charles J. Hynes, "Hynes Answers Colin Moore," *City Sun,* January 13–19, 1993.
66. Robert D. McFadden, "Black Marchers in Protest at Hynes's Summer Home," *New York Times,* September 8, 1991.
67. *Jewish Week,* September 27–October 3, 1991.

68. *City Sun*, September 11–17, 1991.
69. Sharpton claimed that Lifsh had left for Israel before the grand jury returned a verdict. "How did he know he wasn't going to be indicted? There's something suspicious there." Sharpton and Walton, *Go and Tell Pharaoh*, 199.
70. Frances McMorris, "Summons for the Rebbe?" *Daily News*, September 21, 1991.
71. *Jewish Press*, September 27, 1991; Clyde Haberman, "Sharpton Tries to Serve Summons in Israel But Doesn't Find His Man," *New York Times*, September 18, 1991.
72. Utrice C. Leid, "Hasid Involved In Cato's Death is Sought In Israel," *City Sun*, September 18–24, 1991; Goldschmidt, "Peoples Apart," 72–73.
73. *Jewish Press*, September 27, 1991.
74. Basha Majerczyk, "Sharpton Barks at 770," *Algemeiner Journal*, October 11, 1991.
75. *New York Times*, October 10, 1991; Jonathan Mark, "Catos Suing Rebbe for $575 Million," *Jewish Week*, October 11–17, 1991.
76. Mitch Gelman, "Kin to Sue in Death of Jewish Man," *Newsday*, August 31, 1991.
77. On August 30, 1991, Andrew J. Stein, president of the New York City Council, called upon Raymond D. Sweeney, director of the Office of Health Systems Management in the state's Department of Health, to investigate the death of Rosenbaum. Stein to Sweeney, August 30, 1991, Bush Papers.
78. Josh Barbanel, "State Assails Hospital's Care in Crown Heights Stabbing," *New York Times*, September 24, 1991.
79. Josh Barbanel, "Doctor's Past Is Questioned Over a Death," *New York Times*, September 27, 1991.
80. Barbanel, "Doctor's Past Is Questioned." See also Nick Ravo, "Resident Surgeons Chief Investigated in Crown Heights Death," *New York Times*, September 29, 1991.
81. Basha Majerczyk, "Emergency Room Doctor Had No Licence," *Algemeiner Journal*, October 4, 1991.
82. Mitch Gelman, "Poor Care for Hasidic Victim?" *Newsday*, August 30, 1991; *New York Times*, September 24, 1991.
83. Majerczyk, "Jews All Over the World Shaken by Crown Heights Anti-Semitic Explosion."
84. Utrice C. Leid, "Yankel Rosenbaum and Annie Winston: Victims of Negligence," *City Sun*, September 25–October 1, 1991; Leid, "Negligence, Not Wound, Killed Hasid, Says Doctor," *City Sun*, September 4–10, 1991.
85. Vinette K. Pryce, "Rosenbaum's Tragedy: It Happens to Blacks Everyday at Kings County, Say Activists," *Amsterdam News*, September 28, 1991; Joan Shepard, "Nelson's Battle for Freedom," *City Sun*, August 17–23, 1994. For

another view of the problems at Kings County, see the *New York Times* editorial "The Emergency Room's Emergency" (October 7, 1991).

86. "Remarks by Mayor David N. Dinkins at a Press Conference Concerning the Quality of Medical Care Provided by Kings County Hospital Center to Yankel Rosenbaum," September 24, 1991, Bush Papers.
87. Mireya Navarro, "Dinkins Orders Review of Hospital in Brooklyn," *New York Times,* September 25, 1991; Josh Barbanel, "Criminal Query is Begun in Care Given to Hasid," *New York Times,* September 26, 1991.
88. "The Report of Stanley H. Lowell, Special Counsel to the Health and Hospital Corporation of New York" (New York: November 1, 1991), 16–18, 53 (copy in the files of the New York Jewish Community Relations Council).
89. *Algemeiner Journal,* November 15, 1991.
90. Shmuel Butman, "Rabbi Butman's Statement on Crown Heights Affair," *Jewish Press,* September 20, 1991.
91. Laura Deckelman, "2,000 Jews Rally at Gracie Mansion," *Jewish Press,* September 6, 1991.
92. Steve Lipman, "Seeking Justice," *Jewish Week,* August 21–27, 1992.
93. Goldschmidt, "Peoples Apart," 289–90.

2

DAYS OF RAGE

Although media reports linked the deaths of Gavin Cato and Yankel Rosenbaum and the three days of rioting that ensued, they were in fact separate events. The riot was not an inevitable result of the killing of Cato. Had the riot never occurred, the events of that August night in Crown Heights would today be a footnote in the history of the city, remembered chiefly for the murder of Rosenbaum. Not even the most pessimistic observers of the city could have anticipated such a riot or envisioned such a tentative response by the city's political leadership. Once the riot occurred, however, there emerged a host of instant experts eager to ponificate on what the riot signified for New York City and for the future of urban race relations.

One of the buzzwords used to describe the rioting was "rage." Newspapers ran articles titled "Grief and Rage," "Public Rage," and "Streets of Rage," and the word served as a dramatic and concise way to describe these days of turmoil for readers impatient with more sophisticated and nuanced explanations. The meaning of "rage," however, was ambiguous and of little help in understanding the rioting. Was the rage felt by blacks equal and morally equivalent to that felt by Lubavitchers? Was the rage on either side justified? Was the rage spontaneous or had it been incited by provocateurs from outside Crown Heights? Was rage—a psychological term—the source of the rioting? Or could the rioting be better explained by social, political, and economic factors? Was rage a substitute for other words, such as "anti-Semitism"?[1]

The anger felt by blacks was at first unfocused. The crowd that gathered on the evening of August 19, 1991, at the scene of the Gavin Cato accident indiscriminately condemned Jews, the police, the press, and the city government. Initially some people assumed that the major target of any riot would be the police. A headline in the *New York Times* of August 20 read, "Fatal Crash Starts Melee with Police in Brooklyn." On Monday night three policemen were assaulted. A headline that same day in the *New York Post* took a different tack: "Traffic Death Sparks Race Riot in B'klyn." It soon became clear, however, that the Lubavitch and not the police or whites in general were to be the major targets of the rioters.

Charles Price, who would be indicted for the murder of Yankel Rosenbaum, was crucial in defining the enemy. The thirty-seven-year-old Price, a heroin addict and petty thief, was in the throng that had gathered at Utica Avenue and President Street after the accident. He was deeply shaken by Gavin Cato's death, and at around 11:00 P.M. he began talking to the crowd. "There were so many people up there that motherfuckin' night," Price recounted. "Man, it was like—God, I thought I was in the '60s." There are several accounts of what Price said. One person recalled that he said, "Do y'all feel what I feel? Do y'all feel the pain?" Another reported he stated, "I'm going up to the Jew neighborhood! Who's with me?" Riled up by Price, some of his listeners began moving in groups west along President Street into the heart of Jewish Crown Heights. They hurled rocks and bottles at the police and the homes of Lubavitchers, overturned and burned cars, including a van owned by a yeshiva, and beat two Jewish men. One of the groups encountered Rosenbaum.[2]

By the morning of Tuesday, August 20, the police leadership and city hall believed the worse was over and the situation was under control. Three hundred and fifty additional police officers had been dispatched to Crown Heights, and it was assumed that they would be sufficient to keep the peace. The rioting of the previous evening had been a spontaneous response to the accident, the police believed, and it was unlikely that it would continue into Tuesday. There were more important things in the newspapers that morning to concern New Yorkers, particularly the coup against the Gorbachev regime that led to the breakup of the Soviet Union.

The violence on Monday evening, however, was a mere prelude to far more serious rioting on Tuesday. While blacks walked the streets of Crown Heights, pleading in vain for an end to the rioting, Lubavitchers complained to city hall about inadequate protection. Some blacks, however, complained that the excessive number of police in Crown Heights made them feel that they were living in a police state. Twice on Tuesday afternoon, groups of blacks and Hasidim numbering in the hundreds threw rocks and bottles at one another. All the while blacks marched through Crown Heights chanting, "No justice, no peace!" "Whose streets? Our Streets!" and "Death to the Jews!" Twelve hundred additional police officers were dispatched to the neighborhood to restore order. Assigned to fixed positions, they were largely ineffective. Police looked on from these positions while four stores on Utica Avenue were looted, automobiles were overturned and burned (including eight police cars), pedestrians were assaulted, and police were shot at.[3]

After a rally on Tuesday addressed by Al Sharpton and Lenora Fulani of the anti-Semitic New Alliance Party, a crowd composed mainly of teenaged blacks advanced on a line of police. They taunted and spit at the police and threw bricks and bottles. The police advanced on the crowd, but then had to retire when the crowd received reinforcements. Two hundred police officers retreated rapidly south on Utica Avenue under a barrage of bottles, rocks, bricks, and gunshots from the crowd and persons stationed on rooftops on Utica Avenue. The sight of New York City police literally running away to escape the onslaught was one of the most embarrassing moments in the history of the force. The police believed the intersection of President and Utica, where Gavin Cato had been killed, had assumed symbolic importance for blacks, and that any attempt to disperse the crowd would exacerbate the situation. Instead, their impotence incited the mob. Later that day the police did reclaim Utica Avenue. The rioting on Tuesday ended around midnight when a heavy rain drove people indoors. Some within the police department believed the riot had ended with the rain. The police made only twelve arrests on Tuesday, four for looting, six for assaulting police officers, and two for refusing to disperse. At least twelve policemen and three journalists were injured that day, most by bricks and bottles.[4]

Tuesday produced the riot's most famous photograph: the award-winning picture of terrified twelve-year-old Yechiel Bitton, crouched besides his father, Isaac, who lay barely conscious on the sidewalk after being hit by bricks, stones, bottles, sticks, and fists. The attack on the Bittons occurred around 6:00 P.M., shortly after Isaac Bitton got off work as a reception manager at a Crown Heights hotel. Bitton, the father of eleven children, was a Moroccan immigrant, a former drummer in a rock group, and a fan of West Indian and soul music. (He coined the term

"Moroccan roll.") Because of the riot, Bitton had called for a taxi to drive him and his son to their President Street home. The driver refused to take the Bittons all the way because of the presence of a large group of demonstrators on President Street. Instead, he dropped the Bittons off at Schenectady Avenue and Carroll Street, one block south of President Street. Police were stationed at both ends of Schenectady at Carroll and President, and Isaac asked one whether it was safe to walk along Schenectady to his home. He was told that it was, and no police accompanied the Bittons as they proceeded north on Schenectady. The couple were attacked by a mob after walking less than a block. The police saw the attack and, instead of coming to the Bittons' rescue, radioed for reinforcements. When the police finally came to the aid of the Bittons, they were met by bottles and rocks. None of the perpetrators were arrested.[5]

The Bittons were saved by local residents and reporters covering the Crown Heights story. Several of the rescuers were black, including Peter Noel, a West Indian journalist for the *Village Voice*.[6] Isaac Bitton suffered a torn rotator cuff and a head wound requiring ten stitches. Yechiel Bitton sustained hearing loss and psychological damage. "I'll always think about it. It will stay with me," he said.[7] The *New York Post*, a tabloid, put the photo of the Bittons on its front page, and it came to symbolize what had happened in Crown Heights. The image of the Bittons on the sidewalk in their Orthodox garb reinforced the popular interpretation of the riot as an example of Jewish victimization at the hands of violent blacks. The photo also implicitly asked the question, Where were the police?

The level of violence and marching peaked on Wednesday and forced the city to send additional police to the area. At a press conference on the steps of city hall that day, Al Sharpton and attorney Alton J. Maddox, Jr., warned the city that it had seventy-two hours to arrest Yosef Lifsh. If it didn't, they would make a citizens' arrest. The Hasidim continued to protest the ineffectiveness of the police. Thursday's *New York Post* reported "Anarchy Grips Crown Heights," and the New York *Daily News* spoke of "Streets of Rage" and "Blood Feud in Crown Heights." Wednesday's events included the wounding of eight police officers by shotgun pellets, the slashing of a Lubavitch man and the beating of others, including individuals pulled from cars, the overturning of four more police cars and the setting on fire of others, the injuring of many cops, the shooting of two civilians, and the burning of an Israeli flag. Marchers continued tramping through the streets of Crown Heights carrying anti-Semitic signs. One group hurled stones and bottles at Lubavitch headquarters on Eastern Parkway while shouting "Heil Hitler." While the Hasidim did not stage counter-demonstrations, they did throw rocks and bottles in response. Violence continued into the evening with shootings, beatings, the pelting of police with rocks and bottles, the overturning of police cars, and confrontations between groups of blacks and Hasidim. At 7:52 P.M. a firehouse on Saint John's Place was stormed by thirty protesters. One fireman was injured and a fire car was damaged.[8]

On Wednesday, Police Commissioner Lee P. Brown praised the restraints placed on the police and told reporters that the situation was under control. These restraints, he maintained, had prevented the violence from escalating. The state investigation of the riot viewed the situation differently. "Unruly mobs were rampaging on surrounding streets," while "eyewitnesses said the police were disorganized and scared, and . . . there appeared to be chaos in the ranks." A delegate of the Patrolmen's Benevolent Association, the police union, threatened a job action if the shackles were not removed from its members.[9]

The policy of restraint would soon change. At 5:11 P.M., less than a half hour after Brown had said that things were under control, a crowd of several hundred in Crown Heights pelted his car with rocks. Nine officers were injured when they came to his rescue, and the police and reporters had to seek protection in P.S. 167 on Eastern Parkway. Mayor David Dinkins arrived in Crown Heights twenty minutes later for a meeting with Brown and Crown Heights residents and community leaders. After the meeting, held at P.S. 167, he attempted to speak to those gathered outside the school. The crowd booed the mayor, called him a traitor, and threw bottles at him. Although using a bullhorn, he was unable to make himself heard. The mayor then left to pay a call on the Cato family, accompanied by several police cars and fifty cops. He met the same hostile reception when he entered and left the Cato residence. The mayor later claimed that Wednesday's events convinced him of the seriousness of the situation.[10]

Helping to make up his mind was the visit that he and the police commissioner made to Coney Island Hospital on Wednesday night to meet with eight police officers. They had been injured by shotgun blasts from a sniper on a Schenectady Avenue apartment rooftop a few hours earlier. By early Thursday morning, Dinkins and Brown concluded that the situation was out of control and that the police would have to crack down. "Under no circumstances," Dinkins said, "are we going to tolerate lawlessness and violence."[11] People who break the law were now going to be treated as lawbreakers. "We are not going to permit thugs to take over the city," the mayor stated.[12]

The police sent more patrolmen to Crown Heights on Thursday, used mounted and motorcycle police, exerted tighter crowd control, and adopted a get-tough policy toward the rioters. By now eighteen hundred police were assigned to Crown Heights to put down the violence, and the police saturated the neighborhood with foot patrols. They were instructed to disperse crowds at the first sign of trouble and not to hesitate in making arrests. It was hoped that these measures would preclude having to call in the National Guard, which Jewish leaders were demanding, or imposing a curfew. "Cops Mass; Area Calms," proclaimed Friday's New York *Daily News*.[13]

Order was quickly restored during the daylight hours, although there were scattered acts of violence Thursday evening. At one rally at the scene of the Cato accident, the police outnumbered the protesters two to one. In contrast to the marches of Tuesday and Wednesday, there was no throwing of rocks and bottles during Thursday's march along Eastern Parkway in front of Lubavitch headquarters. Instead, the marchers were restricted to yelling anti-Semitic slurs for twenty minutes. Thursday's calm was not due merely to the efforts of the police. Also helpful was a meeting between the Lubavitchers and representatives of the Cato family held at the office of the National Committee for the Furtherance of Jewish Education, a Lubavitch institution. At the meeting two candles were lit, one for Gavin Cato and the other for Yankel Rosenbaum.[14]

Quiet returned to the streets of Crown Heights on Friday, and no arrests were made that day. There were fears, however, that this respite was only temporary, and the mayor wanted a moratorium on marches by blacks and anyone else. This hope was unlikely: a march organized by Al Sharpton and Alton H. Maddox was scheduled for Saturday on Eastern Parkway beginning at 1:00 P.M. The march could exacerbate tensions if the Lubavitch concluded that it was designed to disrupt the Jewish sabbath, particularly as it was to pass by Lubavitch headquarters, which contained the main Lubavitch synagogue. Despite the entreaties of the mayor, the organizers of the march refused to cancel it. They did assure him, however, that it would be peaceful. The march began more than an hour late, and by then the Lubavitch were in their homes enjoying their sabbath afternoon meal or a nap. During the march, a helicopter circled overhead and motorcycle patrols kept pace with the marchers. The city also stationed fourteen hundred police along the route of the march. Only four hundred persons marched, and two hundred and fifty of them had been bused in from Harlem. The marchers did not include any members of the Cato family. There were no incidents during the march, even though the marchers shouted anti-Semitic slurs along with the mantras "No justice, no peace" and "Whose streets? Our streets!"[15]

THE RIOT'S AFTERMATH

For all intents and purposes, the Crown Heights riot had ended by Saturday, although scattered acts of violence continued for several weeks. In one incident a bullet was fired into an empty synagogue on Maple Street. This was hours before the Jewish New Year was to commence on September 8 at dusk. The bullet broke a window and damaged two pews. The synagogue's members immediately renamed part of the building in memory of Yankel Rosenbaum during a ceremony attended by Jewish communal leaders and New York City Comptroller Elizabeth Holtzman. The police were puzzled by the shooting as the synagogue, located a half mile south of Eastern Parkway, had not been a target of vandalism previously. The Lubavitch were less hesitant in explaining it. "It seems the actual war may have stopped, but the guerrilla warfare and sniping is continuing," Rabbi Joseph Spielman, chairman of the Crown Heights Jewish Community Council, declared.[16] The Crown Heights riot took place over four days and in a ninety square-block area covering approximately one square mile. But the violence was concentrated within a thirty square-block zone encompassing a third of a square mile. The riot resulted in Rosenbaum's death, significant damage to a half-dozen businesses and to dozens of private residences, injuries to one hundred and fifty-two police officers (including eight hit by buckshot), wounds to at least thirty-eight civilians, and municipal expenditures of nearly seven million dollars for police overtime and for the twenty-seven police vehicles damaged or destroyed. The police attributed two hundred and twenty-five cases of robbery and burglary to the riot. The riot also was a factor in the suicide of Brokha Estrin, an elderly Holocaust survivor.[17]

To these damages must be added the psychological costs of the riot. Brooklyn District Attorney Charles J. Hynes called the four days of the rioting among "the most chilling" in New York City's history. The anti-Semitic slogans of the rioters, he declared, "were the most vile incitement to hatred, destruction and murder that Brooklyn has ever witnessed."[18] The effects of the riot were particularly felt by the merchants in the area. The Utica Gold Exchange was burned to the ground. Its owner was an immigrant from Iran. "This," he exclaimed, "was worse than Iran. There, if someone tries to burn your store, the people wouldn't allow them to do it."[19] "You see all the gray hair?" asked Sang Han, an immigrant from South Korea who owned Sneaker King on Utica Avenue. "All I do is worry, worry, worry." The city responded to such concerns by offering loans ranging from five thousand to fifty thousand dollars at a low interest rate to the store owners on Utica Avenue whose businesses had been looted or destroyed. Loan applications from the store owners, the mayor promised, would be handled as quickly as possible. The mayor's offer was due in part to reports that police had stood passively by while these shops were looted and burned.[20]

A total of one hundred and twenty-nine persons were arrested, and another forty-six were issued summonses as a result of the riot. More than 90 percent of these were black males under the age of twenty-five. Six of the arrested were Hasidim. Those arrested were charged with a variety of offenses, including unlawful assembly, criminal mischief, rioting, assault, disorderly conduct, criminal possession of a weapon, and reckless endangerment. Fifteen of the arrested were charged with a felony, and the rest were charged with misdemeanors. Six of the fifteen charged with a felony were found guilty. Four were placed on probation and the other two were convicted of burglary and were sent to prison for one to three years.[21]

Even though radicals frequently referred to the riot as an "insurrection" and a "rebellion," there was no evidence that those involved in the rioting and looting saw themselves as the vanguard of a revolutionary movement. They did not articulate political goals, except for anti-Semitism, and their spokesmen never related their actions to social, political, and economic concerns in a way that made sense. Crown Heights in 1991 did not resemble Paris of 1789 or Petrograd of 1917. The most important correlative of the young rioters, many of whom did not even live in Crown Heights, was their estrangement from communal norms and restraints. They had little respect for the city's black mayor, black police commissioner, other black political figures, or anything that symbolized authority, particularly the police.[22] Dinkins had few illusions about the rioters. He attributed their actions to the collapse of parental authority and their susceptibility to incitement by racial provocateurs.[23]

The journalist Mike McAlary agreed with the mayor. The riot, he wrote on August 23, had "become a kind of freewheeling caper for black teenagers. Kids know about limitations. They know how to test them. . . . And the word is out. You can get away with flipping cop cars like bottle caps and throwing the occasional rock now in Crown Heights."[24] Not everyone in the mass media, however, believed that the young black males caught up in the Crown Heights rioting were hooligans acting out their infantile fantasies. Felicia Lee, a reporter for the *New York Times,* said the "rage" of these young persons "transcended the accident." Their "grievances were not the well articulated one of the middle-class, who still had faith in the ability of government to solve problems." But the black rioters were not simply nihilists. Rather, Lee claimed, their participation in the riot stemmed from anger over police brutality, joblessness, and inferior schools. Lee left unsaid how rioting and attacks on Jews would resolve any of these conditions, nor did she present any evidence that the rioters sought a more challenging education. If these young blacks had no faith in government, then whom did they want to rein in the police, provide jobs, and fix the schools? Lee quoted approvingly the praise of Councilman Sal Albanese for Mayor Dinkins's efforts to calm the situation. "I think the Mayor did the best he could. Just being out there conveyed the feeling that he cared," Albanese said. But is this what the rioters needed? To have someone say he cared for them? If the problem with the rioters was a sense that no one cared for them, then it is very difficult to see how the city could fill this void.[25]

The police listed twenty-seven bias crimes in the 71st Precinct, which was responsible for most of the area affected by the riot. Of these crimes, twenty-one were anti-Semitic, three anti-black, and three anti-white. The police also listed sixty-six cases of assault and robbery, seven cases of harassment or menacing, and five instances of criminal mischief resulting from the riot. The Crown Heights riot was a significant municipal disorder, and its importance was magnified by the fact that it occurred in New York City, the media center of the United States, if not the world. But the property damage, loss of life, and size of the area affected was far smaller than that of other recent American riots.[26]

While the riot in Brooklyn was concentrated in a one-third square mile area, the 1980 riot in Dade County (Miami), Florida involved fifty square miles, and the riot in Los Angeles in 1992 took place in a one hundred square mile stretch. The Crown Heights riot was also shorter than these other two riots. It lasted for fewer than four days, while the disorder in Dade County continued for nine days and the riot in Los Angeles lasted for six days. The killing of Yankel Rosenbaum and perhaps that of Brokha Estrin were the only deaths directly attributed to the rioting in Crown Heights. By contrast, eighteen people were killed in Dade County, and fifty-five were killed in Los Angeles. While the rioting in Crown Heights affected six businesses and had property losses mounting to perhaps a million dollars, in Los Angeles seven hundred businesses were burned, property damage amounted to a billion dollars, and parts of the city were left without public transportation, mail service, and electricity. The riot in Miami destroyed sixteen homes and damaged or wrecked more than three hundred businesses. As the Girgenti Report concluded, the Crown Heights tumult "was much more limited in scope and caused less harm than the other highly publicized large-scale riots recently experienced around the country."[27]

The Crown Heights riot was also far from being the most important riot in the history of New York City. That dubious honor rests with the draft riot of July 1863 during the Civil War. The Crown Heights riot was not even as important as the riots of 1964 and 1967. The rioting in July 1964 in Harlem and the Bedford-Stuyvesant neighborhood in Brooklyn was precipitated by the fatal shooting of a fifteen-year-old black boy by a white policeman. Two hundred stores were damaged or destroyed, and four hundred and sixty-five persons arrested. The disturbances three years later in East Harlem and the South Bronx broke out after a police officer shot and killed an Hispanic man. During the resulting turmoil, three civilians were killed by gunfire, and dozens of stores were looted and burned. Trains traveling through the affected areas had to turn off their lights. In July 1992, eleven months after the Crown Heights riot, a riot occurred in the largely Dominican community of Washington Heights in upper Manhattan. One person was killed, seventy-two police officers were injured, and fourteen buildings were set on fire. "Compared to other disturbances in New York City's recent past," the Girgenti Report concluded, "the events in Crown Heights resulted in at least as much personal injury, but significantly less property damage."[28]

The city's Jewish newspapers and the leadership of Jewish organizations were critical of historical comparisons that downplayed the significance of the Crown Heights riot. They were more impressed with what they considered to be the riot's most salient feature. In contrast to other recent riots, which involved the looting of stores or were directed primarily at the police and other symbols of authority, the violence in Crown Heights targeted primarily one sector of the population: Jews. And this was a sector that, because of its history, was extremely sensitive to such acts. The Crown Heights riot hearkened back to earlier American riots that pitted ethnic and religious groups against one another. In nineteenth-century riots, Protestants fought Catholics, and whites attacked blacks during riots in the early twentieth century in Chicago, Tulsa, Detroit, and East Saint Louis.[29] The importance of the Crown Heights riot lay not in the specific events of August 19–22, 1991 (as horrific as these were to the Lubavitch community), but in the fact that anti-Semitism had seemingly escalated and attained a modicum of legitimacy among certain blacks. This aggression against Jews, the Girgenti Report said, "was systematic, intense, and injurious."[30]

In this respect, the riot was unique to American history. One indication of this was *American Violence,* a book edited by Richard Hofstadter and Michael Wallace which appeared in the wake of the campus violence, urban riots, and political assassinations of the 1960s. This anthology contained readings on violence directed at blacks, Indians, Italians, Quakers, Roman Catholics, Mormons, Chinese, Germans, and Mexicans. But there was not one entry on anti-Jewish violence, the word "Jews" was not listed in the book's index, and the lynching of Leo Frank was not discussed. *American Violence* reflected an optimism about the American Jewish condition that, Jews now feared, seemed less secure in the wake of the Crown Heights riot.[31]

DISSECTING THE POLICE

There is no more controversial aspect of the events in Crown Heights than the failure of the police to restore law and order immediately in the wake of the rioting on the night of August 19. This failure, more than anything else, was responsible for New Yorkers whipping themselves into what one person called "a froth of accusation and counteraccusation."[32] One detective in the 71st Precinct said the police "could have wrapped this thing up Monday night, but there was no game plan."[33] The riot was followed by a wave of buck-passing, recriminations, and mea culpas emanating from city hall and police headquarters.

In 1993, during congressional hearings on his appointment as the nation's drug czar, Police Commissioner Brown strenuously denied accusations from Jews that he or the mayor had been derelict in protecting the Jews of Crown Heights in August 1991. These denials came shortly before the release of the Girgenti Report, which presented a different picture.[34] Raymond W. Kelly, who had been the first deputy commissioner of the Police Department in 1991 and had then succeeded Brown as police commissioner, was more willing to admit his mistakes during the riot. Kelly had once headed a precinct in Crown Heights, and he faulted himself for not recognizing the seriousness of the situation until August 21. Until then he had been out of the operational loop and was reluctant to break the chain of command.[35]

The residents of Crown Heights, Jews and blacks alike, were surprised by the initial passivity of the police, even though the police and police vehicles were targeted by the rioters. The Lubavitchers concluded that city hall had consciously held back the police and had left the Hasidim to fend for themselves. They offered a variety of explanations for the mayor's inaction: anti-Semitism, racial solidarity with fellow blacks, and fear of a political backlash if the police cracked down hard on the rioters. Relations between the mayor and the Hasidim became venomous. Particularly notorious were accusations that Dinkins was responsible for the death of Yankel Rosenbaum. One Crown Heights resident called Dinkins "the mayor who made a pogrom against Jews in America," and Norman Rosenbaum said that "the blood of Yankel Rosenbaum is on Dinkins' hands." Posters circulated at Jewish rallies with photographs of the mayor and the caption, "Wanted for the Murder of Yankel Rosenbaum." These posters angered Dinkins, who had gone out of his way to respond to Jewish concerns and had appointed many Jews to high-ranking positions within his administration.[36]

Jews noted that while Dinkins had attended the funeral of Gavin Cato, he did not attend the services for Yankel Rosenbaum held on Eastern Parkway prior to the shipment of Rosenbaum's body to Australia for burial. The mayor responded that he had not been invited to participate. He had been told that Rosenbaum's funeral would be in Australia, and he assumed that any ceremonies in Crown Heights would be quiet and brief. "I clearly would have attended the ceremony," he said, "had I known and had I been invited." Dinkins could not have predicted that, instead of a drive-by past Lubavitch headquarters, a thousand persons would march behind Rosenbaum's casket and that microphones would be set up outside 770 Eastern Parkway to broadcast eulogies. Besides, he had sent Herbert Block, his liaison to the city's Jews, to represent him and the city. Dinkins said that criticisms directed at him regarding the Rosenbaum ceremonies illustrated impossibly high and unfair standards.[37]

Jews throughout the city conluded that the mayor had made a deliberate decision to sacrifice their interests in order to curry favor with the city's minority population. They pointed to the famous "day of grace" statement attributed to the mayor that he supposedly uttered in a conversation with New York Governor Mario Cuomo on August 20. The statement surfaced in an interview with the governor by Arnold Fine that appeared in the September 6, 1991, issue of the *Jewish Press.* "The Mayor," Fine quoted Cuomo, "said that the night before had been a sort of day of grace to the mob, and that wouldn't happen a second day because it was abused and because there were crimes perpetrated that were not prevented." This proved, the mayor's critics charged, that he was unwilling to stand up to black lawbreakers and was unsympathetic to the anxieties of Jews regarding their safety.[38] The quotation was one reason why federal judge Reena Raggi refused to dismiss the lawsuit filed by the estate of Yankel Rosenbaum, the Crown Heights Jewish Community Council, and twenty-nine Jewish residents of Crown Heights against the mayor, the police commissioner, and the city government for not protecting their civil rights during the riot. In view of the statement, Raggi said, "I don't know how I can throw the case out of court."[39]

The tempest over the quotation raised several questions. The most important was whether Dinkins ever said it in the first place. He adamantly denied it, and he claimed he never ordered the police to show restraint.[40] The evidence supported him. Governor Cuomo also denied ever having heard the mayor speak about a day of grace, and he also said that he never heard any of the mayor's advisers or anyone in the police department claim that Dinkins had ordered a day of grace. Officials within the police department and Milton Mollen, the deputy mayor for public safety, confirmed this.[41] Nor did the Girgenti investigation uncover any evidence that the mayor had spoken about a day of grace or had ordered the police to stand down in the face of violence.[42]

The second question regarding the "day of grace" quotation was why it ever surfaced in the first place. The governor denied that he had told Fine that Dinkins had used this expression. The mayor's supporters, however, believed Fine and accused the governor, whose relations with

Dinkins were not warm, of acting out of spite. Another explanation attributed the origin of the quote to partisan politics. The *Jewish Press* was close to New York Republican Senator Alphonse D'Amato, a bitter political enemy of the mayor. The paper was also a harsh critic of the mayor, and Dinkins suspected that the newspaper's use of the spurious quotation was part of an attempt to deny him reelection in 1993.

THE MAYOR AND THE POLICE

The police ranks were also bitter toward the mayor. Their hands had been tied from the beginning of the riot, they believed, and the responsibility for this rested with city hall and not with the police brass. As a result, the riot had been prolonged and the lives of the police put in danger. Relations between the police rank and file and the city's first black mayor, which had been awkward from the beginning of his administration, were now strained even further. Early in his term, Dinkins had arranged for the city to pay for the funeral of a Washington Heights drug dealer killed by an undercover cop and to fly his family to the Dominican Republic for the burial. Other incidents during Dinkins's first two years in office—including his weak response to the boycott of a Korean grocery store in Brooklyn led by the black demagogue Sonny Carson—strengthened the impression of the police that the mayor was weak on crime and had a racial double standard when it came to enforcing the law.

The mayor, many police officers concluded, was either ignorant of or unsympathetic to their mission. During the 1989 mayoral campaign, Dinkins promised to be "the greatest mayor against crime this city has ever seen," and he was elected in part because some whites believed that as a black man he could better deal with the high black crime rate. After Crown Heights, he appeared to the police to be soft on crime and a racial panderer. The police became openly contemptuous of Dinkins, and there was hardly an element within the city more hostile toward the mayor.

Dinkins, of course, knew even before the Crown Heights riot that he had a problem with the police. To mollify them, he had made more public appearances with members of the police department than with members of any other city agency. He was constantly photographed with the police, frequently praised New York's finest, and described Lee Brown as "the greatest police commissioner of the country."[43] The mayor continually denied holding back the police in August 1991, and he strongly denounced the accusation that he had allowed the rioters to vent their rage. There was never any evidence of a plan by the mayor to gain favor within the black community at the expense of Jews, or that the mayor ever instructed the police not to enforce the law and not to arrest rioters. While the mayor and his police commissioner undoubtedly made mistakes, they were just that, mistakes, and they were made under the pressure of a crisis for which no one was prepared, least of all the police.

The riot could not have taken place at a worse time for the police department. The riot occurred during the summer when some key Brooklyn police officials were on vacation, and their temporary replacements had to improvise. Also, some officials were new to their jobs and inexperienced. The uniqueness of the riot also complicated any rapid resolution. As the Girgenti Report noted, the Crown Heights riot was "the most widespread racial unrest in New York City in over twenty years," and both the police and the politicians were unprepared for such a singular and unexpected event.[44] On August 19, the Brooklyn police commanders were reluctant to invoke a citywide mobilization plan. "The department," a history of the New York City police stated, "had not actually attempted such a thing in twenty years, and since officers would not even have understood the radio codes necessary to set it in motion, the brass feared mass confusion."[45] The lack of preparedness was also indicated by the mayor's not being informed about the rioting until two hours after the Cato accident, and by the failure to transfer additional police officers to Crown Heights until four hours after the Cato accident. Even then the police, members of what they would like to believe was the finest police department in the world, were unable to stop the violence.[46]

The major fear of Dinkins and Brown was that overreaction by the police could increase the violence. Their strategy was to contain the rioting and hope that cooler minds would prevail.[47] Containment was one of the principal lessons learned from the riots of the 1960s and 1970s. A study of the 1980 riot in Miami, Florida suggested that the police should immediately "limit the area of the disorder by establishing a perimeter around the area."[48] By 1991 this fear of excessive force had become canonical within the New York Police Department. "New York City police tradition has leaned toward restraint and it's a philosophy that has served them well,"said Thomas Reppetto, the head of the Citizens'

Crime Control Commission, a law-enforcement watchdog organization.[49] A good case can be made, however, that the situation in Crown Heights required more force and less restraint right from the very beginning. Once the police got serious on Thursday, August 22, making sixty-one arrests, the riot quickly fizzled out.[50] "The increased police presence and different tactics, coupled with a new get-tough policy," the Girgenti Report concluded, "let area residents know that rioting and lawlessness would not be tolerated."[51]

Lee Brown had earned a doctorate in criminology from the University of California at Berkeley and was familiar with the recent literature on how to handle a riot. He had been the police chief in Atlanta and Houston before coming to New York, and he was considered an innovative and careful administrator.[52] His strategic decisions during the Crown Heights riot, noted Mitch Gelman, a *Newsday* reporter, followed "the textbook police response to riot control." The procedure was "to contain the problem area, don't let the disturbance engulf a wider area, disperse crowds and protect 'hot spots,' such as roofs and subway exits. Officers are told to man physical (sawhorses, trucks, etc.) and personal (human) barricades, ensure the security of dignitaries and never break ranks. Above all, they are told to simply stay cool." Gelman quoted Jerry Wilson, the former police chief of Washington, D.C., and a veteran in handling riots. "If a measured approach fails to get the community calmed down, you have to go in and take it back by force." For Dinkins and Brown, this point was reached in the evening of August 21 when sniper fire wounded six patrolmen and two sergeants. "Once you have people shooting at officers," Wilson said, "you have to move in."[53]

The strategy of containment meant, however, that those living within the area that had been isolated would temporarily be at the mercy of the rioters. After the riot, the lawsuit filed by the estate of Yankel Rosenbaum, the Crown Heights Jewish community, and a group of Crown Heights residents alleged the existence of a conspiracy to "withhold police protective services on a discriminatory and selective basis." It further claimed the city had failed to protect the civil rights of the Lubavitchers by not putting down the riot immediately. A lawyer for the city called these allegations "wholly unsubstantiated and, frankly, outrageous."[54]

Second-guessing the decisions made by the police regarding the deployment of their resources and holding the mayor personally responsible for the failures of the police were inevitable. Even so, there was nothing to indicate that Dinkins ever concerned himself with the question of how the police department should have utilized its manpower during the riot. Maybe he should have. Lee Brown strongly denied that Dinkins ever proposed refusing police protection to the beleaguered Hasidim, and he declared that if the mayor had made such a suggestion he would have resigned. "I am a police official," Brown said, "and under no circumstances would I obey an order which would require me not to carry out my responsibilities. I took an oath to uphold the law." As a black man, he noted, he was personally familiar with "unequal enforcement of the law."[55] Yet it seems incontrovertible that the police in the trenches in Crown Heights were told by their superiors to go on the defensive and to adopt a policy of containment. If this restriction deprived the Jews of Crown Heights of police protection, the responsibility rested with the police and not with city hall.

For the Lubavitch community, the major problem with the policy of containment during the Crown Heights riot was that it seemingly had left them at the mercy of the rioters. "My car windows were broken and the police stood there and did nothing," one Lubavitcher remarked, "and that means it's open season on Jews. You're giving the streets over to the hoodlums, like the Holocaust."[56] Some blacks believed there was a more serious police problem: discriminatory and excessive enforcement of the law and the close relationship between the police and the Lubavitchers. A headline in the *Amsterdam News* read "Many Blacks, No Jews Arrested in Crown Heights." The subtitle was "Racial Double Standard Causes Unrest, Activists Say." The accompanying article quoted Al Sharpton regarding the "preferential treatment" accorded the Hasidim in Crown Heights and the "continued harassment of Blacks by Hasidim," and it included the words of a resident in Crown Heights: "If we don't get justice, we will call for Black power, then revolution."[57]

BROKHA ESTRIN AND ANTHONY GRAZIOSI

The riot continued to affect the Jews of Crown Heights after August 22. One of the more puzzling aspects of the post-riot days occurred in the morning of August 26 with the death of sixty-eight-year-old Brokha Estrin. Estrin fell to her death from her third-floor apartment at 1650 President Street, an apparent suicide. Her son, Alexander, was baffled by her action. Others in the Lubavitch community were not so mystified.

Estrin, a widow, was a Lubavitcher and a Holocaust survivor from the Soviet Union. She lived near the Cato apartment house, which had become the gathering place for agitators, and for a week she had been subjected to anti-Semitic harangues. Estrin had reportedly told neighbors that she could not endure what was taking place in the neighborhood; she feared blacks, and wanted to move. It was natural, some Lubavitchers said, that the riot caused her to relive her horrific experiences during World War II, to believe that anti-Semites were coming after her once again, and to collapse emotionally under the pressure. Her suicide, Rabbi Shmuel Butman claimed, "was a direct result of fear placed on her by strangers outside of the community using Nazi tactics." While Butman was not specific as to the identity of these strangers, there was little doubt that he was referring to people such as Al Sharpton and the Reverend Herbert D. Daughtry, Sr., both of whom lived in New Jersey.[58]

The speculations of Butman and other Lubavitchers that blacks were to blame for Estrin's suicide were mere conjectures, and there was no way to determine their accuracy. She did not leave a suicide note, and there was no mention in the news reports that she had been having mental problems. But there was also little likelihood that her family and the close-knit Lubavitch community would have admitted this to the outside world. Others preferred to believe that Estrin had simply become emotionally unbalanced. The police, not wanting another death to inflame Crown Heights, downplayed the suicide and claimed it was an isolated event. While the cause of Estrin's death remained a mystery, for the Lubavitchers it was another indication of the lethal effects of black anti-Semitism.

The other major post-riot incident in Crown Heights occurred on September 5. Anthony Graziosi, a sixty-seven-year-old salesman of batteries and other electronic equipment, was traveling through Crown Heights on business when he stopped for a red light at approximately 11:00 P.M. at the intersection of Rogers Avenue and Lincoln Place. His car was surrounded by four black men, and one of them shot him. The death certificate said that Graziosi died from a "gunshot wound of back with perforations of lung, spleen, stomach and pancreas."[59]

The Graziosi family assumed the murder was a bias crime and a continuation of the Crown Heights riot. The shooting took place six blocks from the stabbing of Yankel Rosenbaum. Graziosi's wallet was not taken even though it contained one hundred and twenty-five dollars, and the electronic equipment in his car was left undisturbed. Graziosi, the family surmised, was possibly mistaken for an Orthodox Jew since he had a white beard and was wearing a dark suit. At the very least, they surmised, he was killed because he was white. The police believed the same group that killed Graziosi had earlier that night robbed two blacks without physically harming them. To the Graziosi family, the only explanation for the gang having treated Graziosi differently was the color of his skin or his resemblance to a Hasid.[60]

Carl Jeffrey Daniels was the only one charged with Graziosi's murder. Daniels told the police he had participated in the attempted robbery of Graziosi, but that another man had done the shooting. Daniels was indicted on four counts, ranging from murder to attempted robbery. He was acquitted by a jury of ten blacks and two whites in June 1992 after a one-week trial.[61] The primary witness against Williams was a prostitute who used cocaine, and her testimony was not credible to the jury. The other three suspects in the murder were known only by nicknames supplied by Daniels, and the police were unable to positively identify them. Detectives suspected that Daniels might even have invented the nicknames to divert attention from himself, and the authorities concluded that they lacked evidence to indict anyone else. The investigation of the murder was further hampered by the refusal of witnesses to cooperate and by the relocation of Daniels out of the state to an unknown city after he was shot in an unrelated incident. Further investigation, the police believed, would likely be fruitless.[62]

The Graziosi family wanted the death of Anthony Graziosi to be classified as a bias crime and to be treated with the same seriousness that the city displayed in prosecuting the suspects in the murder of Yankel Rosenbaum. The police, however, thought the shooting was simply a bungled robbery attempt. It had occurred outside the area of the riot, the suspects were believed to have committed other robberies that evening in what appeared to be a crime spree, and Daniels denied that Graziosi was accosted because he appeared to be a Jew. Mayor Dinkins accepted the judgment of the police that the murder was unrelated to the Crown Heights riot, and he maintained that the Graziosi case was being exploited by his political enemies.[63]

The mayor's attitude infuriated the Graziosi family. On June 16, 1993, Robert J. Miller, the family's pro bono attorney, told a rally protesting the city's indifference toward the Graziosi murder that it "has turned its back on Mr. Graziosi and his family. . . . The anger of the family . . . is heightened by the knowledge that no one seems to care and that the

City does not want to learn the truth about his death." Miller claimed the police and the Dinkins administration were in a state of denial. They didn't want to face the reality that another person had been killed because of the riot. Why, Miller asked, did the city fear the truth? "What is the City afraid of learning? There can never be justice unless we start with the truth," Miller said. And what was this truth? "Yankel Rosenbaum was killed because he was a Jew. Anthony Graziosi was killed because he looked like a Jew."[64] Miller believed additional arrests might result if the police continued the investigation, and he demanded that the mayor post a reward for information regarding Graziosi's murder.[65]

The Dinkins administration was not forthcoming. Miller concluded the mayor was a coward and feared alienating his political base, which included black radicals. Miller and his allies then turned to the federal government. The Graziosi family; Andrew Stein, the president of the New York City Council; U.S. Senators Alfonse D'Amato and Daniel Patrick Moynihan; and a host of Italian-American organizations, including the Order of the Sons of Italy in America, the National Italian-American Foundation, the Italian American Legal Defense Fund and Higher Education Fund, and the National Organization of Italian American Women, demanded that the federal government's investigation into the Crown Heights riot and the death of Yankel Rosenbaum be expanded to include the Graziosi murder and that it be treated as a bias crime.[66]

D'Amato, in particular, took an active interest in the Graziosi case. In March 1993 he asked Attorney General Janet Reno to direct the Federal Bureau of Investigation to look into the murder, claiming that it probably was a bias crime and part of the "Crown Heights Pogrom." Graziosi, D'Amato asserted, was killed because he resembled an Orthodox Jew. "This is proof of what I've said repeatedly, that no citizen is safe from mob violence left unchecked." D'Amato's motivation was not simply to convict Graziosi's attackers, but also to discredit the Dinkins administration. "Anthony Graziosi's death is a further indictment against the handling of the mob violence that erupted in August, 1991," D'Amato continued. "He should not be forgotten because it is convenient to some. We must seek a full measure of justice for his horrible death." There was no doubt as to the identity of these "some." Reno acceded to D'Amato's request, and in April 1993 she ordered the FBI to determine whether the murder of Graziosi was a bias crime. No federal indictments were ever handed down, and Miller and the Graziosi family believed the Justice Department's efforts had been perfunctory.[67]

The Graziosi family remained in limbo. "I don't want my husband to be forgotten," Minnie Graziosi said in 1996. "I want people to know that just like Yankel Rosenbaum's family is aching, Anthony Graziosi's family is aching, also." By then Graziosi had become the "forgotten man" of Crown Heights.[68] Except for the *Jewish Press*, the city's newspapers took little interest in the Graziosi tragedy.[69] One exception was Mike McAlary's column in the *Daily News* of May 7, 1993. It accused Miller of being a "rabble-rouser" and a race-baiter, and it attacked Senator D'Amato and other "idiot politicians" for dwelling on the Graziosi case. McAlary predicted that if Miller was successful in his "misguided" efforts to transform the robbery-murder of Graziosi into a cause célèbre, it would exacerbate the city's racial tensions.

After McAlary's column appeared, Miller informed Howard L. Adelson, a professor at the City University of New York and a columnist for the *Jewish Press*, on the particulars of the Graziosi case. The Graziosi family, he said, did not accept the killing as just another murder and would not rest until the guilty were brought to justice. McAlary's mean-spirited column, Miller told Adelson, reflected the city's current "studied insensitivity to people's pain and an unbelievable acceptance of a level of violence (regardless of its cause) which is unimaginable in a civilized city."[70] Adelson answered McAlary in his column in the *Jewish Press*. Graziosi's murder, Adelson wrote, was "a bigoted killing" of an Italian-American who was presumed to be a Jew. Why, Adelson asked, did "people in power cooperate with a journalist who is going to condemn those who speak the truth about bias-related crimes while refusing to cooperate with the families of the victims of such crimes? Why do these officials lose vital cases because of poor presentations, and refuse even to investigate others? These are questions begging for an answer!" New Yorkers, Adelson concluded, should be grateful to Robert Miller and Beth Gilinsky, the founder of the Jewish Action Alliance, for their efforts on behalf of the Graziosi family.[71]

The difference between the response of Jews to the killing of Yankel Rosenbaum and that of Italian-Americans to the slaying of Graziosi was dramatic. The Lubavitch community mobilized support for a federal investigation into the Rosenbaum murder, transformed Rosenbaum into a symbol of anti-Semitism, and kept the city's newspapers interested in the repercussions of the riot. The Graziosi case, by contrast, was not that significant to Italian-Americans. Part of the reason is that it was never clear whether the murder of Graziosi was a bias crime or merely a random robbery gone bad. More important, Italians, in contrast to Jews, never believed that they were part of a brotherhood of the persecuted (which included blacks). The killing of Anthony Graziosi did not create a crisis in black-Italian relations in the way that the killing of Yankel Rosenbaum created a crisis in black-Jewish relations because there were no black-Italian relations to begin with. Italian-Americans never assumed, as did many Jews, that a liberal stance on race relations was central to their ethnic identity.

Although forty-five Italian-American organizations ultimately joined together in demanding justice for the Graziosi family, many of these were merely letterhead organizations. With the exception of D'Amato and Miller—both Italian-Americans—the most important support for the Graziosi cause came from Jews. And the most prominent of these were Beth Gilinsky and her Jewish Action Alliance, which Howard Adelson claimed in May 1993 was "rapidly becoming the most effective of the defense organizations for the Jewish community."[72] Gilinsky had reached out to the Graziosi family soon after the murder. "When the family showed me his photograph and we heard the details of this case," she said, "it was clear that the Jewish community should be involved. In our opinion, the lack of proper action on the part of city officials in this case is an extension of the problems of the entire Crown Heights story."[73]

Gilinsky convinced Miller to become the lawyer for the Graziosi family, and she arranged the June 1993 city hall rally at which Miller spoke. Gilinsky was also behind a press conference on July 1, 1993, on the steps of the Department of Justice in Washington where a massive "Petition for Justice" containing more than fifty thousand signatures demanding justice in the Graziosi and Rosenbaum cases was handed over to Justice Department officials. Among the signatories were former New York Mayor Ed Koch and former New York State Attorney General Robert Abrams. Gilinsky's efforts brought together bitter political foes. Abrams and D'Amato, opponents in the 1992 senatorial election, politely shook hands at the Washington press conference. By linking the fates of Rosenbaum and Graziosi, Gilinsky broadened her organization's influence beyond the Jewish community.[74]

Gilinsky first came to public attention in April 1992 when she organized a demonstration in City Hall Park to protest the failure of the police to find any suspects in the murder of Yankel Rosenbaum other than Lemrick Nelson.[75] More events followed, including a demonstration in

1993 outside a Manhattan hotel hosting a Democratic fund-raising dinner attended by President Bill Clinton and Mayor Dinkins.[76] Gilinsky's most successful undertaking was an economic boycott of the black-oriented radio station WLIB, which was partially owned by the Dinkins family. WLIB had angered the city's Jews by its daily racist harangues and its dabbling in anti-Semitism. Gilinsky wanted the mayor to stop appearing on the station, to disassociate himself from the "hatemongering" of this "garbage radio," and to sell his family's stock in the station, if it did not change its programming.[77] The JAA picketed the radio station, and Gilinsky wrote letters to a score of national companies informing them of the station's bias and asking them to stop advertising on it. If they did not, she promised, she would organize a nationwide boycott of their products and services.[78] Her efforts were partially successful. The Wrigley chewing gum company, MasterCard, and the Republic National Bank stopped advertising on WLIB.[79]

City Council President Andrew Stein and former deputy mayor Herman Badillo, possible challengers to Dinkins in the 1993 Democratic mayoral primary, supported Gilinsky in her campaign against WLIB. Dinkins naturally concluded that the attack on the radio station was being fomented by his political rivals. On January 10, 1993, shortly after Gilinsky's campaign against WLIB had begun, the mayor issued a broad condemnation of "hate radio." The mayor did not single WLIB out by name, and the identity of the offending radio stations was not clear. The mayor's statement did not mollify his critics. Stein accused the mayor of being hypocritical in condemning hate radio as long as his family remained part owners of WLIB.[80]

JEWISH DIVISIONS

The JAA helped crystallize the resentment of Jews living in beleaguered neighborhoods in the Bronx, Queens, and Brooklyn toward the Jewish establishment headquartered in Manhattan. This resentment involved not merely issues of race but also matters of class, religious affiliation, and political ideology. Jews living in the outer boroughs tended to be less educated, poorer, and more religious than the leaders of the Jewish establishment, who mainly resided in Manhattan and the affluent suburbs of New Jersey, Westchester County, and Long Island. Living among or near blacks and in nonaffluent neighborhoods, Jews in the outer boroughs were often wary if not fearful of blacks, and were skeptical of the Jewish establishment's liberal stance regarding black-Jewish relations. They suspected that the establishment valued its relationship with blacks over the interests of less affluent Jews, and that it had shown its true colors during the Crown Heights riot when it failed to aid the Lubavitchers.[81]

Some Jews craved personal involvement in what they perceived to be a matter of Jewish survival. They disdained the quiet diplomacy, the filing of legal briefs, and the scholarly work of the defense organizations. "The ADL is just a bunch of indifferent yuppies, and we need some real leadership," said one Bronx resident.[82] Others compared the Jewish establishment to the Jewish leaders of the 1930s and 1940s who supposedly were deaf to the plight of European Jewry. An article by the journalist Sidney Zion said the performance of the defense agencies was reminiscent of the 1930s and 1940s "when Jewish organizations joined in the conspiracy of silence dictated by the Allied powers with Franklin Roosevelt at the watch." In light of Crown Heights, Zion asked, "why the hell do we need these great Jewish organizations?"[83] David A. Harris, the executive vice president of the American Jewish Committee, called Zion's article "scurrilous" and claimed that, instead of being indifferent, "Jewish groups . . . worked feverishly behind the scenes in order to try to end the violence."[84]

The belief that mainstream Jewish organizations had been absent without leave during the Crown Heights crisis became part of the conventional wisdom of many American Jews. The writer Cynthia Ozick asserted that these organizations had been "silent" during the riot "in order not to appear to be putting pressure of any kind on blacks. It was the dread of giving hurt that prevailed, even in the face of a murder."[85] In an op-ed piece in the *New York Times* titled "Ghosts of Crown Heights," Arthur Hertzberg, a rabbi, historian, and Jewish activist, described the Jewish establishment as simply "irrelevant."[86]

Jerome A. Chanes, a Jewish community relations specialist, speculated that the establishment's slow response to the riot was partially due to the fact that "mainstream Jewish organizations were generally distant from the Hasidim and ambivalent toward them. They also hesitated to disrupt the already fragile black-Jewish coalition in the city."[87] In a mea culpa shortly after the riot, Abraham H. Foxman of the Anti-Defamation League claimed that the ADL and other Jewish organizations suffered from "a strange sort of color-consciousness [that] may begin to function when the problem is anti-Semitism." Foxman believed the Jewish establishment would have acted earlier and more effectively had Yankel Rosenbaum's assailants been white.[88]

In November 1992 the *Forward,* a Jewish weekly published in New York City, accused the defense agencies of responding "sluggishly" to the riot. They displayed "at best an unwillingness to revise sentimental notions about black-Jewish relations" and "at worst an aversion to the plight of so conspicuous and fervent a population of Jews as the Chasidim."[89] A week later the *Forward* published the salaries of ten heads of Jewish organizations, including those of Foxman of the ADL, Henry Siegman of the American Jewish Congress, and Harris of the American Jewish Committee. The cynical caption below the list read "Jews Pay Hefty Price for Leaders."[90]

Criticisms of the defense organizations were not limited to Jews or to Jewish publications. Perhaps the most important of these criticisms was Lucette Lagnado's article "The Jewish Non-Defense League," which appeared in the *Village Voice* in August 1993. The article's subtitle is "How Mainstream Jews Failed the Hasidim of Crown Heights." This harsh critique of the ADL, the American Jewish Committee, the Jewish Community Relations Council, and the American Jewish Congress asserted that the organizations had "failed horribly during the riot." They provided no substantive assistance to the Lubavitchers and seemed befuddled by the riot. Lagnado quoted one Jew to the effect that mainstream Jewish groups had "slept through this crisis."[91]

Lagnado's piece struck a sensitive chord. Kenneth J. Bialkin, a past president of the JCRC, wrote the editor of the *Village Voice* to protest the article's inaccuracies. In 1993, Bialkin, along with Judah Gribetz, the president of the JCRC, also wrote a six-page statement titled "Looking at History." The letter and the statement argued that the JCRC had been actively involved from the beginning of the riot in aiding the Jews of Crown Heights.[92]

The JCRC did, in fact, respond promptly to the crisis. A representative from the JCRC arrived in Crown Heights a few hours after the Cato accident, and the next day the JCRC issued a statement to the press calling on the mayor to restore order, insisting that the National Guard be called in if the police could not do its job, and denying that the deaths of Gavin Cato and Yankel Rosenbaum, both tragic events, were morally equivalent.[93] The JCRC continually conveyed to city officials, including the mayor, the growing concern of New York's Jews about the escalating violence in Crown Heights. The JCRC also kept local and national Jewish organizations informed as to what was taking place in Brooklyn, and in August 1991 it offered a $10,000 reward for information leading to the arrest and conviction of those responsible for the murder of Rosenbaum. The JCRC supplied a document drawn up by a major New York law firm that provided legal justification for a full investigation by the federal government into the Crown Heights riot. This document was an important factor in the Justice Department's decision to become involved. It is difficult to imagine what else the JCRC could have done at that time considering its limited resources.

The JCRC was deeply disappointed that its work on behalf of the Jews of Crown Heights was not widely known and acknowledged, and that many Jews continued to believe the accusation that it had done little during the crisis.[94] Other New York Jews, however, read this history differently. "The JCRC wasn't there in confronting the false allegations made by the mob," said Marvin Shick, "and they weren't there in confronting the media which broadcast the falsehoods and gave them credence. Nor was the JCRC there in giving comfort to Jews."[95]

The anger toward the Jewish establishment was most deeply felt by the Jews of Crown Heights. Lubavitchers expressed dismay that New York rabbis who had traveled to Selma, Alabama, in the 1960s to march on behalf of civil rights for blacks, could not find the transportation and time to take them to Crown Heights.[96] Jews in Crown Heights believed the Jewish establishment viewed them with disdain because of their religious beliefs and distinctive lifestyle, and Lubavitchers reciprocated this supposed contempt.[97] This stormy relationship between the Jews of Crown Heights and the Manhattan-based Jewish defense agencies would continue into the twenty-first century.

Lubavitchers were seemingly impervious to any evidence that challenged their deeply held belief that the agencies had failed them in August 1991.[98] And yet the Lubavitchers were partially responsible for the organizations' not responding as rapidly as they would have liked. Lubavitchers had argued from the inception of the riot that it was the work of outside agitators, and that their relationship with their black neighbors was cordial. If this argument were true, there would have been no need for the defense organizations to become involved in what promised to be a temporary flare-up caused by a small group of outside provocateurs.[99]

The defense agencies believed that the outrageous accusations of indifference directed at them came from frustrated individuals looking for scapegoats. Phil Saperia, a Jewish aide to Mayor Dinkins and a former official of the American Jewish Congress, put it bluntly: Beth Gilinsky and her Jewish Action Alliance were "a bunch of grandstanders who are [working] for their own ambitions." Harriet Bogard, the director of the New York office of the ADL, agreed: Gilinsky's major agenda, she claimed, was "garnering publicity."[100] Saperia and other Jews blamed the Lubavitchers' insularity for their failure to appreciate the activities of the defense agencies. The Lubavitchers supposedly did not understand the nature of community relations work and refused to cooperate with those Jewish organizations that did.[101]

David Dinkins was fond of using the phrase "a gorgeous mosaic" to describe New York City. A different view was expressed by a headline of August 23, 1991, in *Newsday.* It said simply, "Mosaic Crumbles."[102] The residents of Crown Heights had never used such romantic terms as "a gorgeous mosaic" to describe their gritty neighborhood. At best, a live-and-let-live attitude marked the relationship between the Jews and blacks and between African Americans and Caribbean blacks. But even this guarded tolerance seemed unrealistic after the riot. The Crown Heights riot was a unique event in the history of New York City, but the history and sociology of the neighborhood provided hints that such an event had never been out of the realm of possibility.

Notes

1. It was not until August 29 that the *New York Post* became the first New York newspaper to use the word "anti-Semitism" in an editorial discussing the riot, and it was not until a day later that the Anti-Defamation League of B'nai B'rith characterized the riot as anti-Semitic and called for an investigation by the Department of Justice. "Transcript of Remarks Made by Abraham H. Foxman, National Director, Anti-Defamation League at August 30th Press Conference," Anti-Defamation Papers, New York; William Douglas and Clara Hemphill, "Crown Heights Anti-Semitism Probe Sought," *Newsday,* August 31, 1991.
2. Henry Goldschmidt, "Peoples Apart: Race, Religion and Other Jewish Differences in Crown Heights" (Ph.D. diss., University of California at Santa Cruz, 2000), 57–62; Richard H. Girgenti, *A Report to the Governor of the Disturbances in Crown Heights,* vol. 1, *An Assessment of the City's Preparedness and Response to Civil Disorder* (Albany, N.Y.: New York State Division of Criminal Justice Services, 1993), 64–65 (hereafter cited as Girgenti Report, vol. 1).

3. Girgenti Report, 1:5–6, 66–72.
4. Ibid., 1:6, 15, 73–88; Joseph A. Gambardello, Wendell Jamieson, and David Kocieniewski, "Hundreds Battle Cops in 2nd Night of Clashes," *Newsday,* August 21, 1991; "Goldschmidt, "Peoples Apart," 78; Miguel Garcilazo et al., "Race Riot in B'klyn," *New York Post,* August 21, 1991; Larry Celone, "Inside the War Zone: Reporter Relives the Night B'klyn Was on the Brink," *New York Post,* February 11, 1997; John Kifner, "Death Ignites Clashes in Crown Heights," *New York Times,* August 21, 1991.
5. Girgenti Report, 1:79–81.
6. For Peter Noel's role, see Noel, "Word to My Brother: A Crisis of Conscience in Crown Heights," *Village Voice,* 38 (July 5, 1993), 10–11. Noel quoted Isaac Bitton, "I don't know why the reporters . . . never mentioned the fact that a black guy, who was not with the mob, saved Yechiel and me."
7. William Neuman, "Photo Pair Recall Nightmare: Beaten Dad Sad—Son Scared," *New York Post,* June 24, 1993; Stewart Ain, "Chasid 'Still Recovering' from Beating," *Jewish Week,* September 6–12, 1991; Ain, "Still Scared: The Psychological Pain Remains for Father and Son Beaten in Riots," *Jewish Week,* August 21–27, 1992. Six and a half years after the attack the Bittons received a six-figure settlement from the City of New York. *Jewish Press,* January 23, 1998.
8. Girgenti Report, 1:89, 99; *Newsday,* August 22, 1991; John Kifner, "Clashes Persist in Crown Heights for 3d Night in a Row," *New York Times,* August 22, 1991.
9. Girgenti Report, 1:7–8.
10. David Kocieniewski, "Brown Praises Cops' Restraint," *Newsday,* August 22, 1991; Girgenti Report, 1:65, 93–94; Todd S. Purdum, "Dinkins, Seeking Peace, Finds Menacing Crowd," *New York Times,* August 22, 1991; James Lardner and Thomas Reppetto, *NYPD: A City and Its Police* (New York: Henry Holt, 2000), 304.
11. *Newsday,* August 22, 1991.
12. Rose Marie Arce et al., "Fourth Night Turns Violent," *Newsday,* August 23, 1991.
13. Joel Siegel and Dick Sheridan, "Cops Mass; Area Calms," *Daily News,* August 23, 1991; Girgenti Report, 1:102–105.
14. Girgenti Report, 1:8–9; John Kifner, "Dinkins Vows Tough Tactics in Race Strife," *New York Times,* August 23, 1991; *New York Post,* August 23, 1991.
15. John Kifner, "Police Brace for Protest in Brooklyn: Mayor's Plea Rebuffed for End to the Marches," *New York Times,* August 24, 1991; Kifner, "Blacks March by Hasidim Through a Corridor of Blue," *New York Times,* August 25, 1991; Will Brunch et al., "Can't Stop March: Sharpton Will Lead Protest Despite Plea," *Newsday,* August 24, 1991; Melinda Henneberger, "Angry, Peaceful Protest: Sharpton's March Avoids Violence," *Newsday,* August 25, 1991;

Charles M. Sennott, "Sharpton Shunned by Residents," *New York Post*, August 25, 1991.

16. *Algemeiner Journal*, September 7, 1991; David Gonzalez, "Bullet Is Shot Into a Synagogue in Crown Heights," *New York Times*, September 1, 1991.
17. Stephen McFarland, "Big Problem: Crown Heights, 1991," *Daily News*, December 4, 1998; Girgenti Report, 1:125–31; *New York Times*, September 7, 1991; Eli B. Silverman, *NYPD Battles Crime: Innovative Strategies in Policing* (Boston: Northeastern University Press, 1999), 76–79.
18. *Jewish Press*, May 1, 1992.
19. *Newsday*, August 22, 1991.
20. "Bonfire in Crown Heights," *Newsweek* 118 (September 9, 1991), 48: *Newsday*, August 22, 1991; Seth Faison, Jr., "Looted Crown Heights Store Reopens," *New York Times*, October 20, 1991; Michael Powell, "Aid for Crown Heights Stores: City Program to Provide Small Loans," *Newsday*, August 27, 1991.
21. Virginia Breen, "Most Arrests Have Been Black Males," *Newsday*, August 23, 1991; Mark Mooney, "Only Two Crown Hts. Rioters Got Serious Jail Time," *New York Post*, December 24, 1991; *New York Times*, August 29, 1991.
22. The historian William M. Tuttle, Jr. noted that in previous American riots, "the preponderance of the rioters of both races were teenagers and young adults, typically unattached males with fewer inhibitions and responsibilities than their elders." William M. Tuttle, Jr., *Race Riot: Chicago in the Red Summer of 1919* (New York: Atheneum, 1971), 264–75.
23. Todd S. Purdum, "A Frustrated Dinkins Appeals for Peace: 'I Alone Cannot Do It," *New York Times*, August 23, 1991. Deputy Mayor Bill Lynch called the rioters "disconnected youth." Earl Caldwell, "The Fire Next Time Is Alarmingly Near," *Daily News*, August 23, 1991.
24. Mike McAlary, "Dave Lets City's Wounds Fester," *New York Post*, August 23, 1991.
25. Felicia Lee, "Differing Demands of Black Groups Challenge Dinkins," *New York Times*, September 1, 1991.
26. Girgenti Report, 1:129.
27. Ibid., 1:125–33.
28. Ibid., 1:132–34.
29. Robert Fogelson, "Violence as Protest," in *Riot, Rout and Tumult: Readings in American Social and Political Violence*, ed. Roger Lane and John J. Turner (Westport, Conn.: Greenwood, 1978), 327–48; Elliott Rudwick, *Race Riot at East St. Louis, July 2, 1917* (New York: Atheneum, 1964); Tuttle, *Race Riot: Chicago in the Red Summer of 1919*.
30. Girgenti Report, 1:136.
31. Richard Hofstadter and Michael Wallace, eds., *American Violence: A Documentary History* (New York: Vintage Books, 1971).
32. Lardner and Reppetto, *NYPD*, 305.

33. Seth Faison, Jr., "Police Official Is Critical of Lack of Preparation," *New York Times,* August 24, 1991.
34. Marilyn Rauber, "Brown Told Senators He Never Held Cops Back," *New York Post,* June 24, 1993. For another view, see Paul Schwartzman and Frank Lombardi, "Blame It on Brown: Ex-Dave Aide Rips Lee on Riots," *Daily News,* August 18, 1993. Brown was approved unanimously by the Senate committee and then the full Senate to be the federal drug czar.
35. Anne E. Murray, "Kelly: I Should Have Stepped In," *New York Post,* June 13, 1993; Wendell Jamieson, Bob Liff, and Joseph A. Gambardello, "Commish Calls for Release of Crown Hts. Report ASAP," *Newsday,* June 23, 1993.
36. Roger Biles, "Mayor David Dinkins and the Politics of Race in New York City," in *African-American Mayors: Race, Politics, and the American City,* ed. David R. Colburn and Jeffrey S. Adler (Urbana: University of Illinois Press 2001), 143; Laurie Goodstein, "Dinkins Caught in Racial Cross-Fire," *Washington Post,* December 6, 1992.
37. Michael H. Cottman and Jennifer Preston, "Dinkins Walks Through Racial Fire," *Newsday,* August 22, 1991.
38. Arnold Fine, "An Interview with Gov. Cuomo on the Crown Heights Issue," *Jewish Press,* September 6, 1991.
39. Wayne Barrett, "With Friends Like These . . . Mario's Mouth Puts His Pals on the Crown Heights Hot Seat," *Village Voice* 38 (August 10, 1993), 13.
40. Girgenti Report, 1:appendix D, 17.
41. Alan Finder, "A Crown Heights Remark Returns to Trouble Cuomo," *New York Times,* August 1, 1993; Joseph P. Fried, "Cuomo Testifies on Crown Heights Rioting," *New York Times,* November 19, 1995; Martin Gottlieb, "Police in Crown Height: 'A Holding Approach,'" *New York Times,* November 19, 1992.
42. Girgenti Report, 1:315. See also Joseph P. Fried, "Police File Affidavits on Melee," *New York Times,* February 2, 1993.
43. Andy Logan, "Never Again," *New Yorker* 69 (August 2, 1993): 32–33.
44. Girgenti Report, 1:10–12, 132.
45. Lardner and Reppetto, *NYPD,* 303.
46. Girgenti Report, 1:9, 59–62. This failure to anticipate urban disorder was not restricted to New York City. See H. Jerome Miron and Robert Wasserman, *Prevention and Control of Urban Disorders: Issues for the 1980s: A Monograph for Law Enforcement Executives,* A Report Prepared by the Police Technical Assistance Project for the Enforcement Division, Office of Criminal Justice Programs, Law Assistance Administration of the United States Department of Justice (Washington, D.C.: University Research Corporation, 1980), 18–19. The higher echelons of the New York Police Department would have been well-served had they taken these words of Miron and Wasserman to heart: "The reason for hesitancy in admitting the possibility of controlling a small

disorder with existing shift personnel is . . . likely due to uncertainty about the organizations' policy for mobilizing and controlling disorders. It appears that, except at the highest levels of the police organization, there is an unwillingness to initiate a build-up of police forces. But such a build-up at an early stage can determine whether an escalating disorder is brought under control quickly or whether it will continue" (46).

47. Jonathan Kaufman, *Broken Alliance: The Turbulent Times Between Blacks and Jews in America* (New York: Scribner, 1995), 288; Lardner and Reppetto, *NYPD*, 303–304.
48. Miron and Wasserman, *Prevention and Control of Urban Disorders*, 57.
49. Mitch Gelman, "Above All Else, Cops Stay Cool," *Newsday*, August 23, 1991.
50. Girgenti Report, 1:16. Six arrests were made on Monday, twelve on Tuesday, and thirty on Wednesday. More than half of the arrests on Wednesday occurred at the corner of Utica Avenue and President Street.
51. Girgenti Report, 1:105.
52. Lardner and Reppetto, *NYPD*, 296–97.
53. Gelman, "Above All Else, Cops Stay Cool." For Brown's praise of the policy of restraint, see David Kocieniewski, "Brown Praises Cops' 'Restraint,'" *Newsday*, August 22, 1991.
54. Basha Majerczyk, "Policy Deny Failure to Respond During Crown Heights Riots of 1991," *Algemeiner Journal*, February 5, 1993.
55. Rauber, "Brown Told Senators."
56. Kocieniewski, "Brown Praises Cops' 'Restraint.'"
57. Vinette K. Pryce, "Many Blacks, No Jews Arrested in Crown Heights," *Amsterdam News*, August 24, 1991. See also Pryce, "Community Activists in Crown Hts. Charge Hasids, Police Insulted Blacks," *Amsterdam News*, November 28, 1991; Carolyn Butts and Colin Miner, "Media & Cops Bear the Brunt of Blame from Brooklyn Blacks," *New York Post*, June 14, 1993.
58. T. J. Collins and George E. Jordan, "'Suicide Try' Blamed on Local Tensions,"*Newsday*, August 27, 1991.
59. "Certificate of Death of Anthony Graziosi," September 7, 1991, Robert J. Miller Papers, New York. A copy of the autopsy of Graziosi is in the Miller Papers.
60. "Statement of Diane Braccia," undated, Miller Papers. Braccia was a daughter of Graziosi. Early press reports said that Graziosi was able to flee in his car after being shot. This might explain why his attackers did not take his wallet.
61. "Anthony Graziosi," July 1, 1993, Miller Papers.
62. Charles J. Wells to Robert J. Miller, March 4, 1994, Miller Papers. Wells was the commanding officer of the 14th Detective Division.
63. David N. Dinkins to Vincent Romano, February 19, 1993, Miller Papers; Milton Mollen to Minnie Graziosi, January 29, 1992, ibid.

64. "Statement of Robert Miller, Attorney for the Graziosi Family at the June 16—City Hall Rally," June 16, 1993, Miller Papers.
65. Margaret Ramirez, "Forgotten Man: Kin Seeks Justice in 2nd Crown Heights Slay," *New York Post,* September 4, 1996; Robert J. Miller to Alfonse M. D'Amato, October 6, 1993, Miller Papers; Miller to Fritz W. Alexander II, July 20, 1993, ibid.; Raymond W. Kelly to Miller, August 9, 1993, ibid.; Miller to Kelly, August 10, 1993, ibid. Alexander was the deputy mayor of New York City, and Kelly was the police commissioner. After Rudolph Giuliani became mayor of New York City in 1994, the police reopened the investigation into Graziosi's murder. Miller to Dear Friends, March 22, 1994, Miller Papers. Miller and the Graziosi family opposed the nomination of Lee Brown to be the nation's drug-policy czar. Miller to Arlan Specter, June 4, 1993, Miller Papers.
66. Author's interview with Robert J. Miller, March 14, 2002, New York.
67. Andrew Stein to Janet Reno, April 29, 1993, Miller Papers; United States Senator Al D'Amato Press Release, "D'Amato Demands Justice for Italian-American Slain in Crown Heights Riots," March 16, 1993, ibid.; United States Senator Al D'Amato Press Release, "D'Amato Announces FBI Probe in Graziosi Murder,"April 30, 1993, ibid.; Dennis Duggan, "Killing Just 'a Simple Murder'?" *Newsday,* August 15, 1993.
68. Ramirez, "Forgotten Man: Kin Seeks Justice in 2nd Crown Heights Slay"; Robert J. Miller letter, "Crown Heights Pogrom: The Other Victim," *New York Post,* May 3, 1993.
69. See esp. Robert J. Miller, "Crown Heights—A Failure of Leadership," *Jewish Press,* January 1, 1993.
70. Miller to Adelson, May 7, 1993, Miller Papers.
71. Adelson, "Bigotry and Murder," *Jewish Press,* May 21, 1993.
72. Adelson, "Bigotry and Murder"; Beth Gilinsky, "Crown Heights: Too Little, Too Late," *New York Post,* February 12, 1997.
73. *Jewish Post of New York,* April, 1993.
74. A flier advertising a July 1993 rally organized by the Jewish Action Alliance said, "Yankel Rosenbaum/Anthony Graziosi, Murdered, Crown Heights, 1991. The vicious mobs that killed them have not been brought to justice. We will NOT be silent! We will NOT forget! Join us to *save our city* from criminals, racists & hatemongers." Miller Papers.
75. Richard Steier, "Jews Demand Arrests in Rosenbaum Slaying," *New York Post,* April 6, 1993. Norman Rosenbaum effusively praised the JAA. Rosenbaum to Beth Gilinsky, August 25, 1992, Jewish Action Alliance Papers, New York.
76. Jeff Helmreich, "Taking It to the Streets: A New Kind of Activism Is Born from the Ashes of Crown Heights," *Long Island Jewish World,* October 1–7, 1993.
77. *Jewish Press,* January 8, 1993; Mindo Southgate, "The World According to Radio Station WLIB," *New York Post,* November 11, 1992; Marvin Greisman,

"Slotnick: No Messiah in Washington to Solve Crown Heights Problems," *Jewish Press,* November 19, 1993.

78. Howard L. Adelson, "Problems Here and in Israel," *Jewish Press,* January 29,1993.
79. Jonathan Mark, "ADL to Investigate Ongoing Static Over WLIB," *Jewish Week,* August 9–15, 1993; *Jewish Press,* January 8, 1993.
80. Mary B. W. Tabor, "Dinkins Urging Radio Stations to Curb Talk Show Bigotry," *New York Times,* January 10, 1993.
81. J. J. Goldberg, *Jewish Power: Inside the American Jewish Establishment* (Reading, Mass.: Addison-Wesley, 1996), 306–307; James Barron, "5,000 at Rally Join to Protest Anti-Semitism," *New York Times,* October 14, 1991; Stewart Ain, "Rally to Protest Anti-Semitism Draws 5,000," and Jonathan Mark, "Too Little, Too Late?: Critics of Rally Against Anti-Semitism Question Timing, Funds," *Jewish Week,* October 18–24, 1991.
82. Helmreich, "Taking It to the Streets."
83. Sidney Zion, "First Cut," *New York Observer,* September 16, 1991.
84. Sidney Zion, "Crown Heights and the Failure of Jewish Leaders," *New York Post,* July 30, 1993; David A. Harris letter in *New York Post,* August 13, 1993.
85. Cynthia Ozick, "Literary Blacks and Jews," in *Blacks and Jews: Alliances and Arguments,* ed. Paul Berman (New York: Delacorte, 1994), 71.
86. Arthur Hertzberg, "Ghosts of Crown Heights," *New York Times,* December 21, 1992.
87. Jerome A. Chanes, "Intergroup Relations," in *American Jewish Year Book 1993,* ed. David Singer and Ruth R. Seldin (New York: American Jewish Committee, 1994), 93:92.
88. "Transcript of Question and Answer Session Following Anti-Defamation League Press Conference, Friday, August 30, 1991," American Jewish Committee Papers, New York; Foxman letter in *Baltimore Jewish Times,* September 9, 1991; Ari L. Goldman, "Jews Saying Restraint on Brooklyn Was Mistake," *New York Times,* August 31, 1991.
89. *Forward* editorial "Beyond the Pale," November 6, 1992.
90. *Forward,* November 13, 1992.
91. Lucette Lagnado, "The Jewish Non-Defense League: How Mainstream Jews Failed the Hasidim of Crown Heights," *Village Voice* 38 (August 10, 1993), 11.
92. Kenneth J. Bialkin to Editor, *Village Voice,* August 12, 1993, Jewish Community Relations Council Papers, New York; Kenneth J. Bialkin and Judah Gribetz, "Looking at History," ibid. As a result of the riot, the JCRC decided that its executive director and associate director could not be out of town simultaneously. Both executives had been in Israel when the riot broke out.
93. Jewish Community Relations Council of New York, "JCRC Condemns Bigotry and Violence in Crown Heights," August 22, 1991, JCRC Papers.

94. David M. Pollock, "Where Was the Jewish Community?" *Jewish World*, September 13–19, 1991.
95. Marvin Schick, "Setting the Record Straight," *Jewish World*, September 27–October 3, 1991. Winston Pickett claimed the JCRC was "out of touch with events as they unfolded in Crown Heights, slow to act, and ineffectual when it finally did." Pickett, "The State Looks at Crown Heights: Lessons for Jewish Leadership," *Jewish World*, July 30, 1993. The information in Pickett's article refutes this harsh judgment.
96. Jonathan Mark, "Crown Heights: A Deadly Confrontation," *Jewish Week*, August 22–29, 1991; Yetta Halberstam Mandelbaum, "We Are All Crown Heights," *Algemeiner Journal*, November 15, 1991.
97. Jewish Telegraphic Agency, *Daily News Bulletin*, July 22, 1993; Steve Lipman, "Orthodox Taking Off Gloves to Battle Anti-Semitism," *Jewish Week*, November 7–13, 1992.
98. Rachel Donadio, "How Riots Forced Jewish Groups to Mend Their Fences," *Forward*, August 17, 2001.
99. Goldberg, *Jewish Power*, 301.
100. Helmreich, "Taking It to the Streets."
101. Jewish Telegraphic Agency, *Daily News Bulletin*, July 22, 1993; Stewart Ain, "Mayhem in Brooklyn: Tensions, and Blame, Boil Over," *Baltimore Jewish Times*, August 30, 1991.
102. Jennifer Preston, "Mosaic Crumbles: Some Say Black Respect Declines," *Newsday*, August 23, 1991.

3

A SUNDERED NEIGHBORHOOD

The Crown Heights riot cannot be understood without considering the distinctive history and sociology of Crown Heights itself and its residents. Those involved in the riot were not simply Jews and blacks, but people with distinct characteristics, backgrounds, and values who lived in a neighborhood like none other in America. Crown Heights was the only place in the United States where a large and growing number of Jews lived in the midst of an even larger number of blacks. The Jews of Crown Heights, however, were not simply Jews, but members of an Hasidic sect known for its missionary work among nonreligious Jews and for its good relations with Gentiles. In contrast to Jews who lived near or among blacks in what were frequently called "declining neighborhoods," the Jews of Crown Heights had no intention of deserting Crown Heights, the headquarters of the worldwide Lubavitch movement. They did not perceive Crown Heights to be an area in decay, and their numbers grew rapidly during the 1980s and 1990s. The black population of Crown Heights was also atypical. It comprised not merely Afro-Americans but an even larger number of black West Indians, and was the cultural center of West Indian life on mainland North America.

From the early twentieth century until the 1950s, Crown Heights was an upscale middle-class and overwhelmingly white neighborhood for economically and socially mobile Brooklynites. Its numerous churches and synagogues, tree-lined boulevards, parks, elegant houses, and spacious apartments attracted first- and second-generation immigrants from Italy, Ireland, Eastern and Central Europe, and Scandinavia after

World War I. The attractiveness of Crown Heights increased with the opening of a subway line in 1920. Of Crown Heights' ethnic groups, the most numerous were Jews, and by 1940 they comprised 42 percent of the white population of Crown Heights. Most of these Jews had migrated from the heavily Jewish Brooklyn neighborhoods of Williamsburg to the west and Brownsville to the east and from Manhattan's Lower East Side. Less affluent Jews lived in the area's modest apartment houses and attached houses, while Jewish professionals and successful businessmen lived in the spacious homes on President Street and the elegant apartments on Eastern Parkway. For these "alrightniks," Eastern Parkway had the same cachet that the Grand Concourse had for Bronx Jews. During and after World War II, Jews continued to settle in Crown Heights, and by 1957 they constituted 52 percent of the neighborhood's white population. By then Crown Heights had thirty-five synagogues ranging from Reform to Hasidic. The most imposing of these was the Brooklyn Jewish Center on Eastern Parkway.[1]

Beginning in the 1950s, however, three developments rapidly changed the demography of Crown Heights. The first was "white flight," as the expanding black population of the Bedford-Stuyvesant ghetto, which abutted Crown Heights on the north, pushed southward. The area's racial composition also changed due to the migration of black families from the South and to the decision of the city to move some black families on welfare into Crown Heights. In 1957, Walter O'Malley moved his Brooklyn Dodgers to Los Angeles in part because he feared that whites were becoming reluctant to attend the team's home games at Ebbets Field, located in Crown Heights, as the area became increasingly black. The settling in Crown Heights of poor, single-parent, welfare families was blamed for an increase in vandalism and crime. Jews and other whites fled the area for other neighborhoods in Brooklyn or the suburbs of Long Island. Not all the black newcomers to Crown Heights, however, were poor. Just as it had attracted upwardly mobile whites, Crown Heights also lured black civil servants, judges, doctors, and lawyers. This black bourgeoisie shared the middle-class values of the whites of Crown Heights and sought a safe, clean, and harmonious neighborhood.[2]

The second demographic change resulted from the passage of the Hart-Celler Immigration and Nationality Act of 1965, which reformed America's immigration policy. Signed by President Lyndon Johnson on Ellis Island, Hart-Cellar resulted in a sharp increase in the number of immigrants admitted to the United States and a change in their ethnic makeup. Whereas prior to 1965 immigrants to America came primarily from Europe, after 1965 more than 80 percent were from Asia, South and Central America, Africa, and the Caribbean. The new immigration law helped boost the flow of immigrants from the islands of the Caribbean into New York City. "The Caribbean is to New York what Mexico is to Texas and California," wrote urbanologist Louis Winnick in 1990.[3] Large numbers of newcomers from the Dominican Republic, Guyana, Haiti, Jamaica, Trinidad, Tobago, Grenada, Saint Kitts, and Barbados settled in the city after 1965.[4]

Brooklyn was a popular destination for the West Indians. After 1965, the cultural center of America's West Indian population shifted from Harlem and Bedford-Stuyvesant to the Flatbush, East Flatbush, and Crown Heights neighborhoods of central Brooklyn. By 1980, more than half of New York's West Indian population, and almost one-fourth of the nation's, lived in Brooklyn.[5] They included many of the one hundred thousand Guyanese who had immigrated to New York City since 1965, including the families of Gavin and Angela Cato. Attesting to the importance of Brooklyn to the West Indian diaspora was the annual West Indian American Day Parade. Beginning in 1969, the parade, known also as Carnival, has taken place every Labor Day on Eastern Parkway in Crown Heights. It attracts nearly a million marchers, spectators, and aspiring city and state politicians. It is by far the largest ethnic parade in New York City as well as the largest annual gathering of blacks in North America.[6]

By 1991, more than half the residents of greater Crown Heights were of West Indian background, and they were a majority in the blocks immediately south of Eastern Parkway, the heart of Lubavitch Crown Heights. Stores and churches in Crown Heights catering to the West Indians flourished. An English heavily marked with West Indian idioms was heard on the streets; cricket games scores were a favorite topic of conversation; and restaurants and stores featured codfish cakes, spicy jerk chicken, and Jamaican pastries. The West Indians, by and large, wished to live in an integrated community alongside the Lubavitchers; they shared many of their concerns such as crime and property values.[7]

The third factor in the transformation of Crown Heights was the growth of the Lubavitch community. By the 1970s, few non-Orthodox Jews lived in Crown Heights. Although there were a small number of Lubavitch Hasidim living in Crown Heights during the 1920s and 1930s, the Lubavitch population became a community in March 1940 with the arrival of the family of Joseph Isaac Schneerson, Menachem Mendel Schneerson's father-in-law. Irwin Steingut, an influential Jewish politician who lived in Crown Heights, had used his influence with President Franklin Roosevelt to secure a visa for the elder Schneerson so that he could leave the Soviet Union. Steingut encouraged the rabbi to transplant his Hasidic court to Crown Heights.[8] Schneerson purchased the building at 770 Eastern Parkway, which became the Lubavitch headquarters, and his daughter and son-in-law settled in an apartment on President Street. With the death of his father-in-law in 1950, Schneerson became the seventh Lubavitch "rebbe." He proceeded to supervise an amazing expansion of Lubavitch institutions throughout the world, and he became a significant figure on the American Jewish scene. Some of his more enthusiastic disciples even considered him to be the long-awaited messiah for whom Jews have been waiting since the time of King David.

After World War II the Lubavitch population was supplemented by thousands of Holocaust survivors, and by the 1960s it had reached a critical mass. The growth of the Lubavitch population was another reason for the exodus of other Jews and whites from Crown Heights. The presence of the Lubavitch diminished the prestige of a Crown Heights address, and it changed the area's image from that of an upscale neighborhood to one inhabited by poor and exotic European Jews. Acculturated Jews had not moved from Williamsburg and Brownsville in order to reside in an immigrant Jewish ghetto in which men walked around in long black coats talking in Yiddish, women wore unstylish long dresses, and children attended schools in which they were taught subjects more appropriate for prewar Poland than America. As they fled Crown Heights, these Jews abandoned dozens of synagogues and cultural institutions or sold them for a pittance to the Lubavitch.[9]

The crucial decade for the demographic transformation of Crown Heights was the 1960s, just as it was for Jewish urban neighborhoods throughout the country. In 1960, some 71 percent of Crown Heights' approximately two hundred thousand residents were white. By 1970, only 27 percent of Crown Heights' inhabitants were white. This transformation of Crown Heights from a white to a predominately black neighborhood was responsible in part for the sense of beleaguerment and isolation that Lubavitchers frequently expressed during and after the riot of 1991.[10]

By the late 1960s, the Lubavitchers faced the same issue that had confronted other whites in Crown Heights: to stay or to leave. The increase in neighborhood crime and assaults on Jews were of particular concern. In 1964 a group of yeshiva students had been attacked by a throng of blacks, a rabbi's wife was dragged at knifepoint out of her apartment and slashed in an attempted rape, and a young schoolteacher was raped and murdered in her apartment building's elevator. These incidents led Rabbi Samuel Schrage, the principal of a Lubavitch school, to establish the Maccabees, a local private anticrime patrol. The Maccabees cruised the streets of Crown Heights from midnight to five A.M. They alleviated but did not eliminate the fear of crime, and some Lubavitchers believed it imperative that the community leave Crown Heights. The decision to remain or leave would be made by the Rebbe. Lubavitchers considered his religious, social, and political pronouncements to be canonical and reflective of his superior knowledge of Torah. They would be accepted without protest.[11]

Despite the entreaties of those of his followers who were anxious to move out of Crown Heights, Schneerson, during the 1969 Passover holiday, made an unequivocal statement before three thousand of his followers on the necessity of remaining in Crown Heights. Passover, which commemorated the exodus from Egypt, seemed an appropriate time to decide whether the Lubavitchers should undertake a mini-exodus of their own. This "shchuna sicha," or "discourse on the neighborhood," was printed in a pamphlet that was widely distributed among the Lubavitch. Schneerson argued that Jewish law mandated staying in Crown Heights, and that this mandate transcended sociological and economic realities. He cited the book of Deuteronomy—"Do what is right and good in the sight of the Lord, so that all may go well with you and that you may be able to possess the good land that the Lord your God promises on oath to your fathers, and that all your enemies may be driven out before you, as the Lord has spoken" (6:18–19)—as well as rabbinic rulings forbidding Jews from selling or renting property in a Jewish neighborhood to Gentiles if this would damage the lifestyle or economic status of Jews, and from selling synagogues to Gentiles except under the most extenuating circumstances. Schneerson also declared that the abandoning of Jewish neighborhoods would be catastrophic to Jewish institutions, which could not be so easily relocated, and to those poorer Jews who would be left behind.[12]

Another advantage of remaining in Crown Heights was that it would be easier to maintain a separate Lubavitch community there than elsewhere. The cultural gap between the Lubavitch and their black neighbors was so wide that there was little danger younger Lubavitchers would absorb the values of the majority population. The world of the blacks was seen as hostile and dangerous, not welcoming and seductive. If they stayed in Crown Heights, the Lubavitch would undoubtedly remain a people apart. But there was less assurance of this insulation should the Lubavitch relocate to other parts of New York City or suburbia. There the allure of acculturation and assimilation would be more powerful. For the Lubavitch, the sociologist Samuel C. Heilman noted, the risks in Crown Heights were physical but the risks elsewhere "were religious and cultural. The former risks seemed to them small in comparison with the latter."[13]

Schneerson emphasized the virtues of a stable Jewish community. "In the old neighborhoods, people had found their own particular circles, had sunk roots into their particular Jewish environment. Each person belonged to an organization devoted in some measure to studying Torah, maintained an active synagogue membership and attendance, and supported charitable organizations." All this would be sacrificed if the Lubavitchers were to follow the path of least resistance and flee Crown Heights. To maintain the community, he suggested that the Lubavitch establish a housing-loan society that would make loans to Lubavitchers for the purchase of homes in Crown Heights. He further urged that pressure be put on the city government to provide better police protection for the neighborhood.[14]

THE LUBAVITCH REMAIN IN CROWN HEIGHTS

Outside observers considered Schneerson's pronouncement unrealistic, and they predicted that he eventually would be forced to reverse his decision as Crown Heights continued to become increasingly inhospitable to whites. But Schneerson had been prescient, and the Lubavitch community flourished. Lubavitch families were large, and younger generations wished to remain in Crown Heights to be close to the Rebbe, their families, and Lubavitch religious institutions.[15] Converts to Lubavitch Hasidim also settled in Crown Heights during and after the 1960s, and by the 1980s the Lubavitch were the fastest-growing segment of the local population. Local Lubavitch organizations worked to increase the Lubavitch population of Crown Heights. They purchased several apartment buildings in Crown Heights for Lubavitch families, and they became skillful in using government loan and subsidy programs to help Lubavitch families purchase houses and rent apartments in the neighborhood.[16]

One sign of the growth of the Lubavitch population was the opening of the Crown Palace Hotel on Crown Street in Crown Heights in 1984. This hotel was established to provide lodging for the many Lubavitchers who came to visit their families or to be near the Rebbe. Each of its rooms contained a wall clock with a color representation of Lubavitch headquarters and a sink for the obligatory morning washing of hands. One of the hotel's employees was Isaac Bitton, who was injured during the August 1991 riot.[17]

This growth in Lubavitch numbers occurred despite several ugly incidents of crime and anti-Semitism in Crown Heights during the 1970s and 1980s. In July 1970, during a struggle over the allocation of local antipoverty funds, two dozen fires were set on Jewish-owned property, and a firebomb destroyed the storefront office of the Crown Heights Jewish Community Council.[18] In September 1975, Israel Turner was shot and killed by a black man while returning to his home on Friday night after a religious celebration. Both he and his wife had been inmates in Auschwitz. Black bystanders taunted the funeral procession carrying Turner's body with cries of "Heil Hitler" and "Hitler was right," and a ruckus involving blacks and Lubavitchers broke out.[19] In June 1977, Abraham Goldman, the son of a rabbi, was stabbed to death in Crown Heights, and one year later a group of young Lubavitchers beat Victor Rhodes for allegedly knocking the skullcap off the head of a Hasid. Rhodes lay in a partial coma for two months.[20]

The writer Dorothy Rabinowitz concluded in 1978 that "the public expression of anti-Semitic sentiment, as a means of conveying political antagonism, seems now to have become normal" in Crown Heights. "So much so, that virtually no public notice could be taken of the explicitly anti-Jewish tirades of Crown Heights leaders, the threats to burn down Jewish houses, the enlistments to riot and commit mayhem against Jews." That anti-Semitism, Rabinowitz wrote, "may now be flaunted openly and with apparent impunity is the real significance of New York's latest black-Jewish conflict."[21]

Jews were joined by blacks in protesting the anti-Semitism that had surfaced in Crown Heights. Twenty-four New York City black Baptist ministers publicly disassociated themselves from the anti-Semitic remarks of speakers at a rally on July 16, 1978, organized by the Reverend Herbert A. Daughtry, pastor of the House of the Lord Pentecostal Church, a church located miles from Crown Heights. At the rally, speakers attacked the Lubavitch as "terrorists" and "oppressors," accused them of exercising "reckless" political influence, and charged that the police were subservient to the Hasidim.[22] Daughtry sought to keep the Crown Heights' pot bubbling, and in 1978 he and the Guyana-born Reverend Heron A. Sam, the rector of Saint Mark's Episcopal Church in Crown Heights, helped create the Crown Heights Black Community Coalition to stop what Sam called "Jewish expansionist aggression" in Crown Heights.[23] "The situation in Crown Heights is simmering," Daughtry said, and "this area is destined to explode."[24]

Verbal and physical attacks on Jews in Crown Heights continued after 1978, and the Lubavitchers continually complained about a lack of police protection and the kid-glove treatment accorded delinquents and muggers. In 1979, Rabbi David Okunov, a recent immigrant from the Soviet Union, was murdered by a black man while walking to a synagogue.[25] A 1984 report by the Carnegie Corporation described Crown Heights as "awash in a sea of ethnocentrism, prejudice, and violent conflict."[26] In 1986, Israel Rosen, a Hasid from Australia visiting his son, was killed by a gang of young blacks. Two months later Shlomo Fishman, a homeless man, was murdered. No arrests were made for either murder. Also in 1986 a black teenager was beaten with a bat, hammer, and hose by three members of a Lubavitch anticrime patrol.[27] In April 1987 more than five hundred blacks participated in a march on Eastern Parkway during which the Lubavitchers were compared to the whites of South Africa. In January 1988 a Hasidic man was slashed, black teenagers attacked a group of yeshiva students, and two hundred Lubavitchers stormed the 71st Precinct demanding more protection. In March 1989 a Hasidic woman's face was slashed by a black mugger. In the decade and a half prior to the 1991 riot, at least ten Lubavitchers were murdered in Crown Heights; by 1991 crime was generally viewed by the Lubavitch community as the neighborhood's most serious problem.[28]

Attacks on Lubavitchers in Crown Heights continued after the riot. It was of little comfort to them that the police considered most of these to be felonies rather than bias crimes. A particularly horrific incident was the murder of Phyllis Lapine, a thirty-eight-year-old mother of four, on the afternoon of February 6, 1992. Lapine, who had moved to Crown

Heights from Texas with her husband after they became Lubavitch Hasidim, was stabbed more than thirty times while carrying groceries into her apartment on Lefferts Avenue. Her credit card was taken by her assailant. A Brooklyn assistant district attorney called the murder of Lapine "the most heinous crime in recent years in this county."[29]

Lubavitchers were outraged by the murder of Lapine. While some said it was a continuation of the violence of the previous August's riot, others argued that it was simply a robbery-murder. During the evening of March 6, 1992, two hundred Lubavitchers marched through Crown Heights, chanting "No more welfare! Go back to Africa!" and carrying signs saying "Jewish Blood Is Not Free." Bottles, eggs, and flowerpots were thrown at the demonstrators from apartments occupied by blacks, and the Lubavitchers responded by throwing stones. One policeman was slightly injured during the melee, and two Lubavitchers were arrested.[30] Blacks strongly denounced the Lubavitch demonstrators for turning the Lapine murder into a racial incident. "This kind of rhetoric and anger is not grief, sorrow or a call for justice," said Michael Meyers, the black executive director of the New York Civil Rights Coalition. "It is scapegoating, a vicious, racial unadulterated ignorance. It must be condemned, and we urge others of good will to do likewise."[31]

Hundreds of police patrolled the streets of Crown Heights during Lapine's funeral the day after her murder, and city officials prayed that there be no repetition of the events of the previous August. The four thousand mourners at the funeral, which included the Brooklyn borough president and prominent black ministers, heard Rabbi Shea Hecht declare, "We have given enough sacrifices. Enough Jewish blood has been spilled on the streets of New York." Mayor David Dinkins did not attend the funeral. Aides said he feared his presence would transform the Lapine murder into a racial crime. Six people a day were murdered in New York City, the mayor noted. Undoubtedly the mayor also realized that he was detested by many Lubavitchers and would receive a hostile reception should he show up.[32]

Great pressure was put on the police to solve the case, and the Lubavitchers were planning to make daily protests until arrests were made. Four days after the murder the police arrested Romane LaFond on two counts of second-degree murder, robbery, and criminal possession of a weapon. The police emphasized that the arrest was made possible by the assistance of both white and black residents of Crown Heights.[33] The twenty-three-year-old LaFond was an unemployed and mentally disturbed Haitian who lived with his parents on President Street. He had a lengthy criminal record and had been released from prison the previous April after serving a six-year term for robbery. He was arrested twice in August 1991 for possession of burglary tools. The police suspected LaFond might be involved in the Lapine case while they were questioning him regarding a sexual assault on a Hasidic woman that had occurred in December 1991. In November 1992, a jury found LaFond guilty of murder and robbery after a trial of six days and after deliberating for less than a day. The decision came shortly after Lemrick Nelson was found not guilty of the murder of Yankel Rosenbaum, and the difference in the two decisions was noted by the Lubavitch community.[34]

As the 1990s unfolded, the Lapine murder was followed by other assaults on Lubavitchers in Crown Heights, reinforcing their sense that their community was under siege and that the authorities were incapable of protecting them. On the same day that Lapine was killed, a Lubavitch couple in Crown Heights was beaten and robbed by two black men. One of them told the couple, "Hey Jew, give me your wallet." The police classified this as a bias crime because of the use of the word "Jew."[35] Two weeks later a school bus carrying Lubavitch children was attacked with rocks and a brick by two black teenagers as it waited at a traffic light in Flatbush. "What is going to stop this?" one Lubavitch woman asked. Nothing, it appeared. [36]

THE NIMMONS CASE

For blacks, the most controversial post-riot incident occurred on December 1, 1992, when Ralph Nimmons was beaten by a group of yeshiva students. According to the students, Nimmons, a twenty-five-year-old homeless black man with six prior convictions for robbery, petty larceny, criminal trespass, and drug-related charges, was observed attempting to break into the yeshiva on Union Street just behind Lubavitch headquarters on Eastern Parkway. The students claimed they tried to detain him for the police, that he resisted, and that in the ensuing scuffle he was injured. Nimmons asserted that he had done nothing to provoke the attack, although he admitted that he had been carrying a set of tools that could be used in a burglary.[37]

The Lubavitch adamantly denied the contention of the police department and Mayor Dinkins that the assault on Nimmons was a "bias crime" and that they had yelled racial slurs at him. Rather, the Lubavitch claimed, Nimmons was injured while being held for the police, and they severely criticized Dinkins's statement on the incident. The mayor described the attack on Nimmons "repugnant," "intolerable," and the result of "ugly racist anger," but he failed to mention the circumstances surrounding the confrontation between Nimmons and the students or that Nimmons was well known in Crown Heights for being a burglar. Why, Jews wondered, did Dinkins and Police Commissioner Raymond W. Kelly immediately conclude that the excessive force used to apprehend Nimmons resulted from bias and not because he was a burglar?[38] Dinkins, they charged, was acting as judge and jury before all the facts were in. "We don't think the mayor is an antisemite," Harriet S. Bogard, director of the New York regional office of the Anti-Defamation League, said. "But he is either getting very bad advice, or he really doesn't understand. And I'm beginning to think he really doesn't understand."[39]

The police arrested Moshe Katzman, a twenty-four-year-old yeshiva student, and claimed that he had incited the yeshiva students to assault Nimmons. Katzman was charged with second-degree assault, second-degree aggravated harassment, violation of the Federal Civil Rights Act, unlawful possession of noxious material (mace), and fourth-degree criminal possession of a weapon (the rock he used to hit Nimmons). Katzman declared that he was home with his bride at the time of the attack. In May 1993, the charges against Katzman were dismissed, largely because Nimmons, on the advice of his attorney, Michael W. Warren, had refused to testify before a grand jury and to cooperate in other ways with the office of the Brooklyn district attorney. The Lubavitchers assumed that Nimmons's decision not to testify before the grand jury was due to fear that he would implicate himself under cross-examination.[40]

Blacks saw the Nimmons case differently. The beating of Nimmons, they believed, illustrated the vigilantism of the Lubavitchers and their belief that Lubavitch lives were more valuable than those of blacks. Blacks claimed that Nimmons was innocently walking through an alley by the yeshiva scrounging for used clothes, as he claimed, when he was accosted by the yeshiva students, that the students called him a "nigger," and that his beating was in retaliation for the decision in the Lemrick Nelson case.[41] Police Commissioner Kelly agreed. "It's clear that he was assaulted," Kelly said. "It's also in our judgment clear, that there was no burglary that had taken place." There was no evidence of a forced entry into the yeshiva, nothing was missing from the yeshiva, and, despite what the yeshiva students claimed, there was no record of a call from the yeshiva to 911 or to the local police precinct informing the police that the students were holding a burglar. Finally, there were no Lubavitchers around when the police arrived, disproving the students' contention that they were simply holding Nimmons for the police.[42]

Blacks pointed to the Lubavitch civilian anticrime patrols as another example of vigilantism and contempt for black people. The patrols, begun in the 1960s, had ignored the guidelines for patrols laid down by the police. These guidelines forbade the patrols from exercising police powers. The Lubavitch patrols escorted persons from subway stations to their homes and patrolled the streets at night, but they also kept watch on suspicious persons and even tracked down suspected criminals. The patrols were mainly, but not exclusively, manned by the Hasidim. The Lubavitchers thought the patrols were necessary to control crime, and that the local blacks should be grateful because the activities of the patrols, although exceeding the police guidelines, were helping preserve Crown Heights as an oasis of safety in comparison to the crime-ridden slums of adjacent neighborhoods.[43]

For blacks, however, the patrols evoked memories of anti-black vigilantism and night riders in the South. Blacks in Crown Heights particularly resented being asked by the patrols to show identification when walking at night, while the Lubavitch thought this was a reasonable way to keep track of outsiders bent on making trouble. In July 1977, fourteen years before the riot, five hundred blacks in Crown Heights protested in front of the 71st Precinct station and 770 Eastern Parkway. They claimed that the Lubavitch anticrime patrols were brutalizing young blacks. The protest was sponsored by the Coalition of People of African Descent, an organization led by the Reverend Heron Sam.[44] Rabbi Yehuda Krinsky, a Lubavitch spokesmen, denied that those manning the patrols were a vigilante group. They protected everyone, he asserted, blacks as well as Jews. Sam's group, Krinsky said, consisted of a few rabble-rousers seeking "self-aggrandizement and publicity."[45]

Politicians, both black and white, attempted to capitalize on racial discontent within Crown Heights. A flier circulated by Clarence Norman, Jr., during his 1988 reelection campaign for the New York Assembly and for state committeeman in the 43rd Assembly District was typical. It stated that his opponents were "controlled by and represent only the interests of 7% of the population in our district"; that Norman opposed "the preferential treatment given to 7% of the population at the expense of 93% of the population in areas such as housing, police protection and distribution of government resources"; and that he had spoken out against the discriminatory policies of the Jewish Community Council in distributing public monies.[46]

GROWTH OF THE LUBAVITCH COMMUNITY

The Lubavitch population continued to increase during the 1980s. By 1991, the remaining white population of greater Crown Heights—the area between Atlantic Avenue and Empire Boulevard and Washington and Ralph Avenues—consisted almost entirely of the area's nearly twenty thousand Lubavitchers. The Lubavitchers constituted 6 percent of Crown Heights' inhabitants, and in the heart of Lubavitch Crown Heights—the twenty-six-block area between New York and Troy Avenues and Eastern Parkway and Empire Boulevard—they were 40 percent. This growth in Lubavitch numbers stemmed from the high Lubavitch birthrate and the settling in Crown Heights of Lubavitch families from Europe, Canada, Latin America, and other parts of the United States.[47]

The development of the Lubavitch community exacerbated the tense relationship between the Lubavitchers and the Satmars, a rival Hasidic group located in Williamsburg, a Brooklyn neighborhood across the East River from the Lower East Side of Manhattan. The Satmars came from Satu Mare (Saint Mary) in the remote Carpathian Mountains in northwest Romania, and their outlook reflected their more isolated geographical origin. The Satmars were far more insular in religious ideology and far more hostile to outsiders than the Lubavitch. The Lubavitch sought converts to the Lubavitch way of life, and they engaged in missionary activities among non-Orthodox Jews to bring them closer to Orthodox Judaism. The Satmars disdained such activities because they feared it would dilute the distinctive Hasidic message, and because they thought the non-Orthodox were beyond redemption. Another point of difference between the Lubavitchers and Satmars concerned the state of Israel. The Lubavitchers believed the establishment of Israel indicated the imminence of the messianic era and was of great religious significance. Lubavitchers living in Israel played an important role in the country's politics, and Lubavitchers living in the United States lobbied on behalf of policies regarding Israel as favored by Schneerson. The Satmars, by contrast, opposed the state of Israel, and those living in Israel refused to have anything to do with the state, including using its money. They saw the founding of Israel as an act of blasphemy because it had resulted not from God's actions but from the efforts of secular and even antireligious Jews, and they were indignant that the state often violated their understanding of Jewish law.

During the 1970s, hostilities between Lubavitchers and Satmars led to physical confrontations on the streets of Brooklyn and the burning of effigies of Schneerson in Williamsburg. Lubavitchers were reluctant to venture into Williamsburg for fear of being assaulted. The police became so concerned by the threats emanating from Williamsburg that they began protecting Schneerson and Lubavitch headquarters around the clock. When Edward I. Koch, a Jew, became New York's mayor in 1978, he eliminated the police presence in front of 770 Eastern Parkway. This policy change evoked the protests of the Lubavitch who believed a police presence necessary because of the hostility of the Satmars and black radicals. Koch also eliminated the practice of blocking the service road on Eastern Parkway in front of Lubavitch headquarters on Saturday, the Jewish sabbath. When death threats were made against Schneerson in 1981 by Satmar zealots, Koch assigned a patrol car to accompany the Rebbe to the Lubavitch cemetery in Queens. Had blacks been aware of the history of Lubavitch-Satmar relations, they would not have so readily accused the police of favoring the Lubavitch, nor would they have been so prone to see a Lubavitch-police entente directed at blacks.[48]

For blacks, the police car assigned to Schneerson symbolized the special privileges accorded the Lubavitchers by city hall, and the double standards used by the police when it came to the Lubavitch and blacks. Schneerson was the only religious figure in the city with such an entitlement, and blacks (and others) wondered why this was so. If the Lubavitch wanted the Rebbe to be protected, they should pay for it themselves. Lubavitchers replied that Schneerson was a world-famous religious figure and deserved police protection in the same way that the pope deserved police protection when he visited New York. The protection provided the pope, however, occurred only during his rare journeys to New York, while the police protected Schneerson on a regular basis during his frequent trips to the Lubavitch cemetery in Queens. Nor did the police protect the grand rabbis of other Hasidic sects when they traveled in the city. For non-Lubavitchers, the police escort of Schneerson seemed unwarranted and a result of political pressure.

There were other issues besides the question of police protection that complicated relations between the Lubavitch and their black neighbors and influenced the blacks' understanding of Crown Heights "realities." Of these issues, the most important involved housing. The high Lubavitch birthrate and the desire of younger Lubavitchers to settle in Crown Heights put upward pressure on the prices of homes and set off an increasingly fierce competition for the small number of housing units coming onto the market. Higher costs for homes and higher rents for apartments were the result. This competition was beneficial to those who owned homes and apartments in Crown Heights, but it was contrary to the interests of potential homeowners and renters.

Blacks accused Lubavitch apartment homeowners of not renting to blacks and of forcing blacks out of their apartments so that Jews could occupy them. In fact, the Lubavitchers lacked the financial resources to monopolize the housing market in Crown Heights, and the average income of the Lubavitchers in Crown Heights was less than that of their black neighbors. But these truths failed to dislodge the myth common within black circles of vast Jewish wealth. "If the city doesn't control the situation, there is going to be a big, big explosion between blacks and Jews in this community," predicted Segre Demorcy, the black director of a Crown Heights pro-tenants organization.[49] The Lubavitchers "only do housing for the Jewish people," complained Clarence Norman, Sr., the pastor of the First Baptist Church in Crown Heights. "They do a lot of private development. The Hasidim are discriminatory. They're putting up fifty housing units, displacing blacks. . . . They're changing the neighborhood." Norman was not entirely wrong. Jewish real estate entrepreneurs did seek, when possible, to reserve Crown Heights rental units to Lubavitch families.[50]

The most controversial aspect of the struggle over housing was the practice of Lubavitchers knocking on their black neighbors' doors to inquire whether their houses were for sale. These inquiries particularly annoyed the more discreet West Indians, who were unfamiliar with such aggressive behavior. The practice also reinforced the idea that the Lubavitchers wanted to force blacks out of the Lubavitch enclave south of Eastern Parkway. "This type of persistent and unwelcome solicitation of homeowners," Mayor Koch wrote Rabbi Joseph Spielman, chairman of the Crown Heights Community Council, in August 1987, "constitutes a form of harassment that can only lead to increased tension" within Crown Heights.[51] The Lubavitchers, however, did not see this as harassment but simply the way a free market is supposed to operate. They saw nothing wrong in asking their neighbors whether they were interested in selling their homes. If those making the inquiries were polite, where was the harm? If blacks were not interested in selling, they could simply say so.[52] Nor, the Lubavitch claimed, was there any conspiracy to eject blacks from the Lubavitch territory in Crown Heights. Lubavitchers were simply desperate for housing, Rabbi Spielman explained, and "no malice" was intended when they knocked on doors.[53]

There was also competition between the Lubavitch and blacks over public funds provided by antipoverty agencies. This competition was intensified by the emphasis of antipoverty programs on local community participation. In 1977 the Lubavitch had been successful in separating the heart of Lubavitch Crown Heights from Community Planning Board 8, which included the overwhelmingly black areas north of Eastern Parkway, and placing it in Community Planning Board 9, which ran south of Eastern Parkway. Community Planning Board 9 was initially controlled by the Lubavitch, and Rabbi Jacob Goldstein was its chairman. This community board was the conduit for government antipoverty funds, and blacks charged, not without justification, that a disproportionate percentage of these monies was being funneled into the treasuries of Lubavitch-run institutions. By 1991, however, Lubavitch influence on Community Planning Board 9 had dissipated; nonetheless, the creation of the board in 1977 still rankled black activists.[54]

The *perception* of Lubavitch political power, however, was more important than its actual status. "There definitely is a perception in the black community that the Hasidics get preferential treatment," a police spokesman said. "The same perception in the Hasidic community exists, where people think blacks get more police protection."[55] Two weeks after the August 1991 riot, the Reverend Daughtry charged that the Lubavitch were abusing their power and colluding with city hall at the expense of the blacks of Crown Heights. Such collusion was highly unlikely; both the mayor and his first deputy were black, and they would hardly have countenanced such discrimination against their own people. A lengthy article by *Newsday* reporters Michael Powell and Jennifer Preston published two weeks after the riot claimed that, whatever had occurred earlier, by the 1990s blacks in Crown Heights were not being shortchanged in the allocation of government funds for job training, youth and other social programs, subsidized apartments, street paving, and job training.[56]

In the aftermath of the riot, city officials were very sensitive to charges, justified or not, that the Lubavitch were being favored at the expense of blacks. In late December 1991, the city's newspapers published articles that the Dinkins administration had decided for budgetary reasons to funnel funds from the city-administered and federally funded Federal Home Energy Assistance Program through black and Hispanic organizations rather than through Jewish and Irish ones. In Crown Heights the administration of HEAP was moved from the Crown Heights Jewish Community Center on Kingston Avenue (in the heart of the Lubavitch enclave) to the Crown Heights Service Center on Nostrand Avenue (a largely black area).[57]

Powell and Preston believed there was more justification for the charge of favoritism in matters not involving the allocation of funds, such as offering police protection, closing streets temporarily during Jewish holidays and the sabbath, allowing double-parking near Lubavitch headquarters, and sounding a siren on Friday afternoons at the beginning of the sabbath. In response to criticisms that these practices indicated favoritism toward the Hasidim, the police eliminated some of the courtesies it had previously bestowed on the Lubavitch. Among these was the police car and helicopter escort the police had provided on the Friday of Chanukah to Lubavitchers involved in lighting a giant menorah in front of the Plaza Hotel on Fifth Avenue in Manhattan.

For thirteen years the police had provided this escort so that the Lubavitchers could be back in Crown Heights before sunset, which marked the onset of the sabbath. The Reverend Daughtry welcomed the police decision, while the Lubavitchers were outraged and blamed the police for caving in to unjustified assertions of preferential treatment. "Without the ride, I don't know how we're going to do it this year," Rabbi Shmuel Butman said. "We will get stuck in traffic." Other Jews, however, believed the police escort had overstepped the boundary between church and state. They argued that Lubavitchers who resided in Manhattan could light the menorah; or, if Lubavitchers from Crown Heights wanted to light the menorah, they could spend the sabbath in Manhattan.[58]

A more important police matter involved the heavy concentration of police in the area around Eastern Parkway near Lubavitch headquarters. Even before the riot, questions had been raised about whether this disproportion was a sensible use of scarce police resources, and the riot intensified the debate. The Lubavitch believed the anti-Semitism exhibited during the riot demonstrated the need for even greater police protection of Lubavitch institutions and for the closing of streets on days when the Lubavitch congregated on religious holidays. But the riot also increased the complaints concerning supposed police favoritism toward the Lubavitch. On October 17, 1991, Police Commissioner Lee Brown announced an immediate "strategic deployment" that eliminated the heavy concentration of police around 770 Eastern Parkway and increased the number of police foot patrols in other parts of Crown Heights. Brown hoped that this new policy would diminish black complaints of inadequate security and of police favoritism to the Lubavitch.[59]

DEMOCRACY OR PRESSURE POLITICS

The Lubavitchers responded in two ways to the charge that they had benefitted from political favoritism. The first was to deny the accusation. In discussing the way in which his community board had allocated its funds Rabbi Goldstein, chairman of Community Board 9, said: "It's fair the way we dish it out."[60] The Lubavitch denial of favoritism was part of their self-image as residents of Crown Heights. Lubavitchers repeatedly asserted that they were good neighbors of blacks, that Jewish-black relations in Crown Heights were harmonious, and that any troubles in the neighborhood came from outsiders. "Crown Heights," Rabbi Yehuda Krinsky said, "is a model community where white and blacks live in peace together." Black spokesmen, however, were skeptical.[61]

Some Lubavitchers did admit that they had received a disproportionate amount of public funds. But, they claimed, this imbalance was not due to any conspiracy. They had simply worked the political processes more effectively than the blacks. The Lubavitch should be praised and not condemned for understanding how the democratic game is played in New York City. Lubavitchers advised blacks that, instead of complaining about any group's excessive political influence, they should follow the Lubavitch example and become involved in city politics.[62] Such advice was of scant comfort to blacks. Henry Goldschmidt, an anthropologist who wrote his dissertation on Crown Heights, noted that the other residents of Crown Heights, when considering the political success of the Lubavitch, often found it difficult to draw a line "between the hard-won fruits of community organizing and the ill-gotten gains of deceitful politicking."[63]

Unfortunately, the relations between the Lubavitch and the blacks were too formal and distant to overcome their estrangement. Granted, the Lubavitch were by far the least insular of all Hasidic groups. Nevertheless, the religious chasm between the Lubavitch and their neighbors precluded anything but polite and impersonal relationships. Furthermore, black ideologies preaching racial identity and racial unity further thwarted a sense of community that could transcend the racial and religious differences within Crown Heights.

Blacks continually criticized the Lubavitch for wanting, according to the Reverend Clarence Norman, "to live in isolation, but they also want to control the neighborhood. . . . It may be a religious thing for them, but many blacks see it as racial."[64] "People are made to feel like foreigners in this community where they were born and raised," said one black Crown Heights resident. "Just the slightest provocation could start something," predicted Hulbert James, a local black political figure. "It's clear that the housing shortage is at the heart of what's at issue, but it may be a police encounter, a merchant encounter that could trigger a situation." In fact, it would be a traffic accident.[65] The Reverend Heron Sam attributed the attitude of the Lubavitchers toward blacks to a paranoia stemming from their experiences in Eastern Europe. "Now they think they're being persecuted—again by a majority. In this case blacks. They're operating out of a strong case of fear. No wonder they stick to themselves."[66]

BLACK COMPLAINTS

The blacks in Crown Heights continually complained about the insults, real and imagined, they had suffered at the hands of the Lubavitch. "Years ago the Jews who lived here were friendly and we conversed regularly," Dr. Vernal G. Cave said, "but now, only two houses separate my house from some Hasidim property and they don't even nod toward me."[67] "We have discussed the lack of respect with which they relate to us socially, walking six or seven abreast in concrete formation, threatening to sweep us off the common sidewalk," complained the Reverend Heron Sam.[68]

The Reverend Sam was a longtime bitter critic of the Lubavitch, and his comments must be viewed with skepticism. In his 1987 Easter message, he complained that there could be no real Easter celebration as long as there was "racism, aggressive Zionism, [and] the fire-bombing of black homes and detention of blacks by Jews." (He did not provide any evidence that Jews had firebombed black homes or detained blacks.) According to Sam, the buying up of property in Crown Heights by the Lubavitchers was "an aggressive Zionist expansionist policy" in the diaspora and resembled what Israeli settlers were doing in the occupied lands on the West Bank of the Jordan River. The Lubavitch Zionists of Crown Heights, he averred, sought to displace all blacks who lived within a half-mile radius of 770 Eastern Parkway. In the spring of 1987, Sam was battling the Lubavitch over who would build a housing project at the corner of Montgomery Street and New York Avenue, one of the last sites in Crown Heights available for development.[69]

Sam was not the only black cleric who spoke of Jews as imperialists. The Reverend Al Sharpton claimed the Lubavitchers were "dismissive and contemptuous of blacks," and he described the Lubavitch community in Crown Heights as "a Fort Apache in the black ghetto."[70] Protestant ministers in Crown Heights were among the bitterest critics of the Lubavitch community. Their churches were often social as well as religious institutions, and they competed with the Lubavitch community over public monies allocated for housing, job counseling, and other social services within Crown Heights. In addition, many of the ministers and much of the membership of these churches had emigrated from West Indian islands unfamiliar with the American religious paradigm of "Protestant-Catholic-Jew," and they were accustomed to viewing Jews and Judaism as marginal phenomena. They also had a welter of anti-Semitic notions derived from Christianity to explain their problems with the Lubavitchers.

Despite the hostility of many of their black neighbors, the Lubavitch had not taken the easy way out by relocating en masse as had the Bobov Hasidim, a group originally established in southern Poland. Some of its remnants had settled in Brooklyn after World War II. Over the opposition of Schneerson, the Bobovers had left Crown Heights in 1968 for Boro Park, an Orthodox Jewish Brooklyn neighborhood several miles to the southwest. Schneerson also tried without success to dissuade other Jews, Orthodox and non-Orthodox alike, from leaving Crown Heights. When criticized by civil rights supporters for not participating in the civil rights marches in the South during the 1960s, the Lubavitch responded that while it was true that they did not go to Selma, Alabama, neither did they go to Scarsdale or Nassau County. Crown Heights remained one of the very few American neighborhoods where a large and growing number of Jews lived as a minority side by side with blacks. The Lubavitch Hasidim believed that they, and not the leaders of the Jewish defense agencies, safely ensconced in lily-white suburban neighborhoods, were living on the civil rights frontier and contributing to resolving America's race problem. They had put their own lives on the line by deciding to live in a black-majority community, and they had even attracted black converts.[71]

Most amazing of all, Lubavitch Hasidim were moving *into* Crown Heights, contradicting the conventional wisdom regarding black-Jewish relations. When blacks moved into a Jewish neighborhood, the Jews supposedly fled. But not so in Crown Heights. Where else were Jews choosing to live in the inner city where they were greatly outnumbered by blacks? Where else were Jews relocating to a neighborhood that exhibited the typical maladies of the inner city: drug addiction, alcoholism, homicide, crime, infant mortality, public welfare, and female-headed families?[72] Crown Heights, one Orthodox Jew wrote, "represents a kind of integration which has rarely occurred in this country."[73]

Crown Heights, where Jews and blacks lived together in roughly similar economic circumstances, was a test case for the theory that contact between groups diminishes hostility. In Crown Heights, however, the continual contact between blacks and Jews on the street, in stores, and on the subway did not lessen the tensions between the two groups. The preconceptions that blacks and Jews had of one another were more important than these superficial contacts.

The assumption of liberal Jews that Jews and blacks were natural allies in the struggle against prejudice and poverty was challenged during the Crown Heights riot by blacks claiming that the Lubavitchers were hostile to black interests. The riot was the latest in a series of events in New York City during the previous quarter of a century that had pitted Jews against blacks. From the conflicts over the police civilian review board and school decentralization in the late 1960s; to the struggle over public housing in Forest Hills, Queens, and the integration of schools in Canarsie, Brooklyn, in the 1970s; and then through the 1988 presidential campaign of Jesse Jackson (when Ed Koch said that a Jew would have to be "crazy" to support Jesse Jackson), the politics of the city's Jews and blacks often diverged. Blacks, who had fewer illusions regarding the black-Jewish political entente, increasingly viewed Jews less as natural political allies than as privileged whites with a different political agenda.

Liberal Jews, however, were often unable to accept this new political reality and tended to downplay the anti-Semitism within the black community.[74] Liberals lived in a time warp of the 1960s that evoked memories of the philosophy of nonviolence, love, and transracial political alliances espoused by their favorite black, Martin Luther King, Jr. By 1991, however, King had been dead for twenty-three years, and the politics of racial identity had become prominent in New York City politics.[75] And nowhere more prominent than in Crown Heights. In 1978, thirteen years before the riot, Dorothy Rabinowitz had noted that in no other section of the city "have intergroup rivalries been more intense, the contest for political power more vividly defined" than in Crown Heights.[76] And the contest had only intensified since then.

THE WEST INDIANS

The distinction between the Lubavitchers and blacks was not the only significant demographic difference within Crown Heights. Another was between African Americans and Caribbean blacks. Despite their shared skin color and often similar political objectives, there were social differences between the two groups. Political competition between Caribbeans and African Americans intensified tensions between the two groups, with Caribbeans complaining that they did not receive the political offices and other favors that their numbers warranted. These strains came to the fore in the wake of the riot.

African American professionals and businessmen had lived in Crown Heights for decades, but beginning in the 1950s their numbers were dwarfed by the arrival of poorer families, many of whom were on welfare and exhibited the lifestyle associated with the urban underclass. This influx threatened not only the Lubavitch but also the West Indians, who viewed themselves as part of an aspiring middle class, and who respected the norms of behavior associated with being middle-class. The West Indians were more socially and economically upwardly mobile than the African Americans of Crown Heights, their rate of home ownership was much higher, and they had higher educational goals for their children. Conscious of the stigma in America associated with being black, West Indians sought to distinguish themselves from African Americans by zealously holding on to a distinctive West Indian ethnic identity. "Insofar as West Indian blacks are viewed in a more favorable light than are African Americans," the demographers Kyle D. Crowder and Lucky M. Tedrow wrote, "maintaining ethnic distinctiveness may lessen the sting of racism and provide a measure of protection against relegation to America's lowest social position."[77]

Political styles also separated Caribbean blacks from African Americans. The Caribbeans came from societies in which blacks were in the majority and controlled the levers of power. They were not accustomed to thinking of themselves as a victimized minority; neither had they been directly influenced by the American civil rights movement with its moralism, flamboyant rhetoric, protest marches, and nonnegotiable demands. For them, politics was an instrument for personal and group advancement involving compromise and negotiation. It was not an arena for the expression of resentments and the pursuit of utopian social and economic change. The West Indians of Crown Heights were willing to be represented in the New York State Senate by Marty Markowitz, as long as he represented their interests. In 1985, many West Indians, to the dismay of African Americans, voted for Mayor Ed Koch when he ran for reelection against an African American. Local African American politicians complained that West Indian ethnic politics stemmed from ethnic "tribalism" and white manipulation, thus undercutting black unity.[78]

In the wake of the 1991 riot, the West Indian leadership feared the general public would perceive the West Indian population as violent, shiftless, and criminally inclined; they sought to distance themselves from African Americans, whom they believed were responsible for the riot. Prior to 1991 they had resisted the efforts of black radicals to draw West Indians into a coalition revolving around racial resentments, and this dissociation continued after the riot. West Indians leaders resisted the attempt of black radicals to capitalize on the death of Gavin Cato, and they opposed the participation of Al Sharpton and Sonny Carson at Cato's funeral.

The most visible manifestation of the desire of West Indians to distance themselves from African Americans occurred on September 2, 1991 at the West Indian Labor Day parade. For years the Lubavitch had angered the West Indians by seeking to reroute the parade away from 770 Eastern Parkway. The Lubavitch considered it inappropriate that the parade, with its lascivious costumes and boisterous onlookers, should march in front of what they considered to be the most sacred center of world Jewry. The West Indians believed, however, that the attempts to reroute the parade exhibited an insensitivity toward West Indian culture and ceremony and an arrogance and insularity typical of the Lubavitch.[79]

The riot of 1991 gave further reason to the Lubavitch to seek to cancel or reroute that year's parade. They feared it would incite further acts of anti-Semitism, and they sought an injunction preventing it from taking place along Eastern Parkway. In late August 1991 the Lubavitch wisely dropped these legal efforts after receiving assurances from city and state officials and the parade's organizers that everything possible would be done to prevent violence. The slogan for the 1991 parade was "Peace on the Parkway."[80]

Twenty-two hundred police officers were assigned to the parade area to keep the peace (seven hundred and fifty more than usual), and they were largely successful. Although one man died in a scuffle and a police car was set afire after the parade, there were no attacks on Lubavitchers or on other whites. Fear of violence had discouraged many people from attending the parade. It attracted only about seven hundred thousand marchers and spectators, well below the one million persons it normally drew. The only discordant note during the parade was a group of about two dozen young blacks in front of Lubavitch headquarters who shouted anti-Semitic slogans and held signs, one of which proclaimed, "If it's kosher, don't buy it."[81] Bottles and rocks were also thrown at the police guarding the Lubavitch headquarters on Eastern Parkway, and two persons were arrested.[82]

Carlos Lezama, the longtime president of the West Indian American Day Carnival Association, had invited several prominent Lubavitch figures, including Shmuel Butman, and Robert Bush, a member of the faculty at the Hofstra University Law School and a legal adviser to the Lubavitch community, to march in the front of the parade alongside Mayor Dinkins and black West Indian leaders. (One of the rabbis invited to march was Joseph Spielman, two of whose sons were in the car driven by Yosef Lifsh that struck Gavin Cato.)[83] An audience of revelers cheered Butman when he told them that he had marched in a spirit of "brotherhood, camaraderie, friendship and peace. We want the peace that we started today to continue."[84] A joke told at the parade revealed the friendly attitude of the West Indians toward the Lubavitch. "Did you hear what happened to Rabbi Butman?" "No, I heard everything was quiet at Carnival." "Yes, the Rabbi won the best costume award."[85]

The West Indians' invitation to the Lubavitch did not go unnoticed. Newspaper reports suggested that the gesture was simply a response to the request of the governor and the mayor that they reach out to the Lubavitch community. It was more than that, however. West Indian leaders believed the riot had besmirched the good name of the West Indian community, and they wished to restore normal relations with the Lubavitchers. Carlos Lezama wrote Robert Bush a month after the parade that the inclusion of representatives of the Lubavitch community "has opened the road for dialogue and friendly association among our people, which I intend to pursue, and in which I hope, dear Professor, you will continue to join me."[86]

The presence of the Lubavitch at the parade took on symbolic importance for black radicals. Not surprisingly, the *Amsterdam News* of September 7, 1991, criticized the overtures to the Lubavitch community. "Activist Leaders Not Impressed by Show of Black/Jewish Unity: They Vow to Continue Protests in Crown Hts," ran the headline. The article quoted the Reverend Daughtry's negative take on the West Indian–Lubavitch relationship. "We have been down this road before," he said, and "it is a divide-and-conquer tactic being played out to patch up things that are really bad under the surface and give an impression that peace has come." Daughtry then proceeded to insult the West Indian leadership for their overtures to the Hasidim. "Marching, parading, grinning and skinning do not get to the issue of favoritism and preferential treatment for Hasidic Jews in Brooklyn's Crown Heights and Williamsburg communities."[87] The rabble-rouser Sonny Carson agreed. He declared that the West Indian parade was "the last straw" for him and that he planned to move out of the city. "I thought it was a shame before God that people had the audacity to party on Eastern Parkway on the same facility where the boy was killed," he said.[88] Several persons called in to the city's talk-radio shows offering to help pay for Carson's moving expenses. Carson did not take them up on their offer.

West Indian leaders were deeply offended by the words of Daughtry and Carson and accused them of disrespecting West Indians. They particularly resented Daughtry's comments regarding "grinning and skinning." Where did African Americans get the nerve "to tell the Caribbean community . . . how best to conduct struggles for justice?" the *Caribe News* asked. Roy Hastrick, president of the Caribbean-American Chamber of Commerce and Industry, said that Caribbeans were not merely "party people. . . . We do not just 'grin and skin.' . . . We are a serious people."[89]

The attempts by the West Indian leadership to dissociate their community from the riot was symptomatic of the ambivalence of West Indians regarding their identity and place in American society. Were they primarily West Indian ethnics or blacks, they wondered? Did the West Indian middle class share an identity with the black underclass? How West Indians answered that question influenced their understanding of the riot.[90] The West Indian leadership wished to believe that young West Indians had not been involved in the Crown Heights riot. Blame, rather, rested on an African American underclass residing in the projects outside of Crown Heights, who had been spurred on by outside agitators such as Sharpton and Carson. The West Indian families were supposedly too stable and the West Indian community too conservative to spawn a hoodlum element. In fact, tensions between West Indians and Lubavitchers were long-standing; and many of those arrested during the riot were young, American-born West Indians.[91]

The riot revealed a growing generation gap between upwardly mobile West Indians, many of whom were immigrants who had come to New York after the passage of the 1965 immigration reform act and who saw themselves as West Indians, and their increasingly disaffected and radicalized children, who often thought of themselves less as West Indians than as blacks.[92] These young West Indians did not share the elders' disdain toward the black underclass; and they were attracted to the "repertoire of violent reprisals, collective allocation of blame, and communal vengeance" and to the American-style black separatism popular among lower-class black males.[93] Philip Kasinitz, a leading authority on the West Indians of New York City and the author of *Caribbean New York,* emphasized the concerns of West Indian elders regarding their children. "Many Caribbean parents," he wrote, were "shocked at what their children were becoming or—as they see it—what being black has done to their children. 'You're becoming American,' is how disapproving parents scold their kids."[94] The involvement of West Indian youths in the riot only intensified these apprehensions.

The riot gave rise to other worries as well. Residents throughout the city feared that the riot portended a general breakdown of law and order and the unraveling of the city's social structure. Because of their history, Jews were particularly concerned that any dissolution of the social compact would leave them vulnerable to the mob. The riot occurred at a difficult time in the city's history. The city's fiscal situation was then bleak because of a downturn in the securities industry, the engine that drove the city's economy, and this crisis weakened the city's ability to provide basic services, including police and fire protection. These social and economic anxieties for the city's future inevitably found expression in politics.

Notes

1. Henry Goldschmidt, "Peoples Apart: Race, Religion and Other Jewish Differences in Crown Heights" (Ph.D. diss., University of California at Santa Cruz, 2000), 106–108; Eli Lederhendler, *New York Jews and the Decline of Urban Ethnicity, 1950–1970* (Syracuse, N.Y.: University of Syracuse Press, 2001), 80–81; Richard H. Girgenti, *A Report to the Governor on the Disturbances in Crown Heights*, vol. 1, *An Assessment of the City's Preparedness and Response to Civil Disorder* (Albany, N.Y.: New York State Division of Criminal Justice Services, 1993), 40–41.
2. Toby Sanchez, *The Crown Heights Neighborhood Profile* (Brooklyn: Brooklyn In Touch Information Center, 1987), 4–5; Jerome R. Mintz, *Hasidic People: A Place in the New World* (Cambridge, Mass.: Harvard University Press, 1992), 140–41.
3. Louis Winnick, *New People in Old Neighborhoods: The Role of New Immigrants in Rejuvenating New York's Communities* (New York: Russell Sage Foundation, 1990), 30.
4. Philip Kasinitz, *Caribbean New York: Black Immigrants and the Politics of Race* (Ithaca, N.Y.: Cornell University Press, 1992), 54–55.
5. Ibid., 55–56.
6. Winnick, *New People in Old Neighborhoods*, 141–42.
7. Frederick M. Binder and David M. Reimers, *All the Nations Under Heaven: An Ethnic and Racial History of New York City* (New York: Columbia University Press, 1995), 229–30; George Vecsey, "In Crown Heights, an Uncertain Alliance Is Put to the Test," *New York Times*, July 24, 1978; Sheila Rule, "An Air of Aloofness Covers Tensions in Crown Heights," *New York Times*, June 18, 1979. For statistics regarding the flow of West Indians into Crown Heights during the 1980s, see Joseph J. Salvo and Ronald J. Ortiz, *The Newest New Yorkers: An Analysis of Immigration into New York City During the 1980s* (New York: Department of City Planning of New York City, 1992), 100, 199, 207.
8. Goldschmidt, "Peoples Apart," 108.
9. Ibid., 109.
10. Ibid., 111–15; Sanchez, *Crown Heights Neighborhood Profile*, 4.
11. Lederhendler, *New York Jews*, 165.
12. Goldschmidt, "Peoples Apart," 11–12, 112–13.
13. Samuel C. Heilman, "Orthodox Jews, the City and the Suburb," in *People of the City: Jews and the Urban Challenge*, ed. Ezra Mendelson, *Studies in Contemporary Jewry*, vol. 15 (New York: Oxford University Press, 1999), 26–27.

14. Edward Hoffman, *Despite All Odds: The Story of Lubavitch* (New York: Simon and Schuster, 1991), 146–48. Schneerson also opposed the trading of land for peace by the government of Israel.
15. Ari L. Goldman, "Hasidic Group Expands Amid Debate on Future," *New York Times,* September 5, 1988.
16. Mintz, *Hasidic People,* 148–50, 385; Tom Robbins, "Tales of Crown Heights: The Fruits of Harassment," *City Limits* 6 (December 1981): 12–18.
17. Mervyn Rothstein, "New Hotel Is a Symbol of Change in Brooklyn," *New York Times,* January 28, 1985.
18. Kenneth S. Stern, *Crown Heights: A Case Study in Anti-Semitism and Community Relations* (New York: American Jewish Committee, 1991), 11.
19. *New York Times,* September 28, 1975; Robert McG. Thomas, Jr., "'Heil Hitler' Disrupts Rites for Jew Slain in Holdup," *New York Times,* September 30, 1975; Leslie Maitland, "A Guarded Racial Peace Follows Brooklyn Killing," *New York Times,* October 2, 1975.
20. *New York Times,* July 21, 1978; For the trial of the two men accused of the beating of Rhodes, see Peter Kihss, "Two Rabbis Protest 'Smearing' at Trial," *New York Times,* February 29, 1980.
21. Dorothy Rabinowitz, "Blacks, Jews, and New York Politics," *Commentary* 66 (November 1978): 47.
22. Mintz, *Hasidic People,* 147; Keith Moore, Martin Gottlieb, and Thomas Collins, "Protest Is Peaceful," *New York Post,* July 17, 1978; Peter Kihss, "2,000 Assail Police at Black Rally as Off-Duty Officers Meet Nearby," *New York Times,* July 17, 1978.
23. Peter Noel, "Crown Heights Burning: Rage, Race, and the Politics of Resistance," *Village Voice* 36 (September 3, 1991), 39.
24. Sheila Rule, "Some Blacks and Jews Reach Pact on End to Crown Heights Tensions," *New York Times,* May 9, 1979.
25. Robbery and not race or anti-Semitism was the apparent motive in the murder of Okunov. Lubavitchers criticized Mayor Koch for not attending Okunov's funeral. Sheila Rule, "Hasidic Rabbi Shot Dead on Crown Heights Street," *New York Times,* October 26, 1979; Rule, "Black and Hasidic Coalition Planning a 'War on Crime,'" *New York Times,* October 27, 1979.
26. Noel, "Crown Heights Burning," 38; Lydia Chavez, "Racial Tensions Persist in Crown Heights," *New York Times,* April 10, 1987; Jon Kalish, "Crown Heights Simmers with Racial Tensions," *Sunday Democrat and Chronicle* (Rochester, N.Y.), January 31, 1988.
27. Scott Minerbrook and Miriam Horn, "Side by Side, Apart," *U.S. News and World Report* 111 (November 4, 1991): 52.
28. Mintz, *Hasidic People,* 142–45, 151, 242–46; Howard W. French, "Black Demonstrators March Through Hasidic Area," *New York Times,* April 12, 1987; T. J. Collins, "Blacks March to Protest Influence of Hasidic Group,"

Newsday, April 12, 1987; Merle English and Charles Moses, "Fight Prompts Hasidic Protest," *Newsday,* January 19, 1988; Arnold Fine, "Fear and Tension in Wake of Crown Heights Mugging," *Jewish Press,* March 10–16, 1989.

29. Alison Mitchell, "Suspect in Crown Heights Killing Was Released from Prison in October," *New York Times,* February 12, 1992. For the biography of Phyllis and Dennis Lapine, see N. R. Kleinfield, "From Texas to Crown Heights: A Journey of Love and Religion," *New York Times,* February 9, 1992.
30. Ari L. Goldman, "Angry Protests Follow Killing in Brooklyn," *New York Times,* February 7, 1992.
31. Kenneth Meeks, "Caution Urged After Arrest of Haitian in Crown Heights Killing," *Amsterdam News,* February 15, 1992; Kenneth Meeks, "Catholic Clergy Voice Concerns Over Tensions in Crown Heights," *New York Amsterdam News,* February 29, 1992.
32. Alison Mitchell, "An Uneasy Calm in Crown Heights," *New York Times,* February 8, 1992. In an editorial titled "New Outrage in Crown Heights," the *New York Post* severely criticized Dinkins for not attending the Lapine funeral (February 11, 1992).
33. Stewart Ain, "Community Cooperation Cited in Crown Heights Arrest," *Jewish Week,* February 14–20, 1992.
34. Mintz, *Hasidic People,* 346–47; Alison Mitchell, "An Uneasy Calm in Crown Heights," *New York Times,* February 8, 1992; James Barron, "Suspect Is Arrested in Woman's Killing in Crown Heights," *New York Times,* February 11, 1992; Arnold H. Lubasch, "Man Guilty of Murder of Woman in Brooklyn," *New York Times,* November 25, 1992; Murray Kempton, "A Verdict That Transcends Color," *Newsday,* November 25, 1992.
35. James Bennet, "Jewish Couple Is Beaten in Brooklyn Bias Incident," *New York Times,* February 8, 1992.
36. Steven Lee Myers, "Police Classify Attack on Bus as a Bias Case," *New York Times,* February 24, 1992.
37. For Nimmons's version of the events of December 1, 1992, see Mike McAlary, "Nimmons: They Would Have Killed Me," *New York Post,* December 15, 1992.
38. "Statement by Crown Heights Jewish Community Council Regarding Incident in Crown Heights," December 2, 1992, Robert A. Bush Papers, Brooklyn, New York; "Statement of Mayor Dinkins Regarding Bias Incident in Crown Heights Section of Brooklyn," December 1, 1992, Bush Papers; Basha Majerczyk, "Crown Heights Beating Victim May Be Compelled to Provide Palm Print," *Algemeiner Journal,* December 11, 1992; Rocco Parascandola et al., "Hasids Beat Black Man in Crown Heights," *New York Post,* December 2, 1992; Mary B. W. Tabor, "Black Is Victim of Beating by Hasidim in Crown Heights," *New York Times,* December 2, 1993; *New York Times,* December 4, 1992. Bob Liff, "Dinkins Gets Warning from Jewish Allies," *Newsday,* December 4, 1992.

39. Laurie Goodstein, "Dinkins Caught in Racial Cross-Fire," *Washington Post*, December 6, 1992; *Forward*, December 4, 1992; *New York Post*, December 3, 1992; Stewart Ain, "Violence Hounds Dinkins' Pleas for 'Healing,'" *Jewish Week*, December 4–10, 1992; Sidney Zion, "Mayor Spurs Unlikely Allies: Jews and Jews," *New York Observer*, December 14, 1992.
40. Joseph P. Fried, "Black Man Beaten in Crown Heights Is Missing," *New York Times*, December 10, 1992; Fried, "A Dismissal in an Attack in Brooklyn," *New York Times*, May 4, 1993.
41. Vinette K. Price, "Was Crown Heights Beating Victim 'Betrayed' by Hasidim?" *Amsterdam News*, December 12, 1992.
42. Mitchell, "Dinkins Faces New Criticism"; Mary B. W. Tabor, "Hasidim May Cooperate in Crown Heights Inquiry," *New York Times*, December 9, 1992; Ralph Blumenthal, "Crown Hts. Beating Described in 2 Sharply Different Ways," *New York Times*, December 5, 1992; Vivienne Walt et al., "Top Cop Defends the Case," *Newsday*, December 4, 1992.
43. Joyce Purnick, "Crown Heights, One Year Later," *New York* 12 (July 2, 1979): 8–9.
44. *New York Times*, July 10, 1977.
45. *Daily News Bulletin*, July 12, 1977, Jewish Telegraph Agency.
46. Norman election flier in Jewish Community Relations Council Papers, New York City.
47. Goldschmidt, "Peoples Apart," 114–15, 144; Hoffman, *Despite All Odds*, 145–46; Bob Liff, "A Leader Worldly, Mystical," *Newsday*, August 25, 1991.
48. James Lardner and Thomas Reppetto, *NYPD: A City and Its Police* (New York: Henry Holt, 2000), 30; Mintz, *Hasidic People*, 328. The police escort to the Lubavitch cemetery in Queens was eliminated after the 1991 riot.
49. Merle English, "Crown Heights: Harassment or Desperation?" *Newsday*, July 19, 1987. By the 1980s, Crown Heights was considered a poor neighborhood. A higher percentage of its residents were receiving public assistance than the average Brooklyn neighborhood, and its population was concentrated in low-income occupations. Sanchez, *Crown Heights Neighborhood Profile*, 33–38.
50. Mintz, *Hasidic People*, 238; Bib Liff, "Tug-of-War for House and Home," *Newsday*, August 25, 1991.
51. Mintz, *Hasidic People*, 329.
52. Noel, "Crown Heights Burning," 39.
53. English, "Crown Heights: Harassment or Desperation?"
54. Interview with Dr. Vernal G. Cave, "How the 'New' Crown Heights Was Born," *City Sun*, August 28–September 3, 1991; Mintz, *Hasidic People*, 144–46.
55. Mitch Gelman and Pamela Newkirk, "Favoritism Is the Perception," *Newsday*, September 8, 1991.

56. Michael Powell and Jennifer Preston, "Little Proof Inequity Persists," *Newsday,* September 8, 1991; Ruth Landa, "Access Battle in Crown Hts.: Blacks, Hasidim and the Streets," *Daily News,* October 17, 1991. See also Pamela Newkirk, "Black Progress Reduces Charges of Favoritism," *Newsday,* July 19, 1993, for further evidence that the Lubavitch were not receiving a disproportionate share of government funds.
57. Bob Liff, "Dinkins Shifts Grant Program Administration: Says Too Few Minorities Aided," *Newsday,* December 28, 1991; James C. McKinley, "New York Shifts Heating Subsidies," *New York Times,* December 28, 1991.
58. While the police provided the helicopter, the Lubavitchers reimbursed the city for the expense. Wendell Jamieson, "Cops Nix Annual Menorah Dash," *Newsday,* November 2, 1991; Ari L. Goldman, "Police End Annual Escort of Hasidim for Hanukkah," *New York Times,* November 5, 1991.
59. Robert Polner, "Lee: Heavy Patrols for Hasidim Over," *Daily News,* October 18, 1991.
60. Powell and Preston, "Little Proof Inequity Persists."
61. "An Eye for an Eye," *Time* 18 (September 9, 1991): 20.
62. William J. Kephart and William W. Zellner, *Extraordinary Groups: An Examination of Unconventional Life-Styles* (New York: St. Martin's, 1994), 183.
63. Goldschmidt, "Peoples Apart," 131.
64. Jeffrey Goldberg, "Culture Clash Keeps Crown Heights Queasy," *Forward,* August 28, 1992.
65. English, "Crown Heights: Harassment or Desperation?"
66. Purnick, "Crown Heights, One Year Later," 9.
67. Mintz, *Hasidic People,* 146–47.
68. Vinette K. Pryce, "A Crown Heights Priest Recounts the History of Black/Hasidic Relations," *Amsterdam News,*" August 31, 1991. For evidence of the Reverend Sam's anti-Semitism, see David M. Pollock, "Where Was the Jewish Community?" *Jewish World,* September 13–19, 1991.
69. The Reverend Heron A. Sam, 1987 Easter Message, "Crown Heights, 1987 File," JCRC Papers. For Sam's concern with real estate, see Mintz, *Hasidic People,* 148.
70. Al Sharpton and Anthony Walton, *Go and Tell Pharaoh: The Autobiography of Al Sharpton* (New York: Doubleday, 1996), 196–97.
71. Hoffman, *Despite All Odds,* 146.
72. Sanchez, *Crown Heights Neighborhood Profile,* 16–17, 33–38.
73. Marvin Schick, "Crown Heights: More and Less than Meets the Eye," *Jewish World,* December 11–17, 1992.
74. Ben Halpern, *Jews and Blacks: The Classic American Minorities* (New York: Herder and Herder, 1971), 33–34, 130–31.
75. Mark Featherman, "Death of a Dream," *Forward,* September 20, 1991; Jerald E. Podair, *The Failure to "See": Jews, Blacks, and the Ocean Hill-Brownsville Con-*

troversy, 1968 (New York: American Jewish Committee, 1992), 6. "New Yorkers no longer vote their ethnicity," the historian Richard Wade wrote, "They vote their race." Richard Goldstein, "The Politics of Hate: Crown Heights and the Future of New York," *Village Voice* 37 (December 15, 1992), 12.

76. Dorothy Rabinowitz, "Blacks, Jews, and New York Politics," 44–45. See also Peter G. Sinden, "Anti-Semitism and the Black Power Movement," *Ethnicity* 7 (1980): 34–46.

77. Kyle D. Crowder and Lucky M. Tedrow, "West Indians and the Residential Landscape of New York," in *Islands in the City: West Indian Migration in New York*, ed. Nancy Forner (Berkeley and Los Angeles: University of California Press, 2001), 112. For recognition by one black of the split between African Americans and Caribbean Americans, see Andrew W. Cooper, "The Two Nations of Crown Heights," *New York Times*, January 6, 1993.

78. Philip Kasinetz, *Caribbean New York: Black Immigrants and the Politics of Race* (Ithaca, N.Y.: Cornell University Press, 1992), 154–57, 235–38.

79. For West Indian anger over Lubavitch opposition to the parade, see Nick Chiles, "Culture of Pride, Energy," *Newsday*, August 25, 1991.

80. Merle English, "Caribbean Parade Causes 'Concern,'" *Newsday*, August 29, 1991; Paul Schwartzman, "B'klyn Jews Fear Carib Fest Violence," *New York Post*, August 30, 1991; Andrew L. Yarrow, "Brooklyn Prepares, and Braces for a Parade," *New York Times*, August 30, 1991; John Kifner, "Hasidim Won't Try to Step a West Indian Celebration," *New York Times*, August 30, 1991; Robert Polner, "Beating Peace Drum," *Daily News*, September 2, 1991; Jonathan Rieder, "Crown of Thorns," *New Republic* 205 (October 14, 1991): 28–29. In 1994 the Lubavitch community attempted to get the West Indian parade moved back one day because the Jewish New Year began at sundown on Labor Day. The West Indians firmly resisted this request.

81. John Kifner, "In Brooklyn, Steel Drums and a Truce," *New York Times*, September 3, 1991; Ari L. Goldman, "Anxiously, Brooklyn Is Awaiting Holy Days," *New York Times*, September 7, 1991; Stern, *Crown Heights*, 5.

82. Naadu I. Blankson, "Dinkins, Other Leaders Praise Peaceful, Healing Event," *Amsterdam News*, September 9, 1991.

83. According to Jerome Mintz, the six Lubavitchers wore bulletproof vests under their suit jackets. Mintz, *Hasidic People*, 339.

84. Merle English and Manuel Perez-Rivas, "Dinkins, Rabbis Lead Festival with Theme of Camaraderie," *Newsday*, September 3, 1991; Miguel Garcilazo, Paul Schwartzman, and Michael Shain, "No Rain on Parade in Crown Heights," *New York Post*, September 3, 1991.

85. Jonathan Rieder, "The Tribes of Brooklyn: Race, Class and Ethnicity in the Crown Heights Riots," in *The Tribal Basis of American Life: Racial, Religious, and Ethnic Groups in Conflict*, ed. Murray Friedman and Nancy Isserman (Westport, Conn.: Praeger, 1998), 77–78.

86. David Gonzalez, "Hasidim Say They'll Join Parade Line: Good-Will Gesture in Crown Heights," *New York Times,* September 2, 1991; Carlos Lezama to Robert Bush, October 4, 1991, Bush Papers.
87. J. Zamgba Browne, "Activist Leaders Not Impressed by Show of Black/Jewish Unity: They Vow to Continue Protests in Crown Hts.," *Amsterdam News,* September 7, 1991.
88. William Douglas, "Sonny Got Blue," *Newsday,* September 4, 1991.
89. *New York Carib News,* September 17, 1991. See also Jonathan Rieder, "Reflections on Crown Heights: Interpretive Dilemmas and Black-Jewish Conflict," in *Anti-Semitism in America Today,* ed. Jerome A. Chanes (New York: Birch Lane Press, 1995), 360–61; Rieder, "Tribes of Brooklyn," 70–71.
90. Rieder, "Reflections on Crown Heights," 359; Kasinitz, *Caribbean New York,* 35–36, 234–35.
91. Rieder, "Reflections on Crown Heights," 363; Kasinitz, *Caribbean New York,* xiii.
92. Peter Noel, "Crown Heights Burning: Rage, Race, and the Politics of Resistance," *Village Voice* 36 (September 3, 1991), 37–38.
93. Rieder, "Tribes of Brooklyn," 66.
94. Kasinitz quoted in Rieder, "The Tribes of Brooklyn," 67.

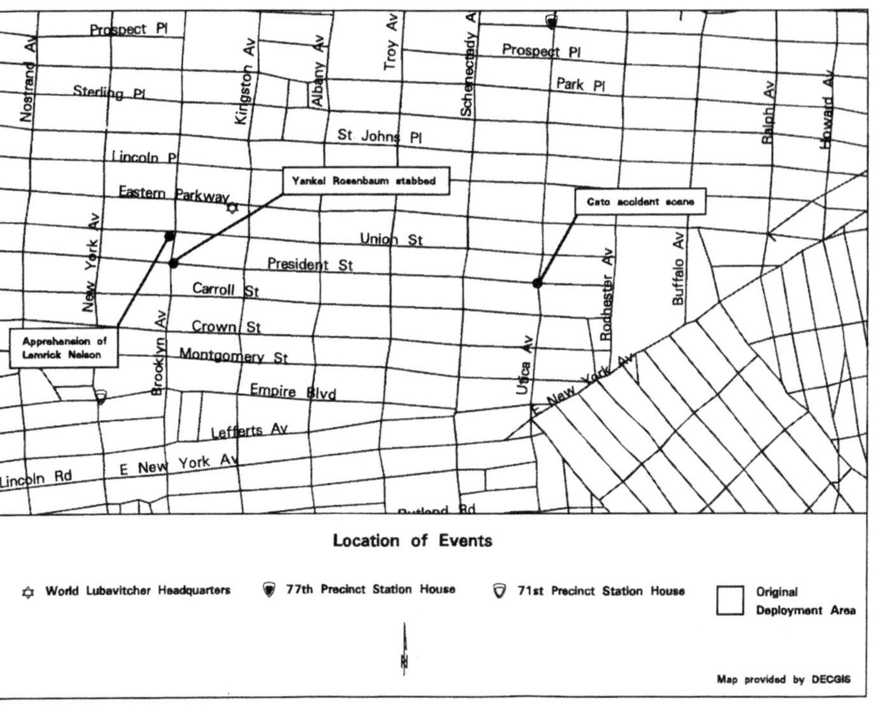

The location of events on the evening of August 19, 1991, in Crown Heights. Map by the New York State Department of Environmental Conservation, reprinted from *A Report to the Governor on the Disturbances in Crown Heights,* as copyrighted by the New York State Division of Criminal Justice Services. Permission to use this map was granted by the Division of Criminal Justice Services.

An automobile accident involving a car accompanying Rabbi Menachem Mendel Schneerson, spiritual head of the Lubavitch community of Crown Heights, set off three days of rioting.

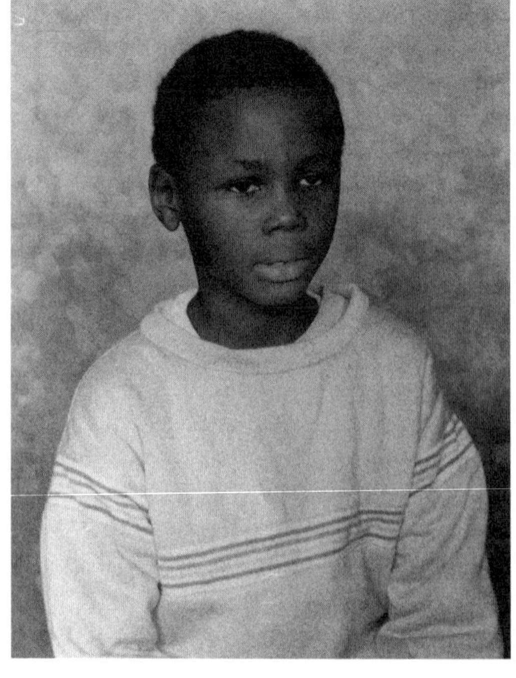

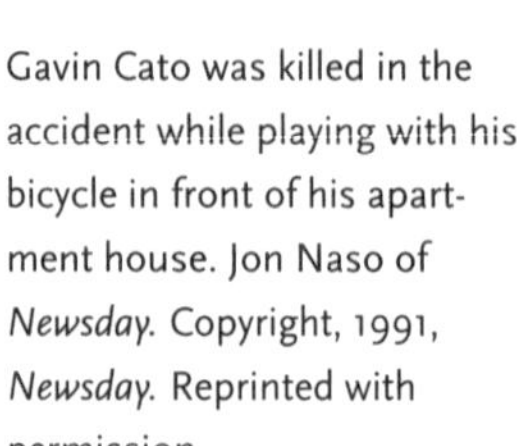

Gavin Cato was killed in the accident while playing with his bicycle in front of his apartment house. Jon Naso of *Newsday*. Copyright, 1991, *Newsday*. Reprinted with permission.

The Cato apartment house near the intersection of President Street and Utica Avenue. Author's photograph.

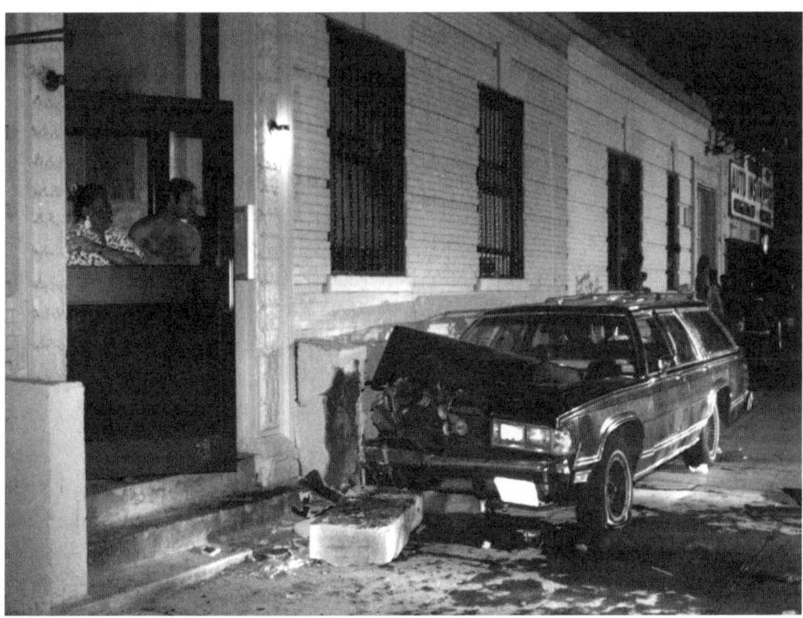

The damaged Mercury station wagon driven by Yosef Lifsh, which struck Gavin Cato. John Paraskevas of *Newsday*. Copyright, 1991, *Newsday*. Reprinted with permission.

Yankel Rosenbaum, an Australian doctoral candidate in history, was murdered several hours after the automobile accident. Copyright, 1991, *Newsday.* Reprinted with permission.

The corner of President Street and Brooklyn Avenue where Yankel Rosenbaum was attacked. Author's photograph.

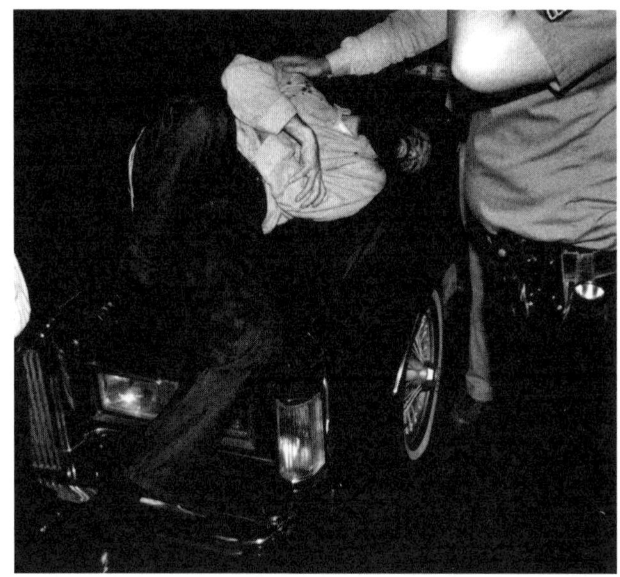

Yankel Rosenbaum lying on the hood of a car shortly after being stabbed. John Paraskevas of *Newsday*. Copyright, 1991, *Newsday*. Reprinted with permission.

Part of the crowd accompanying the casket of Yankel Rosenbaum as it was carried through Crown Heights before being flown to Australia. N.Y. *Daily News*. Copyright by Daily News L.P.

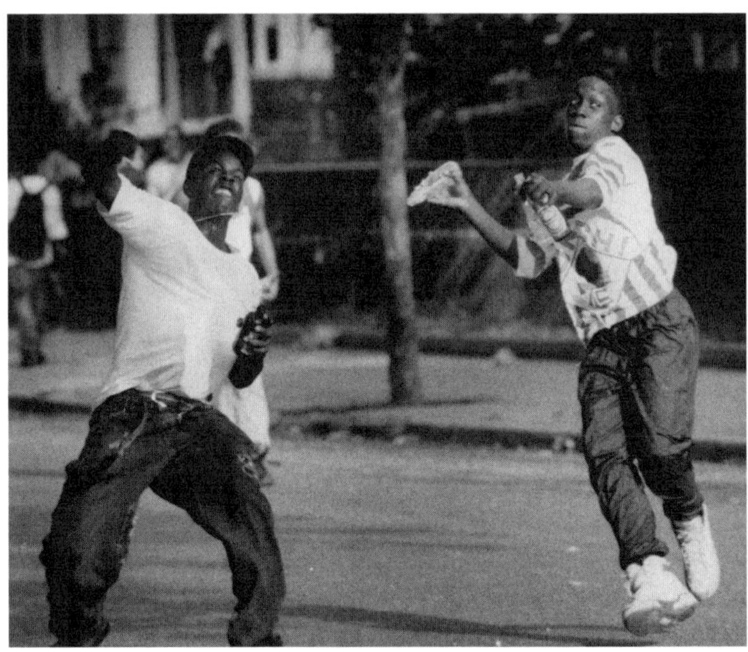

While Mayor David Dinkins pleaded for peace on Wednesday, August 21, angry young blacks hurled bottles and rocks at Jews and other whites. John Paraskevas of *Newsday*. Copyright, 1991, *Newsday*. Reprinted with permission.

Jews under assault in Crown Heights during the riot respond in kind. John Paraskevas of *Newsday*. Copyright, 1991, *Newsday*. Reprinted with permission.

Mayor Dinkins and other city officials at the funeral of Gavin Cato. Ozier Muhammad of *Newsday*. Copyright, 1991, *Newsday*. Reprinted with permission.

Sonny Carson haranguing the throng escorting Gavin Cato's coffin. Copyright, 1991, *Newsday*. Reprinted with permission.

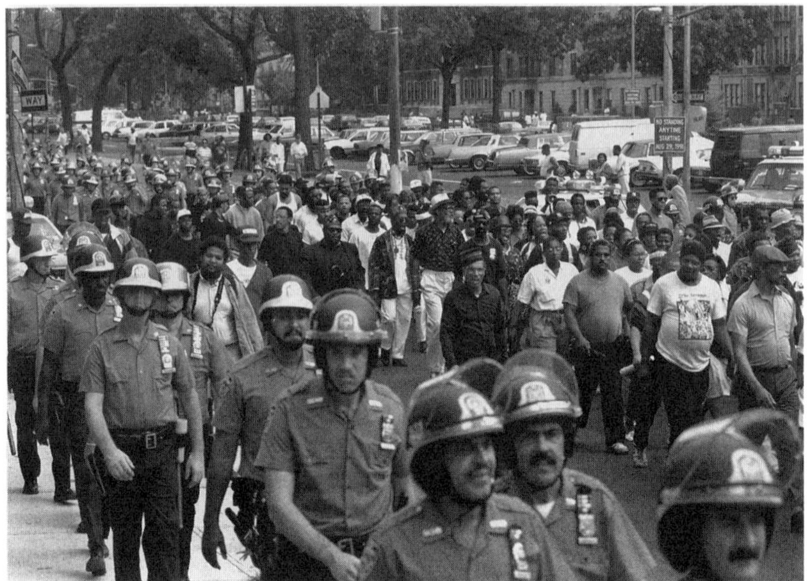

Some of the many police assigned to the August 24, 1991, parade in Crown Heights organized by the Rev. Al Sharpton. The Lubavitch community believed the parade, which occurred on the Jewish Sabbath, was a deliberate provocation. N.Y. *Daily News.* Copyright by Daily News L.P.

Mayor Dinkins at the 1991 West Indian Labor Day parade with Carlos Lezama, the organizer of the parade, and Rabbi Shmuel Butman. Clarence Davis of N.Y. *Daily News.* Copyright by Daily News L.P.

The wife, daughter, and grandson of the murdered Anthony Graziosi hold his photograph at a rally outside of City Hall while Rabbi Yehuda Levin speaks in the background. Jim Hughes of N.Y. *Daily News.* Copyright by Daily News L.P.

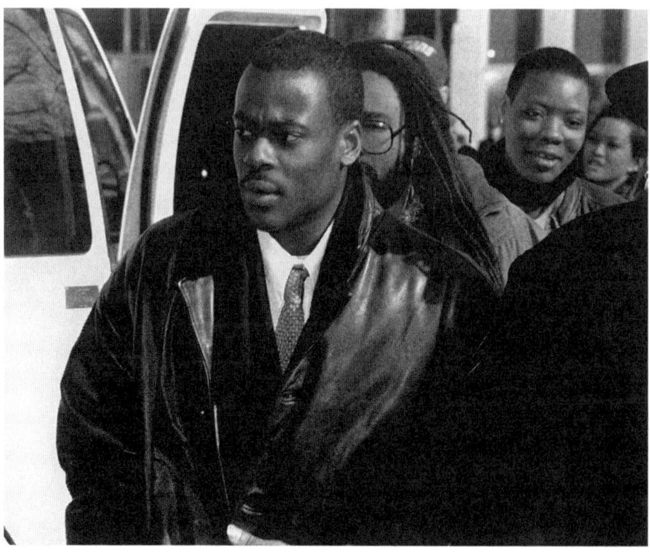

Lemrick Nelson arriving for his trial at the federal courthouse in Brooklyn. Budd Williams of N.Y. *Daily News.* Copyright by Daily News L.P.

Max, Fay, and Norman Rosenbaum meet with Carmel Cato at a kosher restaurant in New York City on August 19, 2003, the twelfth anniversary of the riot. The Rosenbaums were in New York to attend the federal sentencing of Lemrick Nelson. Michael Dabin for N.Y. *Daily News*. Copyright by Daily News L.P.

4

THE POLITICS OF FEAR

During the 1990s a political Gresham's Law seemed to be at work in New York City. The Crown Heights riot strained the entente between the city's Jewish and black political leaders, and it intensified the concern among Jews that their interests were viewed by the city's political leadership as expendable. There was no shortage of politicians willing to capitalize on these fears. Sober proposals to prevent future riots and to improve the performance of the police were often drowned out by highly charged rhetoric catering to narrow ethnic interests, and well-meaning individuals were hounded by demagogues. The riot was an albatross around the neck of Dinkins's administration during its last two years, and it was a key factor in his failure to win reelection.

The riot occurred on the watch of David Dinkins, the city's first and to date its only black mayor. Dinkins was one of the golden boys of the Harlem Democratic establishment. He had married the daughter of Daniel Burrows, a Harlem assemblyman, and he was mentored by J. Raymond Jones, the famous politician known as "the Harlem Fox." A former marine, Dinkins knew the value of loyalty, both given and received, and the importance of the organization. These qualities were respected by his political superiors, and his rise up the political ladder, while not meteoric, was steady and sure. By 1989 he had served one term in the state assembly, ten years as city clerk, and a term as Manhattan borough president. During these years he had earned a reputation for steadfastness and prudence, as well as for timidity, indecisiveness, and lack of imagination. Along the way he was aided by liberal

Jewish politicians and voters. Dinkins considered himself a friend of the Jewish people, and he was supportive of Jewish causes. Few things angered Dinkins more during the Crown Heights controversy than accusations that he had intentionally withheld protection from the Lubavitchers in order to curry favor with blacks.

Supported by the Harlem Democratic organization, Dinkins challenged Edward I. Koch, the three-term incumbent mayor, in the 1989 Democratic primary. Of America's ten largest cities, New York City was the only one not yet to have had a black mayor. Koch was detested by many blacks and by leaders of the city's municipal unions, who were eager to underwrite a credible challenger. The time was propitious: a series of municipal scandals had tarnished Koch, and his abrasive manner had, after twelve years in office, turned off many New Yorkers. Dinkins's courtly demeanor was a welcome contrast to the mayor's irritating and combative personality. The Dinkins camp believed that a coalition of blacks, Hispanics, labor unions, and liberal whites could defeat Koch.

The Achilles' heel of Koch's reelection campaign was the widespread perception that the city's racial situation had worsened during his third term. In two conspicuous incidents, white youths had killed blacks in Howard Beach in Queens in 1986 and in the Bensonhurst section of Brooklyn in 1989. In April 1989 a white female jogger was attacked in Central Park by a group of young black men, and whites feared this could be a harbinger of things to come. Many voters doubted that the caustic Koch could heal the city's racial divisions, pacify restive blacks, and reduce crime. A black mayor, by contrast, was believed more likely to elicit the respect of blacks for political and police authority and to contain black criminal behavior.[1]

Dinkins capitalized on these concerns by portraying himself during the primary and general election campaigns as a racial healer. One of his campaign slogans was "Vote your hopes, not your fears." One of the fears of whites, Dinkins realized, was that a black mayor would be reluctant to confront black crime. His ambiguous campaign slogan "strong enough to hold the line" sought to reassure whites, and he drew a line himself by disassociating himself from black racial provocateurs such as Sonny Carson. Another Dinkins effort to reassure non-blacks was his description of New York City as a "gorgeous mosaic." This term appealed to the city's Caribbeans, Hispanics, Asians, Jews, and other groups who defined their identity in ethnic rather than in stark racial terms. By downplaying the racial cleavage between whites and blacks and by portraying the city as a mosaic of racial, ethnic, and cultural groups, Dinkins sought to mollify whites fearful of their status in a city governed by a black mayor. The Dinkins primary campaign was aided by the implicit endorsement of New York's popular governor, Mario M. Cuomo, who described Dinkins as a "healer" who would bring the city's population together. Dinkins was helped by the fact that the trial of those accused of the murder of Yusuf Hawkins, the black youth killed in Bensonhurst, took place during the primary.[2]

Dinkins easily defeated Koch in the September 1989 primary, with 50.8 percent of the votes to Koch's 42 percent. He carried the Crown Heights assembly district by a margin of eight to one, and he took the heavily Caribbean Saint Albans-Cambria Heights district by nearly fourteen to one.[3] Dinkins also did well in Jewish neighborhoods, even though Koch made much of the fact that he was a Jew. Anywhere from a fourth to a third of Jewish voters supported Dinkins.[4] Dinkins's emphasis on racial healing continued into the general election, where he faced Republican Rudolph W. Giuliani, a renowned former federal prosecutor. Giuliani hired Roger Ailes, a well-known Republican operative, to conduct an aggressive media campaign against Dinkins. Giuliani accused Dinkins of being soft on crime and a captive of the city's municipal unions. Dinkins responded that he would be "the toughest mayor on crime this city has ever seen." He frequently praised the New York City police and was often photographed with police officers.[5] In the closest New York City mayoral election since 1905, Dinkins won by a little more than two percentage points, or 42,450 votes.[6] The *New York Times* called the election of Dinkins a "political coming of age" for blacks, and his majority in black districts was overwhelming.[7] In central Harlem he received 30,600 votes to Giuliani's 1,100; in Bedford-Stuyvesant in Brooklyn 28,400 to Giuliani's 600; and in Brownsville–East New York in Brooklyn 24,700 to Giuliani's 900. Eighty-five percent of Giuliani's voters were white, while 34 percent of Dinkins's voters were white.[8]

Many of the whites who voted for Dinkins were Jews, and Dinkins would not have won without their support. While he received less than a quarter of the votes of white Catholics, he got somewhere between 35 percent to 40 percent of the Jewish vote. The voting in neighborhoods with large numbers of Jews reflected this. In the Riverdale-Woodlawn assembly district in the Bronx, Dinkins got more than 38 percent of the vote, and in the Midwood assembly district in Brooklyn, he received nearly 77 percent of the vote. After the election, Jewish spokesmen continually reminded Dinkins of the crucial role that Jewish voters had played in his margin of victory. Dinkins needed little reminding. An ambitious New York City politician, Dinkins had always been solicitous of Jewish concerns, including support for Israel and opposition to anti-Semitism.[9]

Expectations were high among New Yorkers who took seriously Dinkins's talk about New York City as a gorgeous mosaic. "Dinkins and his allies have been presented with an extraordinary opportunity to renew the ideals of urban liberalism in a way that genuinely incorporates all the various elements of New York City's gorgeous social mosaic and transcends tribal commitments and attachments to any one element," several left-wing academicians wrote in the year of the Crown Heights riot. "Should he meet this challenge, he and his co-workers will have made a signal contribution to American political development."[10] Criticisms of the mayor's performance during the riot would have been more muted and disappointment less widespread had he projected a different image during the 1989 campaign. After August 1991 many New Yorkers reluctantly concluded that the mayor had failed to transcend his own racial attachments. "Dinkins' Mosaic Crumbles" read one headline in the *Daily News* during the Crown Heights riot.

Doubts were raised early in Dinkins's tenure regarding the sincerity of his commitment to fighting crime and to promoting racial reconciliation. A test case for Dinkins occurred in January 1990 at the beginning of his tenure when black "militants" led by Sonny Carson instituted a boycott of a Korean-owned grocery and produce store on Church Avenue in the Flatbush section of Brooklyn. The boycotters said they were protesting the pummeling of Giselaine Felissaint, a black female Haitian immigrant, by Korean employees of the store. The employees and store owner claimed that Felissaint had refused to pay the full price for several plantains and limes, that they attempted to restrain her after she spat at an employee, and that her sole injury was a scratch on the face. Felissaint maintained that she had not stolen anything and was slapped around merely because of her race. Colin Moore, her lawyer, said that she had suffered "trauma of the head, neck, abdomen, some contusions and now has a limp." The police and hospital reported that she had only a slight scratch on the face. The protesters were adamant that the Koreans be prosecuted and the store closed. A municipal court order mandating that picketers stay at least fifty feet from the store was ignored by the boycotters and the police.[11]

The mayor tried to resolve the situation by engaging in behind the-scene negotiations, by denouncing boycotts based on race, and by waiting out the boycotters. Eventually, he believed, they would tire and go home.[12] The strategy made sense at first, but when the boycott continued for several months the mayor's seemingly do-nothing approach appeared to his critics to be a craven caving in to black extremists. The *New York Post* described the mayor's strategy as "Rewarding the Racists."[13] After nine months of the boycott, the mayor entered the grocery store and purchased a few pieces of fruit. But this small offering came too late to shake the growing sense of New Yorkers that he was indecisive, soft on crime, and selective in enforcing the law against blacks. The Korean store imbroglio inflicted a serious blow to Dinkins's reputation as a racial healer.[14]

The impression that race relations had worsened in New York City during the Dinkins administration was not restricted to New Yorkers. A February 1992 report of the United States Commission on Civil Rights strongly condemned the mayor's handling of the boycott. "The Flatbush incident illustrates what can happen when racial tensions are unchecked and racial incidents mishandled by local governments," the report said. "An incident that might have been managed in such a way as to improve racial relations in New York City instead ended up worsening racial relations." Dinkins's unwillingness to become directly involved in the boycott and his reliance on subordinates to resolve the problem presaged his stance during the more serious Crown Heights riot a year and a half later. Here also he stayed on the sidelines for as long as possible. It is unlikely that Ed Koch or Rudolph Giuliani, Dinkins's successor, would have remained out of the loop for so long. During both the boycott and the riot, Dinkins seemed unwilling to confront directly what sociologist Jonathan Rieder called the "torrid brand of resentment politics" and "the angry passions of resurgent black power."[15]

THE POLITICS OF SYMBOLISM

Dinkins also seemed unwilling or unable to perform the symbolic acts that would have helped neutralize criticism from Jews angered by the events in Crown Heights. He could have appointed a nonpartisan commission to investigate the Crown Heights affair either immediately after the riot or right after Lemrick Nelson was found not guilty of murdering Yankel Rosenbaum. He refused even though he could have appointed the members of the commission, influenced its conclusions, and removed the dispute over the riot from the political realm. In lieu of any city inquiry, the principal investigation of the riot would be conducted by the state, and its report would prove very damaging to the mayor.

After the death of Rosenbaum, the mayor could have had the city immediately offer a reward for information leading to the arrest of those who had attacked him. The city did eventually offer a $10,000 reward for information leading to the arrest and conviction of Yankel Rosenbaum's killer or killers, but only after Nelson was found not guilty, more than fourteen months after the murder of Rosenbaum. (The American Jewish Committee offered a $5,000 reward and the Anti-Defamation League of B'nai Brith, a $100,000 reward.) Not only was the mayor tardy in offering the reward (after other bias attacks, rewards had been offered immediately), the timing of this reward implied that the mayor believed Nelson was not the killer and that new suspects had to be found. The mayor was also belated in calling for a federal civil rights probe into the murder of Rosenbaum, even though the Brooklyn district attorney favored such an investigation. New Yorkers suspected that the mayor never fully recognized the concerns raised by the riot regarding him and his administration. Certainly his political response to the riot was maladroit.[16]

Despite all his talk about a gorgeous mosaic, Dinkins seemed oblivious to the fears, anguish, and outrage of the Orthodox Jews of Brooklyn. He appeared uncomfortable in their presence. His reluctance to admit that he and his administration had made serious mistakes during the riot and to offer an apology allowed the debate over the riot to fester and to be dominated by extremists.[17] Of course, it is questionable whether any public figure could have offered sufficient reassurances to these Jews. The riot summoned up deeply painful collective memories of helplessness and victimization that were immune to the bromides offered by politicians. As Rabbi Louis Bernstein noted, "Crown Heights has assumed a broader and deeper meaning" among Jews.[18]

After the Crown Heights riot Jews needed a scapegoat, and Dinkins was the most obvious and available candidate. The mayor was deeply offended by fliers that circulated in Brooklyn charging him with anti-Semitism and responsibility for the death of Rosenbaum. Such accusations, he said, were "horse manure," "outrageous," and "harmful to the city." He repeatedly called upon mainstream Jewish leaders to repudiate the demagogues within their midst.[19] "Sooner or later fair-minded people in this town will realize what's going on," the mayor declared.[20]

But Dinkins had not done enough to prevent such accusations from appearing in the first place, and the more he defended himself the less persuasive he appeared. As *New York Post* columnist Ray Kerrison noted, Dinkins had "a genius for alienating people. . . . He stumbles from one crisis to another, most of his own making."[21] Dinkins's critics charged that, despite his rhetoric about a "gorgeous mosaic," he was simply not up to the job of being mayor of such a heterogeneous city. The problem with Dinkins and Police Commissioner Lee P. Brown, *New York Post* columnist Jack Newfield said, was "incompetence, not conspiracy. It was denial, not malice. It was weakness, not bias. They were two ostriches in a sandstorm." The mayor was not an anti-Semite, nor was he responsible for the death of Rosenbaum. But he was guilty "of doing nothing."[22]

Other New Yorkers, however, believed the Crown Heights riot had lasted for three and a half days not because the mayor was incompetent but because of his calculated policy of appeasing street mobs in a misguided hope that they would fade away. "There is a climate of rigid restraint against the police and it emanates from City Hall," complained Phil Caruso, the head of the Patrolmen's Benevolent Association. "Police were restrained. . . . Police response is not dictated by tactical decisions. They have to wait to get political orders from City Hall." The mayor's strategy, Caruso declared, was a failure: "you cannot negotiate with a mob, which is leaderless, destructive and vicious."[23]

Nowhere was the mayor's handling of the riot more criticized than in the editorial pages of the *New York Post*. Eric Breindel, the editor-in-chief of the paper's editorial page, claimed the riot was needlessly prolonged because Dinkins did not want to antagonize those afflicted with "black rage," and because his administrative style made him reluctant to become personally involved. This resulted in "a stunning and still inexplicable unwillingness on the part of law enforcement authorities to control the violence."[24] *Post* columnist Scott McConnell did not believe it to be so inexplicable. Dinkins's response to the riot in Crown Heights and the boycott of the Korean grocer exhibited a pattern of double standards when it came to race relations. "It is a politically correct, impeccably liberal double standard to be sure," McConnell said, "but a double standard nonetheless."[25]

THE MAYOR'S ENEMIES

Dinkins's political enemies saw the riot as a golden opportunity to bring down the mayor. The primary target for their anti-Dinkins campaign were Jewish voters, a core element in the Democratic coalition in the city and the state. United States Senator Alfonse M. D'Amato, who led the Republican campaign against Dinkins, had personal reasons for involving himself in the Crown Heights imbroglio. D'Amato had been tainted by financial scandals, and he was facing a tough reelection campaign in 1992. His approval rating was less than 40 percent at the time of the riot, and he trailed Democrat Robert Abrams, the state's attorney general and his probable opponent, badly in the polls. A sizable Jewish vote for D'Amato would be devastating to Abrams's chances as it would cut into what was normally a heavily Democratic constituency.

D'Amato continually attacked Dinkins and Abrams, an observant Jew, for being indifferent to the plight of the Lubavitchers, a charge that was patently unfair.[26] Although chided by some Jews for ethnic pandering, D'Amato's attempt to portray himself as the savior of the Jews of Crown Heights was successful. Election analysts estimated that he won as much as 40 percent of the Jewish vote in the 1992 race, an unprecedented figure for a conservative Republican running statewide in New York. The election seemed to indicate that Republican candidates with the proper message could attract significant Jewish support.[27]

D'Amato assailed the mayor more zealously and for a longer period of time than any other politician. These attacks began almost immediately after the riot and continued to the end of the Dinkins administration. Soon after the riot, D'Amato charged Dinkins with being "more interested in playing politics than standing up for what is right." New York City's residents had the right to be protected and to be governed by the rule of law and not mob rule. Instead the mayor had appeased racial agitators such as Al Sharpton, Sonny Carson, and Alton Maddox. "It is high time that the mayor stood up for the people and put the racial racketeers out of business."[28] A headline on the front page of the *New York Post* (September 16, 1991) reflected the relationship between D'Amato and Dinkins. "D'Amato rips into Dinkins: HE'S A COWARD . . . and Hizzoner blasts back: HE'S A CLOWN." Speaking at Park East Synagogue in Manhattan a few weeks after the riot, D'Amato said New York City would be better off if Dinkins took a "long sabbatical" in South Africa.

Dinkins responded that D'Amato was engaging in race-baiting in order to attract support from Jews. "Obviously he's more interested in diatribe than dialogue," Dinkins said. "It does not take a nuclear physicist to understand he goes down this path because of his faltering campaign" for reelection.[29]

The mayor's Democratic rivals also attacked his handling of the riot. The most prominent of these was City Council President Andrew J. Stein, an anticipated opponent of the mayor in the 1993 Democratic mayoral primary. For the ambitious and wealthy Stein, the mayor's handling of the riot provided an opportunity to undermine the mayor's standing among white Democratic voters. For the next twenty-one months he attacked Dinkins over Crown Heights and portrayed himself as a friend of the Crown Heights Jews and a proponent of tough law enforcement. Dinkins viewed Stein as a political opportunist, and he did not disguise his loathing of the city council president. Stein failed to mount a serious challenge to the mayor, and he withdrew from the race on May 27, 1993, leaving Dinkins without a primary opponent.[30]

Dinkins and his advisers realized the political implications of the riot, and they launched a damage control operation to contain its impact. The mayor's reelection campaign, they realized, stood no chance without a significant contribution from Jewish voters, and the mayor sought, to quote Sam Roberts of the *New York Times*, "to persuade Jews that his concern and conciliation goes beyond good intentions."[31] After the exoneration of Nelson, Dinkins enlisted Elie Wiesel, a Nobel Peace Prize winner and the city's most admired Jew, to head a citywide campaign against anti-Semitism. Dinkins also increased his appearances at synagogues and other Jewish venues.[32]

Dinkins's most important overture to Jews in the wake of the Nelson decision was a half-hour speech he gave at the Jewish Theological Seminary on November 17, 1992. Here he denied that he had ever restrained the police during the riot, that his actions during the riot could be explained by his race, and that he viewed black and white rioters differently. "Some people look at this large and very complicated picture and they see only two things—the mayor is African-American and the rioters are African-American—and they conclude that therefore the mayor must have held the police back," Dinkins said. "But there is not a single shred of evidence that I held the NYPD back—and there never will be. And every time this utterly false charge is repeated, the social fabric of our city tears just a little bit more. It must stop."[33]

Dinkins's speech was targeted at such critics of the mayor as Rudolph Giuliani, Andrew Stein, Rabbi Avi Weiss of the Hebrew Institute of Riverdale in the Bronx, and Assemblyman Dov Hikind of Brooklyn. His critics, the mayor charged, were more concerned with seeing him defeated for reelection in 1993 than in bringing to justice those responsible for the killing of Rosenbaum. The predominately non-Orthodox Jewish audience responded enthusiastically to the speech. "I think he has been accused unjustly," one of the listeners said. "I think we have had enough of this baiting and hate-mongering and all of that."[34]

The mayor's critics were unimpressed with his speech. Rabbi Weiss, who was in the audience at the JTS, charged that Dinkins reacted differently to anti-black and anti-Jewish violence, and he called for federal authorities to investigate the instructions given to the police by city hall during the riot. Weiss warned the mayor that the controversy over Crown Heights was not going to go away.[35] Dinkins accused his critics of being politically motivated and described Rabbi Weiss as an "incendiary" racial arsonist and a "demagogue, pure and simple."[36] Weiss responded in kind. "I'm not going to be bullied and intimidated and tainted as a racist because I demand justice for Yankel Rosenbaum. This is unpardonable. Unpardonable." Dinkins, Weiss said, "has got to stop hiding behind the epithets and name-calling and deal with the issues." Some of the city's most prominent rabbis, including Jeremiah Wohlberg, president of the New York Board of Rabbis, defended Weiss. The mayor, Wohlberg charged, was wrong in believing that ad hominem attacks on the motives of his opponents were an effective defense of his own policies. Nor was he correct in believing that only firebrands such as Weiss disagreed with him. The mayor, Wohlberg said, "has not been properly appraised of how estranged certain segments of the Jewish community are."[37]

The Jews of Crown Heights were little inclined to accept any olive branch offered by Dinkins. On November 17, 1992, the same day of his speech at the Jewish Theological Seminary, a federal class-action suit was filed against the city, the mayor, and Lee Brown, the former police commissioner, by residents of Crown Heights. It charged them with needlessly prolonging the riot. The suit was filed on behalf of the estate of Yankel Rosenbaum, individuals who had incurred personal and property damage during the riot, and the Crown Heights Jewish Community Council. That same day Governor Cuomo authorized a state investigation into the response of the New York police to the riot.[38]

THE THANKSGIVING DAY ADDRESS

On Wednesday, November 25, the day before Thanksgiving, the mayor spoke about the Crown Heights riot on the city's local television stations. The *New York Times* called the sixteen-minute speech "[a] stirring holiday sermon," a "timely and masterful" discussion of race relations, and "a welcome antidote to the venom" that the city had suffered recently.[39] Dinkins's address was titled "Reason, Respect and Reconciliation in New York City," and it sought to refute "the politics of distortion and scapegoating" purveyed by "race-baiters and rabble-rousers." "In burying a 7-year-old boy and a quiet Bible scholar," the mayor asked, "did we bury decency too?" Without mentioning names, Dinkins made a thinly disguised attack on Weiss for having "forsaken the prayerbook for the press release."

Dinkins strongly denied that he or anyone else in his administration had decided during the riot to deny police protection to the residents of Crown Heights. "That charge is false, reprehensible and despicable and has been firmly refuted by the police commissioner." While admitting that the police had made mistakes during the riot, Dinkins denied that any erroneous actions were of his making, and he took credit for putting more cops on the beat and for the decline in the rate of crime in the city. Dinkins also outlined the initiatives recently adopted by his administration to increase tolerance.[40]

The mayor's Thanksgiving address was eloquent and forceful, but it was also disappointing to those looking to him to take responsibility for what had taken place in Crown Heights. The *New York Post* noted the "defensive tone" of the speech.[41] Some of Dinkins's advisers as well as political adversaries such as Ed Koch had suggested that he admit he had made mistakes. Michael Tomasky of the *Village Voice* regretted that Dinkins did not use this opportunity to assuage Jews outraged by the decision in the Nelson trial. "A simple, unadorned apology for his initial failure to recognize the hurt and fear Jews felt after the acquittal, and a vow that he understands that fear now, would've made an immeasurable difference," Tomasky said. "I'm confident that if a mostly white jury had gone out to dinner with an alleged white murderer of a black person to celebrate the acquittal, the mayor would've said something."[42]

But Dinkins found it difficult to differentiate between legitimate criticism of his actions during August 1991 and calumny, and he refused to offer any mea culpa to his critics. His description of his critics as "race-baiters and rabble-rousers" infuriated those who believed that sound questions had been raised about the mayor's response to the riot and that Dinkins was stonewalling.[43] As a result, Dinkins's Thanksgiving address failed in its major purpose: to put the Crown Heights controversy behind him. The Monday after Thanksgiving, Dov Hikind and two hundred other Jews picketed a Dinkins fund-raising dinner at the Sheraton Hotel in Manhattan.[44]

Whether the Thanksgiving message would accomplish its political goal would not be determined for another twelve months. It had been directed at the city's Jews, most of whom, the Dinkins camp believed, were politically moderate, eager for peace and reconciliation, and not represented by such fringe figures as Hikind and Weiss. The mayor needed the votes of such moderate Jews if his reelection bid were to succeed. Their immediate response, however, was not favorable. While the mayor had admitted the police response had been inadequate, Manny Behar, executive director of the Queens Jewish Community Council, noted, "he didn't explain why it happened, how it happened, [and] what he will do to see that it doesn't happen again."[45] Franz Leichter, a liberal state senator from New York City who had been invited by Dinkins to city hall to observe the Thanksgiving address, was also skeptical that the mayor had made contact with Jewish listeners. "He could have addressed more the pain and fear that Jews throughout the city feel that a Jew was murdered, lynched," Leichter said.[46]

In response to such criticisms, Dinkins's office issued a nineteen-page account detailing his activities from August 19 through August 21, 1991. Here the mayor said that his goal during the crisis had been to "protect the lives, safety, and property of the residents of Crown Heights, and to quickly restore peace and order to the community." The account also sought to shift blame for the continuing violence onto the police, claiming that they were ill-prepared for such widespread violence, that they did not follow "a comprehensive riot control plan that utilized the maximum police resources and tactics available for responding to a major disturbance," and that such a plan was adopted only after the intervention of Police Commissioner Brown. And the account categorically denied that the city had instructed the police to go easy on the rioters. No one at city hall, it said, "ever gave any direction, either express or implied, that the police department should hold back in any manner whatsoever during this period of time, or in any way act in a manner other than to protect the lives, safety, and property of the residents of Crown Heights and quickly restore peace and order to that community. . . . Had this not been the case, the violence might have been greater and continued unabated for several more days with more arrests and injuries, greater damage to property, and possibly further loss of life."[47]

The mayor's campaign of self-exculpation failed to impress many New Yorkers. A *Daily News* poll conducted by the Louis Harris polling company and released in July 1993 revealed that only 30 percent of New Yorkers gave the mayor's performance during the riot a favorable rating, while 78 percent of whites, 76 percent of Hispanics, and 44 percent of blacks viewed it negatively. More than 60 percent of those polled, including 46 percent of the Jews, blamed incompetence and not racial favoritism for the mayor's inadequacies. "Crown Heights is a potential Achilles' heel for Dinkins," said an employee of the Louis Harris company. The poll also noted that just four months before the 1993 mayoral election, 59 percent of all New Yorkers, including 70 percent of Jews, viewed Dinkins's overall job performance negatively.[48]

Nowhere was antagonism to the mayor stronger than among Brooklyn's Orthodox Jews. They believed the mayor either intentionally or through negligence had failed to protect the Lubavitchers of Crown Heights from the mob. Some Jews, including the Rosenbaum family back in Australia, even claimed Dinkins was responsible for the death of Yankel Rosenbaum. The *Jewish Press,* an Orthodox Brooklyn weekly, said that the mayor should resign and, if he refused, the governor should remove him from office. Such accusations, while understandable, were patently unfair. Dinkins had nothing to do with the murder of Rosenbaum, and there was no evidence that he was hostile to the Jews of Crown Heights.[49] He continually and eloquently attacked racial hatred and violence and defended the rule of law.[50]

THE NELSON DECISION

The Dinkins camp anticipated that the furor over the Crown Heights riot would gradually dissipate and the political alliance that had elected the mayor in 1989 would be resuscitated for the 1993 election. Unanticipated, however, was the furor caused by the exoneration of Lemrick Nelson in state court on October 29, 1992, and by the release of the state investigation report on the riot nine months later. The decision in the

Nelson case was a watershed. More than anything else, it created the chain of events that accentuated Jewish criticism of the mayor, kept the riot on center stage, and ultimately doomed his reelection efforts.

On its face the jury's judgment seemed to defy common sense. Nelson had admitted to the police in the early morning of August 20, 1991, that he had stabbed Rosenbaum; police found in his possession a bloody knife that they assumed was the murder weapon; blotches of blood with the same blood type as Rosenbaum's were on Nelson's pants; and Rosenbaum identified Nelson as his killer. The jurors' bias seemed to be indicated when they—six blacks, four Hispanics, and two whites—attended a postdecision victory celebration hosted by Nelson's attorneys at Callahan's, a restaurant in downtown Brooklyn.

Many New Yorkers were shocked by the decision. Eric Breindel of the *New York Post* attributed it to the reluctance of black and Hispanic jurors to convict any black for murdering a white, and to the pervasive antipolice sentiment within the city's black and Hispanic population that had been instilled by civil rights activists and compliant politicians.[51] Detroit, the *Post* warned, had disintegrated when the middle class left the city after law and order collapsed during the riot of 1967. "We hope this fate isn't what's in store for New York."[52]

Dinkins, who previously had strongly condemned the acquittal of Los Angeles police in the beating of Rodney G. King, now called on New Yorkers to respect the judicial process. "It is always difficult when a terrible crime has been committed and no party is found guilty. It somehow leaves one's sense of justice unfulfilled," he declared a few hours after the jury's decision exonerating Nelson was announced. "I have no reason to doubt that in this case the criminal-justice system has operated fairly and openly. Obviously some will be disappointed with the verdict. But ours is a society of laws, and thus a society requiring that we accept and abide by the decision of the jury system." Dinkins realized that Jews would be incensed by the decision, and he attempted to pacify them. It was crucial to continue the healing process, he said, and not to allow the decision "to remain a source of ongoing strife. The people of Crown Heights have overcome adversity and challenges before, and so they must now."[53] Dinkins's words did not appease Lubavitchers in Crown Heights. "He should have started off by saying, 'I feel for you and understand the pain,' rather than saying this is the verdict and be happy," Rabbi Shea Hecht said. "That's not what he said after the Rodney King verdict."[54]

The attacks on the mayor from Jews became more outlandish. Leading the assault on the mayor was Norman Rosenbaum. Dinkins, Rosenbaum said, was a blatant anti-Semite. The front-page headline of the *New York Post* of October 30, 1992, quoted Rosenbaum: "Yankel's Brother Lashes Out at Jury After Acquittal . . . BLOOD ON THEIR HANDS." ("Their" referred to the mayor and the jury.) Rosenbaum continued attacking Dinkins throughout the remainder of 1992 and 1993. In early November 1992, Rosenbaum addressed a large rally of Jews in Crown Heights. "You have allowed yourselves to be ruled by thugs," he informed his listeners.[55] A few days later Rosenbaum told a Yeshiva University audience that "the Crown Heights pogrom is the most disgusting example of anti-Semitism ever to confront us. Remember that what is occurring here is occurring notwithstanding the so-called lessons of Adolf Hitler, and is occurring with the condoning of the so-called representatives of your people."[56]

Many Lubavitchers agreed with Rosenbaum, and they made their feelings known in a full-page advertisement in the *New York Times* of November 18, 1992. It was headlined: "In New York City Jewish Civil Rights Just Don't Matter." It declared that murder in New York City was not being effectively prosecuted "when the perpetrators are minorities and the victims are Jews," and it claimed the Dinkins administration had deliberately left the Jews of Crown Heights unprotected during the riot. The advertisement ended with an appeal for funds to aid the Yankel Rosenbaum Crown Heights Justice Fund in seeking a federal civil rights investigation into the Rosenbaum murder and the Crown Heights "pogrom."

Even Jews who had little in common with the Jews of Crown Heights protested the exoneration of Nelson. Judah Gribetz, president of the New York Jewish Community Relations Council, called the decision a "a blot on the record of the system of justice."[57] The Anti-Defamation League of B'nai B'rith, the American Jewish Congress, and the American Jewish Committee demanded an investigation of the city's handling of the riot.[58] The New York Federation of Reform Synagogues withdrew an invitation to the mayor to participate in a Crown Heights program featuring a dialogue between Jewish and black teenagers. Rabbi Allen Kaplan wrote Dinkins that it would be inappropriate for him to take part in the event in view of his attitude toward the Nelson decision, which Kaplan called a "travesty of justice."[59]

After the Nelson decision there was seemingly nothing the mayor could do to appease his critics. This implacability was particularly true of Jews in Brooklyn and Queens, who felt more vulnerable and angry than their more affluent coreligionists in Manhattan and the suburbs. To them, Dinkins personified the social forces threatening their hard-earned middle- and lower-middle-class status. The most celebrated encounter between Dinkins and his Jewish critics was on December 3, 1992, at the John F. Kennedy Regular Democratic Club in Flushing, Queens. The mayor was heckled during his half-hour talk, and called a "liar" and a "Jew hater" when he defended his conduct during the riot.[60]

Jewish leaders were embarrassed by these confrontations between the mayor and his Jewish critics; this was not the way Jews were supposed to behave. Even Lubavitch figures such as Rabbi Joseph Spielman protested the rhetoric being directed at the mayor. Calling the mayor an anti-Semite would only worsen relations between the city's Jews and blacks. Rabbi Morris Sherer, president of the Agudath Israel of America, disassociated his organization from the "absurd" personal attacks on the mayor, which, he said, resulted out of frustration stemming from the tense racial situation in the city.[61] The American Jewish Congress published a full-page advertisement in the *New York Times* of December 10, 1992, defending the mayor against the charge of being anti-Semitic. Such an accusation, the organization said, was "symptomatic of a growing mean-spiritedness that threatens to destroy what fragile threads of civility remain between ethnic groups here and in other metropolitan areas." It was "outrageous, utterly repugnant and inexcusable" to call Dinkins an anti-Semite; for Jews to remain silent would be "unconscionable" and "destructive of what hope there is for peace and civility in our city."[62] Most Jewish critics of the mayor, however, believed the charge of anti-Semitism to be a red herring. For them, the real issue concerned his competence.

THE GIRGENTI REPORT

One did not have to be Jewish to be disturbed by the Nelson verdict. Jesse Jackson, a Dinkins political ally, said it was necessary to find the killers of Rosenbaum because the impact of his murder went "to the heart of black-Jewish relations, a sacred struggle that has shed blood in common graves, a coalition that is vital to the future of the struggle for racial justice, religious tolerance, gender equality and world peace."[63] Within days after the Nelson verdict, Attorney General William P. Barr announced that the Justice Department would launch a federal civil rights probe into the killing of Rosenbaum. At the same time, Governor Cuomo ordered Richard H. Girgenti, the Brooklyn-born director of criminal justice and commissioner of the Division of Criminal Justice Services for the State of New York, to conduct an investigation of the riot and of the city's prosecution of the Nelson case.[64] Cuomo refused to second-guess the Nelson jury, and stated that the purpose of the state investigation was to see that justice was done in the Rosenbaum case by helping convict those guilty of his murder, whoever they might be. The governor expressed the hope that a dispassionate and objective investigation of the riot would help calm the emotions inflamed by the Nelson decision. In fact, it did the opposite.

State of New York Executive Order 160, dated November 17, 1992, gave Girgenti the legal authority to proceed with the inquiry and laid out the investigation's rationale and scope. The executive order stated that the primary role of government was to provide for the safety and security of the people, and that the public has the right to expect the criminal justice system to operate justly. The failure to convict anyone for the murder of Yankel Rosenbaum, however, had undermined confidence in the criminal justice system and "polarized communities in the City of New York and elsewhere." It was hoped the investigation would lessen the "feeling of mistrust and suspicion of the criminal justice system by those who are unable to reconcile the verdict with their sense of justice."[65]

The investigation was a major undertaking. Girgenti's people were empowered to review the records of the New York City police, to examine all the files pertaining to *The People of the State of New York v. Lemrick Nelson*, to inspect all evidence regarding the murder of Yankel Rosenbaum, to interview interested parties, and "to offer recommendations designed to restore the public's confidence in the criminal justice system." Girgenti received assistance from the inspector general's office of the Metropolitan Transportation Authority and from pro bono lawyers provided by a Manhattan law firm. The Dinkins administration, the New York City police, and the office of Brooklyn District Attorney Charles J. Hynes cooperated fully with the investigation. More than forty lawyers, analysts, and investigators worked on the report, with many laboring on it full-time. They examined thousands of pages of documents, including printouts of calls to the police department's 911 emergency telephone service, police training manuals, and court records of the Lemrick Nelson trial. They also interviewed more than two hundred witnesses, including Dinkins, Hynes, Brown, New York police officers, jurors on the Nelson trial, leaders of the black and Hasidic communities in Crown Heights, and eyewitnesses to the riot.

The investigation was not authorized to look into the accident that led to the death of Gavin Cato. Gavin's father and other blacks argued that this, along with the failure of Girgenti's investigators to probe the social and economic root causes of the riot, proved that the Girgenti Report was politically motivated, biased toward the Lubavitch, and anti-black.[66] Some blacks, as well as members of the Dinkins administration, believed that Cuomo's motives in authorizing the investigation actually had more to do with his own political future than with the verdict in the Nelson trial.[67] They saw it as a ploy to destroy Dinkins and to firm up support from the state's Jews prior to his reelection campaign in 1994. These suspicions were strengthened when Giuliani endorsed Cuomo for reelection and campaigned with him.[68]

Girgenti predicted that the report, by suggesting remedies for what had occurred during both the riot and the prosecution of Lemrick Nelson, "will bring closure to the concerns of many. This will enable the process of healing wounds, which still exist nearly two years after the disturbance, to begin." The report, he said, "will help to overcome the feelings of mistrust and suspicion in the Crown Heights community, and begin to restore confidence in the criminal justice system and in our government."[69] On July 16, 1993, four days before the report's release, Cuomo circulated a letter to New Yorkers expressing the hope that the report would encourage "reconciliation and renewal" and asking the press not to "sensationalize" its findings. "We can react with intelligence and reasonableness, thereby justifying ourselves and making us all stronger," Cuomo said, "or we can fail. I have confidence, from a lifetime in this place, that we will not fail."[70] The optimism of Cuomo and Girgenti would prove to be unwarranted.

In order to remind the city's Jews of his concern, Dinkins had made a four-day visit to Israel during the first week of July 1993. He was accompanied by thirty-six supporters, including three elected Jewish city officials: Councilman Stanley E. Michels, Queens Borough President Claire Schulman, and Manhattan Borough President Ruth W. Messinger (Giuliani's opponent in the 1997 mayoral election). Other city politicians had been invited but refused, fearing a political backlash by Jewish constituents. Sexologist Ruth Westheimer, Letty Cottin Pogrebin (a liberal

Jewish intellectual), six New York policemen, a photographer, a speechwriter, two press assistants, two official liaisons with New York's Jewish community, and sixteen reporters also made the trip.[71]

While in Israel the mayor took part in thirty-five events, including visiting the Western Wall, Yad Vashem, and a hospital, dedicating a Jerusalem intersection as New York Place, attending a ceremony at which a library room was named in his honor, and schmoozing with Foreign Minister Simon Peres and the mayors of Tel Aviv and Jerusalem, both of whom issued statements endorsing Dinkins's reelection and wore Dinkins Hebrew-language campaign buttons. Photographs of these happenings appeared in New York newspapers. One place the mayor did not visit was Efrat, a settlement in territory Israel had captured during the Six-Day War of 1967. Efrat had been on the original schedule of locations released to the press in June, and some speculated that it had been dropped out of deference to those making the trip who opposed the settling of Israelis beyond the 1967 borders.[72]

While in Israel, Dinkins was dogged by protesters, including Avi Weiss and twenty of Weiss's supporters who had trailed the mayor to the Holy Land. (In Israel, Weiss said he would attempt to change the name of New York Place to Crown Heights Place.) If the mayor had expected he could leave behind the Crown Heights controversy at least for a few days, he was soon to be disappointed. Crown Heights was precisely what the press and New Yorkers he met in Israel wanted to discuss. The mayor responded by acknowledging that the police (but not city hall) had made mistakes during the riot and that "never again" would New Yorkers be subjected to what the Jews of Crown Heights had experienced. "Never again" was a mantra of right-wing Jews signifying that Jews would never again reject violent responses to anti-Semitism as they had during World War II.[73]

Giuliani disparaged Dinkins's trip as a "transparent" and desperate political gimmick.[74] Dinkins denied it was politically motivated, but this claim was hardly credible. It was clear that he was in political trouble. Polls showed him and Giuliani in a dead heat, with the challenger holding a two-to-one lead among Jewish voters. Just days before the mayor left for Israel, members of a Democratic club in a heavily Jewish area of Brooklyn had endorsed Giuliani for mayor, the first time in the club's seventy-seven years of existence that it had endorsed a Republican mayoral candidate.[75]

The executive order to Girgenti authorizing the investigation of the

Crown Heights riot did not specify when the report should be submitted. The governor assumed it would be in the spring of 1993, but its release was delayed because of the scope of the investigation. The two-volume, six-hundred-page document was released on July 20, 1993, less than two weeks after Dinkins's return from Israel, and just as the mayoral campaign between Dinkins and Giuliani was heating up. The report added fuel to the political fire. More than a hundred reporters attended the press conference at which the report was released, and the conference was covered live by all seven of the city's television stations.[76]

THE REPORT AND THE ELECTION

The most politically explosive parts of the report dealt with the performance of the mayor and his police commissioner. While the report exonerated Dinkins of the charge that he had ordered a "day of grace" for the rioters, it severely criticized his behavior during the riot.[77] The mayor, the report charged, "did not act in a timely and decisive manner in requiring the Police Department to meet his own stated objectives; 'to protect the lives, safety and property of the residents of Crown Heights, and to quickly restore peace and order to the community.'" The report also claimed that Dinkins and several of his aides were disingenuous in claiming that it was not until Wednesday afternoon of August 21 that the mayor was told of the seriousness of the situation. In fact, his office had been informed of the deteriorating conditions in Crown Heights during the previous day, and it was hardly credible that the mayor would have been unaware of the newspaper and television reports of what was taking place in Brooklyn. Furthermore, other aides and friends of the mayor told the Girgenti investigators that they had told Dinkins on Tuesday that he had to intervene. The report did not directly accuse the mayor of lying, but many commentators asserted that was the only possible inference one could make.[78]

Giuliani and other foes of the mayor, particularly the editorial writers of the *New York Post*, were ecstatic over the report's description of Dinkins as out of touch and evasive. *Post* columnist Jack Newfield compared the report's description of Dinkins to a Jackie Mason monologue. "I didn't know. I wasn't there. I wouldn't have heard even if I was there. I was asleep in another country."[79] Instead of being the final chapter in the Crown Heights story, the Girgenti Report raised new doubts regarding the competency of the mayor and his aides. Norman Rosenbaum promptly called on Dinkins to resign. "This is a man who has failed to uphold the duties of office—not just during the pogrom, but since then until this day."[80] The mayor, Rosenbaum said, should be prosecuted for "dereliction of duty."[81]

The Girgenti Report was even more critical of Lee Brown, whom Dinkins had frequently described as "the greatest police commissioner in the history of the city." The Girgenti Report, however, described him as inept and indecisive. "The Police Commissioner did not effectively fulfill his ultimate responsibility for managing the Department's activities to suppress rioting and preserve the public peace. . . . In times of emergency, the public can reasonably expect the Police Commissioner to ask probing questions of key aides on the scene, as well as monitor ongoing developments. The Commissioner should assess operational effectiveness and demand changes where needed. There is no evidence that Lee P. Brown provided this kind of leadership during the first three days of disturbances in Crown Heights. Evaluated against these standards, the Commissioner's leadership and performance were inadequate."[82] The police department, according to the report, was slow to mobilize and deploy its resources, lacked a clear plan to deal with the riot, failed to coordinate its manpower, did not keep open the lines of communication between the top brass and the officers on duty in Crown Heights, and failed to change tactics when needed.[83] When the Girgenti Report was released, Brown was living in Washington, D.C., and working as the Clinton administration's point man in the war on drugs. After the 1993 election, Brown moved to Houston, Texas, and in 1997 was elected mayor of the city.

The Girgenti Report embarrassed the mayor. Political analysts close to him had predicted that the worst Dinkins could expect was a mild censure. Cuomo, they assumed, would not wish to alienate black voters during his 1994 reelection campaign. The governor, nevertheless, did not interfere in Girgenti's investigation or exert pressure for an early release of the report (although after its release he did defend the mayor).[84] Dinkins's first response to the Girgenti Report was a press release issued on July 20.[85] Here he thanked Girgenti for "a full and accurate account" of what had and had not happened, expressed the hope that the report would help heal the wounds created by the riot, said that such a riot would "never, ever happen again," and welcomed the report's substantiation of his claim that he never restrained the police. The mayor also said he now supported a thorough and expeditious investigation by the Justice Department of the riot and the Nelson trial. The mayor, however, continued to place the blame for the riot on the police. He had relied on the assurances of the police that they had things under control, and he had no reason to doubt them. "This report concludes that my reliance was misplaced. I accept that conclusion." This grudging admission of responsibility fell far short of what Dinkins's critics were seeking. In his press release the mayor called on all decent New Yorkers to join together and "with the truth as our ally" to see that justice be done and the healing of the city proceed. But Dinkins's enemies believed that the mayor's ally remained not truth but its obfuscation.[86]

The New York City press described the Girgenti Report's criticism of Dinkins as scathing and possibly politically fatal. Among the headlines in the city's newspapers on July 21 were "Out to Lunch" (*New York Post*), "Too Little, Too Late" (*Daily News*), "Dinkins Blew It" (*Newsday*), and "Harsh Light on the Mayor Highlights Longstanding Criticisms" (*New York Times*). Editorials in the newspapers on the same day echoed the headlines.[87] The *Daily News* called the report "a damning indictment of a government that failed to protect its people from grave peril, and then fell far short in the pursuit of justice." The *Post* described the "superb" report as "a stunning indictment" of Dinkins, Brown, and their aides. The *Times* noted the report's "breathtaking" portrait of incompetence during the city's worst racial unrest in more than twenty years. "Mayor David Dinkins failed," the *Times* said. "Former Police Commissioner Lee Brown failed most egregiously. Top police officers and commanders failed. The Brooklyn District Attorney . . . failed. Their respective advisors and aides failed." Nevertheless, the *Times* hoped the city could move beyond this "sorry incident." This hope was unlikely during an election year.

The release of the Girgenti Report, coming less than four months before the November election, ensured that the Crown Heights riot would be an important issue in the campaign.[88] While Dinkins's supporters emphasized that the report refuted the claim that the mayor had restrained the police in dealing with the rioters, his critics claimed the report raised serious questions regarding his competency. Columnist Ray Kerrison believed it was "inconceivable" that Dinkins could still be reelected in light of the revelations contained in the report. "The mayor displays no respect for the law and no will to enforce it."[89]

In his initial response to the report, a statement released to the press on July 21, 1993, Giuliani revealed how his campaign would exploit

Girgenti's findings. "New Yorkers will decide whether this was an isolated instance of failed leadership by the Mayor or whether it was part of a pattern which has serious implications for the city with regard to the budget, schools, health care, jobs, crime, drug control and many other components of our life." The mayor, Giuliani charged, "can't manage a riot, he can't manage a boycott, he can't manage a budget, and he can't manage a campaign to keep it even vaguely in compliance with the law."[90] Giuliani hoped that raising doubts about Dinkins's managerial talents would resonate among all New Yorkers—not merely among Jews, who constituted only 15 percent of the city's population—and would provide a credible rationale to the city's overwhelmingly Democratic electorate for removing an incumbent Democratic mayor.[91] For the three and a half months between the release of the Girgenti Report and the election, Giuliani hammered away at Dinkins as an amiable incompetent, called upon him to dismiss those aides criticized by the Girgenti Report, and claimed that had he been mayor during the riot he would have ended it immediately.[92]

While dismayed by the Girgenti Report's description of the city government's response to the riot, the city's major Jewish organizations were unwilling to burn their bridges to the Dinkins administration. There was a good chance that Dinkins would win the November 1993 election, and the Jewish establishment did not want to find itself on the outside looking in. Thus the American Jewish Congress's press release on the Girgenti Report described the events of August 1991 as a "police failure," but it did not criticize the Dinkins administration, did not even mention the mayor's name, and attempted to place the riot in its proper social and political context.[93] Statements by the American Jewish Committee and the Anti-Defamation League of B'nai B'rith were in the same vein. The lay and professional leadership of these organizations was composed largely of liberal Jews. They were willing to give the Dinkins administration the benefit of the doubt, particularly in light of his previous support for Jewish causes, and they wanted to preserve the political alliance between Jews and blacks.

For the Lubavitchers of Crown Heights, the essence of the Girgenti Report was not about the mistakes of the police but about what the report called the "systemic failures" to contain the riot. For these the mayor, not the police, was to blame. As Rabbi Joseph Spielman said, "The report clearly vindicates our position that the mayor had responsibility that he did not exercise, to the detriment of the Jewish community."[94]

Avi Weiss, an Orthodox non-Lubavitch rabbi from the Bronx, agreed. The report confirmed that Dinkins "was guilty of grievous sins of omission."[95] The mayor's problems with his Lubavitcher detractors could have been dissipated had he come to Crown Heights in the wake of the Girgenti Report, admitted his culpability, and asked forgiveness. But for a person of Dinkins's temperament, this was impossible. In July 1993, Sam Roberts of the *New York Times* wondered whether Dinkins was going to lose the election because of his inability to say six words. "I'm sorry. I made a mistake."[96]

With the exception of the Jews of Crown Heights, no group was more hostile to Dinkins than the city's uniformed police force. Relations between city hall and the police during the early 1990s were arguably the worst in the city's history. The police believed the mayor had prevented them from doing their duty during the riot, and that he had blamed them for his own failures. According to the police, the mayor's performance during the riot combined with his support for a civilian board to review complaints against the police indicated his hostility toward their mission. The police became an important ingredient in the anti-Dinkins political coalition of 1993, and the Patrolmen's Benevolent Association enthusiastically supported Giuliani for mayor. The enmity of the police toward Dinkins further deepened the skepticism of white New Yorkers that Dinkins could be tough on criminals, particularly if they were black.

The major political question raised by the Girgenti Report concerned its impact on the November mayoral election, particularly on Jewish voters.[97] It was assumed that while a significant Jewish vote for Dinkins would not ensure his victory, its absence would surely guarantee his defeat. Both Dinkins and Giuliani assiduously courted Jewish voters. Dinkins went after the votes of the more liberal Jews of Manhattan, who had not been traumatized by the Crown Heights riot. These Jews knew him as a friend, had voted for him in 1989, and were willing to cut him some slack on the Crown Heights issue.[98] Giuliani, by contrast, pursued Jewish votes in Crown Heights and other Orthodox enclaves. He hit Dinkins hard on his conduct during the riot, his attitude toward the police and law enforcement, and his managerial incompetence. Fay Rosenbaum even claimed during the campaign that her son would still be living if Giuliani had been mayor in August 1991.

The Dinkins camp portrayed the election as a referendum on race and accused Giuliani of being unsympathetic to blacks and other minorities. On September 24, President Clinton spoke at a Dinkins $1,000-a-plate fund-raiser at a New York City hotel. Race, Clinton said, was the only possible reason why Dinkins was in such a close contest in an overwhelmingly Democratic city, and that if he lost it would be because "there are too many of us who are still too unwilling to vote for the people who are different than we are." There is little doubt that these words were aimed at Jews; Clinton then reminded his audience that "when the Scud missiles were falling on Israel," Dinkins visited the Jewish state.[99] While Clinton played the race card inside the hotel, hundreds of Jews were outside picketing the dinner.

THE VOTERS DECIDE

Dinkins lost the 1993 election by 44,250 votes. His vote total in 1993 was 2.5 percent less than Giuliani's, roughly the same margin by which he had won in 1989.[100] Some analysts assumed Giuliani's victory was due to the movement of erstwhile Dinkins supporters into the Giuliani camp, with many, if not most, of these being Jews. This shift led them to argue that the Crown Heights issue was a decisive factor in Giuliani's election. The Giuliani camp certainly thought so. It selected Rabbi Morris Sherer of the right-wing Agudath Israel to deliver the invocation at the mayor's inauguration in January 1994.

According to polls conducted by the *New York Times*, the Jewish vote for Dinkins only declined by 3 percent from 1989. In the Midwood section of Brooklyn, for example, Dinkins's margin over Giuliani in 1989 shrank from 11,590 to 10,300. This reduction was partially made up for by an increase in the number of Jews in Manhattan who voted for the mayor. On Manhattan's Upper West Side, the very core of the city's liberal political culture and the home of many of the city's most prominent Jewish liberals, Dinkins's margin expanded from 6,130 to 15,570. It is likely that Dinkins would still have lost even if his support from Jews had remained at the level of 1989.

Other groups were more crucial to Giuliani's victory than lapsed Jewish Democrats. One such group was first-time voters. According to the *Times* poll, first-time voters went 50 percent for Giuliani, 47 percent for Dinkins. An even more important group were Italian-Americans. In heavily Italian Staten Island, the borough with the smallest Jewish population, Giuliani's margin over Dinkins went from 65,900 in 1989 to

88,800 in 1993, a gain of 22,900. This gain was due in part to a 17 percent increase in the number of Staten Island voters in 1993 compared to 1989. Many were drawn to the polling booths because a referendum on the secession of Staten Island from New York City was on the ballot. In Gravesend–Bay Ridge, Brooklyn, an Italian neighborhood made famous as the setting for the movie *Saturday Night Fever,* the Giuliani margin went from 16,700 to 20,440, a gain of 22 percent.

There was also a falling off of support for Dinkins in other ethnic neighborhoods. The Dinkins share of the Hispanic vote declined from 65 percent to 60 percent. In the East Harlem Puerto Rican barrio, Dinkins's margin shrunk from 21,070 to 19,240, and in the heavily Puerto Rican South Bronx it fell from 17,440 to 16,520.[101] There was also a decline in Dinkins's vote among Asian-Americans. Roger Sanjek believes Giuliani carried two-thirds of the Asian vote in 1993.[102] Perhaps the most suggestive voting data on the 1993 election concerns the Lower East Side of Manhattan, a neighborhood containing large numbers of Jews, Chinese, Italians, and Puerto Ricans. In 1989, Dinkins's margin over Giuliani on the Lower East Side was 5,500. In 1993 it was 1,740. The Crown Heights riot was not uppermost in the minds of voters on the Lower East Side. But it was part of the mix that led them, and other New Yorkers, to doubt Dinkins's competence and to fear that the city's social fabric was coming apart.

"Dinkins's failure to convince voters of his ability to deal fairly and evenhandedly with all ethnic groups and races," the historian Roger Biles wrote, "proved to be a lethal shortcoming because of the intense scrutiny inevitably applied to all black mayors when issues of race relations arose."[103] A 1993 poll indicated that a large majority of New Yorkers believed race relations had worsened during Dinkins's tenure, and nothing was more important in this respect than the Crown Heights riot.[104] It assumed symbolic importance for New York voters, even though it claimed the life of only one person, caused a minimal amount of property damage, and by American standards was not a significant riot.

Dinkins was the first black mayor of a major American city not to be reelected after one term, and his defeat embittered his black supporters. Blacks, following the lead of President Clinton, attributed it to racism. Percy E. Sutton, a close friend of Dinkins, blamed it on the defections of white Democrats to Giuliani. "We are an extremely hurt people on this night and we have to make an adjustment," Sutton said on election night.[105] Left unsaid was why racism did not prevent Dinkins's election in 1989. By contrast, the Reverend Herbert D. Daughtry, Sr., a fervent adversary of the Lubavitch community, attributed the loss to a backlash among blacks caused by the mayor's efforts to appease the Hasidim.[106] Dinkins's vote did decline in some black neighborhoods from 1989. It decreased by more than a thousand in central Harlem and by almost 2,400 in Brownsville–East New York. But the percentage of blacks voting for Dinkins also increased from 91 percent to 95 percent. No evidence supports the claim that the decline in the numbers of blacks voting for Dinkins was responsible for his defeat or that it stemmed from resentment over his supposed courting of Jews.

The voting statistics of the 1993 election do not indicate that the Crown Heights riot was "the" issue responsible for Dinkins's defeat. As is true of most elections, there was no single decisive issue in 1993. The political importance of Crown Heights was that it reinforced a growing sense within the city that the mayor was simply not up to the job. So strong was this sense that Dinkins might have lost even if the riot had never occurred. To many New Yorkers, his style of governance appeared too laid-back and aloof. At a time when the city needed a hands-on mayor, Dinkins preferred to delegate authority and to pass the buck. His governmental experience and his personal qualities had not equipped him to govern such a fractious city. Giuliani's approach, as demonstrated on Septemer 11, 2001, would be radically different, and his tenure much more successful.

Even Dinkins's harshest critics acknowledged that he was not an anti-Semite. But neither was he a natural politician. Teddy Roosevelt referred to the presidency as a "bully pulpit." Dinkins, however, was not a sermonizer. Although he tried, his dignified and retiring manner did not allow him to project a sense of empathy for the plight of the Jews of Crown Heights, and he failed to appreciate the importance of symbolic actions. One can only imagine how different things would have been had a Ronald Reagan or a Bill Clinton been mayor of New York City in 1991.

Notes

1. For Koch's unpopularity, see Glenn Thrush, "Mayor Out of Favor with Most New Yorkers," *Newsday*, May 8, 2003; Roger Sanjek, *The Future of Us All: Race and Neighborhood Politics in New York City* (Ithaca, N.Y.: Cornell University Press, 1998), 152–53.

2. After the Crown Heights riot the Lubavitch community viewed talk about a "gorgeous mosaic" skeptically and wondered whether there was any place for Jews in Dinkins's mosaic. One ditty read, "Roses are red / Violets are bluish / You're not part of the mosaic / If you're Jewish."
3. Philip Kasinitz, *Caribbean New York: Black Immigrants and the Politics of Race* (Ithaca, N.Y.: Cornell University Press, 1992), 236–37, 248–49.
4. John Hull Mollenkopf, *A Phoenix in the Ashes: The Rise and Fall of the Koch Coalition in New York City Politics* (Princeton, N.J.: Princeton University Press, 1992), 178. Chris McNickle, *To Be Mayor of New York: Ethnic Politics in the City* (New York: Columbia University Press, 1993), 300–302, estimates that slightly less than one-fourth of the Jewish voters supported Dinkins against Koch and the two other Jewish mayoral candidates, real estate developer Richard Ravitch and New York City Comptroller Harrison J. Goldin. Asher Arian et al., eds., *Changing New York City Politics* (New York: Routledge, 1991), 90, asserts that Dinkins received a third of the Jewish vote in the primary.
5. Andy Logan, "Never Again," *New Yorker* 69 (August 2, 1993): 32.
6. Roger Biles, "Mayor David Dinkins and the Politics of Race in New York City," in *African-American Mayors: Race, Politics, and the American City,* ed. David R. Colburn and Jeffrey S. Adler (Urbana: University of Illinois Press, 2001), 133–39.
7. *New York Times,* January 2, 1990.
8. *New York Times,* November 8, 1989.
9. Arian et al., eds., *Changing New York City Politics,* 96, claims that 35 percent of Jews voted for Dinkins, while McNickle, *To Be Mayor of New York,* 302, believes the figure is 40 percent.
10. Arian et al., eds. *Changing New York City Politics,* 205.
11. M. A. Farber, "Black-Korean Who-Pushed-Whom Festers," *New York Times,* May 7, 1990; Jonathan Rieder, "Trouble in Store," *New Republic* 203 (July 2, 1990): 17.
12. Todd S. Purdum, "Angry Dinkins Defends Role in Race Cases," *New York Times,* May 9, 1990; Purdum, "Dinkins Asks for Racial Unity and Offers to Mediate Boycott," *New York Times,* May 12, 1990.
13. *New York Post,* September 5, 1990. See also Sam Roberts, "Which Mayor Knows Best on the Boycott?" *New York Times,* July 30, 1990.
14. Edward T. Chang, "African American Boycotts of Korean-Owned Stores in New York and Los Angeles," in *Riots and Pogroms,* ed., Paul R. Brass (New York: New York University Press, 1996), 246; Eli B. Silverman, *NYPD Battles Crime: Innovative Strategies in Policing* (Boston: Northeastern University Press, 1999), 73–76.
15. Rieder, "Trouble in Store," 16, 21. For an analysis of Dinkins's "painfully deliberate, measured" administrative style, which made him appear "indecisive and reluctant to lead," see Sam Roberts, "Mayor Dinkins: Every Day a

Test," *New York Times Magazine,* April 7, 1991, 27–28, 44–50. See also Roberts, "Given New York Today, Could Anyone Lead It," *New York Times,* December 29, 1991.

16. Michael Tomasky, "The Backlash Thing," *Village Voice* 37 (December 1, 1992), 19; Melvin Salberg and Pan Schafler to David N. Dinkins, November 18, 1992, and Dinkins to Salberg and Schafler, November 20, 1992, Anti-Defamation League Archives, New York. Congressman Charles Rangel of Harlem, a Dinkins ally, warned the Lubavitchers of a "backlash " should their attacks on the mayor continue. "New Yorkers are not kind to people who talk different, look different and act different from them," he said. One wonders how the typical New Yorker, in fact, talked, looked, and acted. Eric Breindel, "The Congressman Issues a Warning," *New York Post,* December 10, 1992.
17. For criticisms of Dinkins's political response to the riot, see Wayne Barrett, "Dinkins's Dilemma: Transcending the Death That Divides the City," *Village Voice* 37 (December 1, 1992), 11–12, 16; Michael Tomasky, "How Dave Botched Crown Heights," *Village Voice* 37 (November 24, 1992), 14; Marc D. Stern, "The Problem of Crown Heights," *Congress Monthly,* 60 (January, 1993): 12–13; James C. McKinley, Jr., "Dinkins May Have Regrets, But Not on Crown Hts.," *New York Times,* January 3, 1993.
18. Louis Bernstein, "The Mayoralty and Crown Heights," *Jewish Press,* January 22, 1993.
19. Ellen Tumposky and Joel Siegel, "Dave Lashes Critics: Thinks Jews Should Deplore Them, Too," *Daily News,* November 15, 1992.
20. John Harney, "Union Boss: Mayoral Rivals Fan Race Hate," *New York Post,* June 25, 1993.
21. *New York Post,* November 16, 1992; David Seifman, "He Goofed Every Step of the Fray," *New York Post,* November 18, 1992. For additional criticism of Dinkins by the leader of the Liberal Party, see Raymond B. Harding's letter in the *New York Post,* November 25, 1992.
22. Jack Newfield, "Why It's Important to Dig Up the Truth About Crown Heights," *New York Post,* June 24, 1993. For Dinkins's passivity, see Mitch Gelman, "A Passive Hand at Helm of the City?" *Newsday,* June 3, 1993; Jack Newfield, "Dinkins Dithered, Cops Collapsed," *New York Post,* July 20, 1993.
23. Ray Kerrison, "Key Question: Who Held Back Cops?" *New York Post,* June 25, 1993.
24. Eric Breindel, "Race and Riot in New York," *Wall Street Journal,* November 18, 1992.
25. Scott McConnell, "Double Standard," *New York Post,* February 29, 1992.
26. Barrett, "Dinkins's Dilemma," 11. Abrams called D'Amato's comments on Dinkins and Crown Heights "political grandstanding of the worst sort." Lindsey Gruson, "Democrats Call D'Amato's Criticism of Dinkins a Ploy," *New York Times,* September 17, 1991. The *New York Times* described D'Am-

ato's criticisms of Dinkins as "a crass attempt to divide New York City for personal political gain." *New York Times,* September 18, 1991.

27. For a criticism of D'Amato's "inflammatory" role in the Crown Heights controversy, see Newfield, "City Must Shun the Provocateurs." "D'Amato," Newfield said," "thinks that a race-based appeal to white fear is the only way he can get re-elected. . . . He is a hungry vulture circling over people who are feeling authentic torment and anger." See also Wayne Barrett, *Rudy! An Investigative Biography of Rudolph Giuliani* (New York: Basic Books, 2000), 276–77; Elizabeth Kadetsky, "Racial Politics in New York," *Nation* 255 (November 30 1992): 656.
28. Serge F. Kovaleski, "Furious Jewish Throng Masses Outside Gracie," *Daily News,* September 2, 1991; Alfonse M. D'Amato, "It's Up to Dinkins to Speak Out Now," *New York Post,* September 5, 1991.
29. Paul Schwartzman, "Al and Dave in Bitter War of Words," *New York Post,* September 16, 1991.
30. Paul Schwartzman, "Dinkins: I'm Not Going to Denounce Sharpton or Carson," *New York Post,* August 28, 1991; Todd S. Purdum, "Stein, Trailing Badly in the Polls, Quits New York Race for Mayor," *New York Times,* May 28, 1993; Martin Gottlieb, "Campaign Breakdown: Stein's Message Fails to Win over Voters," *New York Times,* May 29, 1993.
31. Sam Roberts, "Passionately, Dinkins Reviews Crown Heights," *New York Times,* November 12, 1992.
32. Ian Fisher, "In Crown Hts., Mayor Presses for Harmony," *New York Times,* November 30, 1992.
33. Richard Steier and Peter Moses, "Dave: Race Played No Role in Riot Handling," *New York Post,* November 18, 1002.
34. James C. McKinley, Jr., "Dinkins Says Critics Distort Facts of His Response to Crown Heights," *New York Times,* November 18, 1992.
35. Joel Siegel, "Dave to Critics: Stop," *Daily News,* November 18, 1992. "It is clear," Rabbi Weiss said, that the mayor "distinguishes between anti-Black racist violence and anti-Jewish racist violence. . . . The conscious holding back of the police when Jews were in danger will live in infamy." Avraham Weiss, "The Lessons of Crown Heights," *Jewish Press,* November 27, 1992.
36. Jonathan Mark, "Crown Heights Fallout: Rabbis Defend Avi Weiss Against 'Racial Arsonist' slur," *Jewish Week,* December 4–10, 1992; *Daily News,* November 15, 1992. Rabbi Ismar Schorsch, Chancellor of the Jewish Theological Seminary, called Weiss "the Al Sharpton of the Jewish community." Ray Sanchez, "He's No Stranger to Controversy: Rabbi Weiss Speaks his Mind," *Newsday,* November 20, 1992. See Mark, "Crown Heights Fallout," for Weiss's response to Schorsch's comment.
37. Mark, "Crown Heights Fallout."
38. McKinley, "Dinkins Says Critics Distort Facts."

39. *New York Times,* November 28, 1992.
40. A complete transcript of the Thanksgiving address is in the *Amsterdam News,* November 28, 1992. The *New York Times,* November 26, 1992, printed excerpts from the address.
41. *New York Post,* November 27, 1992.
42. Michael Tomasky, "What a Mayor Can Do," *Village Voice,* 37 (December 8, 1992), 12.
43. Vivienne Walt and George E. Jordan, "Mayor to Cite Cops," *Newsday,* November 25, 1992.
44. Miguel Garcilazo and Mike Koleniak, "Dave Fears Speech Didn't End Storm," *New York Post,* November 27, 1992; Sam Roberts, "Dinkins's Mission: Trying to Relegate Crown Heights to the Past," *New York Times,* November 24, 1992; James C. McKinley, Jr., "Dinkins, in TV Speech, Defends Handling of Crown Hts. Tension," *New York Times,* November 26, 1992.
45. Joel Siegel, "Cop 'Tactical Errors' Admitted," *New York Daily News,* November 26, 1992.
46. Paul Schwartzman and Richard Steier, "'The Buck Stops Here': Mayor's Words on Crown Hts. Stir Praise and Rebukes," *New York Post,* November 26, 1992.
47. "Statement of Mayor David N. Dinkins Regarding Crown Heights Disturbances," in *A Report to the Governor on the Disturbances in Crown Heights* by Richard H. Girgenti, vol. 1, *An Assessment of the City's Preparedness and Response to Civil Disorder* (Albany, N.Y.: New York State Division of Criminal Justice Services, 1993), appendix D (hereafter cited as Girgenti Report, vol. 1).
48. Frank Lombardi, "Mayor a Dud on Riot: Poll," *Daily News,* July 14, 1993.
49. Dinkins blamed racism for the Lubavitchers' unforgiving attitude toward him. Joyce Purnick, "Quiet No Longer, David Dinkins Finds a Voice, With an Edge," *New York Times,* May 11, 1995.
50. Dinkins's speech on August 25, 1991, at the First Baptist Church in Crown Heights. A copy of the speech is in the Robert A. Bush Papers, Brooklyn, New York.
51. Eric Breindel, "Behind the Crown Hts. Verdict," *New York Post,* November 5, 1992.
52. *New York Post,* November 2, 1992.
53. "Statement by Mayor David N. Dinkins Regarding the Verdict in the Nelson Case," *Jewish Press,* November 13, 1992; Kadetsky, "Racial Politics in New York," 657; Stewart Ain, "Dinkins Delivers 'Message of Healing' to New Yorkers," *Jewish Week,* November 27–December 3, 1992.
54. Ain, "Dinkins Delivers 'Message of Healing' to New Yorkers." For a criticism of Dinkins's response to the acquittal of Lemrick Nelson, see the editorial "Keeping the Mosaic Gorgeous—and Whole," *Daily News,* November 10, 1992.

55. Basha Majerczyk, "Mass Protest in Crown Heights Demands Justice for Yankel Rosenbaum," *Algemeiner Journal*, November 6, 1992.
56. J. J. Goldberg, *Jewish Power: Inside the American Jewish Establishment* (Reading, Mass.: Addison-Wesley, 1996), 309. For Norman Rosenbaum, see Alison Mitchell, "A Brother's Sadness Turns to Anger," *New York Times*, November 15, 1992. Mitchell called Rosenbaum "a wild card in New York's racial, ethnic and political wars."
57. Jerome A. Chanes, "Intergroup Relations," in *American Jewish Year Book, 1994* (New York: American Jewish Committee, 1995), 94:123.
58. "AJCongress Troubled by Jury's Acquittal in Crown Heights Case and Applauds Department of Justice Investigation," October 30, 1992, American Jewish Committee Archives; Anti-Defamation League press release, October 29, 1992, ibid.; "American Jewish Committee Shocked by Crown Heights Verdict," n.d., ibid.
59. *Jewish Press*, November 6, 1992.
60. Alison Mitchell, "Dinkins Faces Name-Calling in Queens," *New York Times*, December 3, 1992; *Daily News*, December 5, 1992; Jessie Mangaliman, "This Housewife 'Just Had Enough,'" *Newsday*, December 5, 1992. For a hostile reception Dinkins received from Crown Heights Jews, including Rosalyn Malamud, during a visit to Crown Heights on December 2, 1991, see Patricia Hurtado et al., "Crown Heights Race Tensions Dog Dinkins," *Newsday*, December 3, 1991. Dinkins called Malamud ignorant and irrational.
61. Morris Shearer to David N. Dinkins, December 4, 1992, Bush Papers.
62. The Anti-Defamation League of B'nai B'rith, the American Jewish Committee, the Jewish Community Relations Council of New York, and the New York Board of Rabbis also disassociated themselves from the "scurrilous" attacks on the mayor. See the *Amsterdam News*, November 21, 1992.
63. Roberts, "Passionately, Dinkins Reviews Crown Heights."
64. For Girgenti, see James Barron, "The Quiet Decision Maker With Crown Hts. Report," *New York Times*, June 24, 1993.
65. Richard H. Girgenti, *A Report to the Governor on the Disturbances in Crown Heights*, vol. 2, *A Review of the Circumstances Surrounding the Death of Yankel Rosenbaum and the Resulting Prosecution* (Albany, N.Y.: New York State Division of Criminal Justice Services, 1993), appendix A (hereafter cited as Girgenti Report, vol. 2).
66. Wayne Barrett, "With Friends Like These . . . Mario's Mouth Puts His Pals on the Crown Heights Hot Seat," *Village Voice* 38 (August 10, 1993), 13; Jessie Mangaliman, "Hardly a Mention: Victim's Dad: What of My Son?" *Newsday*, July 21, 1993; Minoo Southgate, "Hate Radio and Crown Heights," *New York Post*, July 27, 1993; Jonathan P. Hicks, "Boy's Father Assails Study of Slayings in Crown Hts.," *New York Times*, July 26, 1993; J. Zamgra Browne, "Black Response: What About Cato?: Outraged Black Leaders and Politicians Call Re-

port One-Sided, pro-Hasidic Jew," *New York Amsterdam News*, July 24, 1993; Vinette K. Pryce, "Leaders Say Crown Heights Report Leaves Out Cato Story," *Amsterdam News*, July 24, 1993; Herb Boyd, "Crown Heights Report Exonerates Mayor Dinkins From Any Blame," *Amsterdam News*, July 24, 1993; Wallace Ford II, "Crown Heights—The Aftermath," *Amsterdam News*, July 31, 1993; David Paterson, "Paterson Responds to Whites on Crown Heights," *Amsterdam News*, August 7, 1993.

67. Alan Finder, "Crown Hts. Shadow Reaches Past Dinkins Toward Cuomo," *New York Times*, July 24, 1993.
68. Michael H. Cottman, "Dinkins' Backers Seek Guv," *Newsday*, July 14, 1993; *New York Amsterdam News*, June 26, 1993; Frederic Dicker, "Sharpton: Report Could Cost Cuomo Key Black Votes," *New York Post*, July 26, 1993.
69. Girgenti Report, 1:1–2.
70. Cuomo's letter was reprinted in *Newsday*, July 17, 1993.
71. The *Jewish Press* described the Jews accompanying Dinkins as "so-called Jewish 'leaders.'" Logan, "Never Again," 34.
72. Jean Herschaft, "Mayor Dinkins' Visit to Israel Irks Jewish Settlers in Judea and Samaria," *Algemeiner Journal*, July 9, 1993.
73. Logan, "Never Again," 34.
74. Bob Liff, "Rudy: Mayor's Israel Visit Is Political Ploy," *Newsday*, June 30, 1993; Stewart Ain, "Crown Hts.: Dinkins' Unwanted Baggage in Israel" and "Visiting New Yorkers Let Off Steam," *Jewish Week*, July 16–22, 1993; Clyde Haberman, "Specter of Crown Heights Clings to Dinkins, Even in Israel," *New York Times*, July 7, 1993; Haberman, "Dinkins Leaves Israel, Still Hearing About Crown Hts.," *New York Times*, July 9, 1993; Alan Finder, "Dinkins's Olive Branch: Facing Crown Hts. From Israel," *New York Times*, July 11, 1993.
75. Stewart Ain, "It's Milk and Honey For a Beleaguered Dinkins," *Jewish Week*, July 9–15, 1993.
76. Logan, "Never Again," 32. Joel Benenson, Tim Ireland, and Frank Lombardi, "Riot Report Out Today: Crown Heights Findings May Affect Mayoral Race," *New York Daily News*, July 20, 1993; Benenson et al. predicted the report "could help seal Dinkins' political fate."
77. Girgenti said that Governor Cuomo was probably quoted accurately by the *Jewish Press* when he said that Dinkins had spoken about a "day of grace," but that the governor did not want what he said to be taken literally. "What we believe happened is that the Governor was not saying that the Mayor had literally given a day of grace," Girgenti said. "My understanding is that it is not a statement of a conversation that the Governor had with the Mayor. I think it is a statement of what he believed to be the state of affairs at that time, based on many conversations." Alan Finder, "A Crown Heights Remark Returns to Trouble Cuomo," *New York Times*, August 1, 1993. This article is the best discussion of the "day of grace" controversy.

78. Girgenti Report, 1:27–28, 361–63. The most relevant portions of the report were reprinted in the *New York Times*, July 21, 1993.
79. Jack Newfield, "A Classic Case of Buck-Passing," *New York Post*, July 21, 1993. Columnist Mike McAlary wrote that Dinkins's testimony to the Girgenti report investigators was "either a lie or an extremely weak attempt at revisionist history." McAlary, "Riots Rocked City and Ruined Dinkins," *Daily News*, July 21, 1993.
80. Andrea Peyser, "Grief And Outrage Drive Yankel's Brother," *New York Post*, July 21, 1993.
81. Chris Oliver, Rita Delfiner, and Leo Standora, "Hasids: Dave Does Deserve a Drubbing," *New York Post*, July 21, 1993.
82. Girgenti Report, 1:246, 263, 351.
83. Ibid., 1:11–25. For changes in the operations of the police suggested by the Girgenti report reforms, see 1:342–55, and for the reforms instituted by the police in the aftermath of the riot, see 1:297–312. For the failure of the police department's policy of restraint, see 1:234–36.
84. "I wish it were out," Cuomo said in June 1993. "I wish it weren't this close to the election. I wish it weren't the subject of newspaper coverage every day. But I'm not going to tell Girgenti to compromise what he thinks is thoroughness." Alison Mitchell, "Dinkins Is Questioned on Violence," *New York Times*, June 24, 1993. For a more cynical view of Cuomo's involvement in the Girgenti Report, see Wayne Barrett, "Girgenti's Ghostwriter," *Village Voice* 38 (August 3, 1993), 11–12.
85. For Dinkins's attempt to neutralize the impact of the Girgenti Report shortly before it was released, see Alan Finder, "Dinkins Meets With Leaders in Brooklyn: Crown Heights Is Focus on Eve of State Report," *New York Times*, July 20, 1993.
86. "Statement by Mayor Dinkins on Release of Report by Richard Girgenti on Events in Crown Heights," July 20, 1993, Bush Papers. The *New York Times* of July 1, 1993, printed excerpts from Dinkins's press release.
87. The lead article on the Girgenti report in the *New York Times* of July 21, 1993, called it a "scathing portrait of ineptitude and miscommunication that extended from police deployment on the Crown Heights streets to the upper reaches of City Hall." Martin Gottlieb, "Crown Heights Study Finds Dinkins and Police at Fault in Letting Unrest Escalate."
88. For an early analysis of the political implications of the Girgenti Report, see Frank Lombardi, "Don't Write Dinkins Off Just Yet," *Daily News*, July 21, 1993.
89. Ray Kerrison, "What a Riot! Double-Standard Dave Does Himself In," *New York Post*, July 23, 1993.
90. Biles, "Mayor David Dinkins," 143–48.
91. Todd S. Purdum, "Competence Is Campaign Focus After the Crown Heights Report," *New York Times*, July 22, 1993.

92. See, for example, Alan Finder, "Dinkins Counterattacks: Giuliani Hammers Away," *New York Times,* July 23, 1993; Sam Roberts, "The Murky Mix of Race, Competence and Politics," *New York Times,* October 4, 1993; Rudolph Giuliani, "Why I Deserve Your Vote for Mayor," *Jewish Week,* October 29–November 4, 1993.
93. "Police Response to Crown Heights Disturbances: An AJCongress Resolution," *Congress Monthly* 60 (November–December, 1993): 13; Lawrence Rubin to NJCRAC and CJF Member Agencies, July 23, 1993, Jewish Community Relations Council of New York Papers, New York.
94. Debra Nussbaum Cohen, "Crown Heights Jews Feel Vindicated by Report," *Jewish Tribune* (Rockland County, New York), July 23–29, 1993.
95. Adam Dickter, "The Crown Hts. Report: Jewish Reaction Mixed," *Jewish Week,* July 23–29, 1993.
96. Sam Roberts, "Many Questions Linger After Crown Hts. Report," *New York Times,* July 26, 1993.
97. Paul Schwartzman, "Findings May Cost Dave at Polls: Jewish Vote Crucial," *Daily News,* July 22, 1993; J. J. Goldberg, "Disenchanted With Dinkins," *Jerusalem Report* 4 (September 23, 1993): 40–41; N. R. Kleinfield, "Tallying Crown Heights Toll, in Votes," *New York Times,* July 25, 1993. One poll taken a week after the release of the Girgenti Report downplayed its political significance. Frank Lombardi, "Poll: No Major Damage for Dave in Crown Height Report," *New York Daily News,* July 28, 1993. See also Alan Finder, "Crown Height: An Overestimated Mayoral Issue?" *New York Times,* July 29, 1993.
98. Eli Blachman, "Mayoral Campaign Goes into High Gear in Pursuit of Jewish Votes," *Algemeiner Journal,* October 6, 1993; For Dinkins's support from the Jewish establishment, see Jeffrey Goldberg, "Jewish Heavies Backing Dinkins as Grass Roots Go for Giuliani," *Forward,* October 8, 1993.
99. *Forward,* October 8, 1993. For a defense of the Clinton speech, see Lani Guinier, "Clinton Spoke the Truth on Race," *New York Times,* October 19, 1993.
100. Voting statistics are from the *New York Times* of November 9, 1989, and November 4, 1993. The total vote reported in the *Times* in 1989 was 1,791,707 and 1,783,936 in 1993. These figures were unofficial and did not include absentee ballots.
101. For Dinkins's problems with Puerto Rican voters, see Purdum, "Buttoned Up," *New York Times Magazine,* September 12, 1993, 50.
102. Sanjek, *Future of Us All,* 154.
103. Biles, "Mayor David Dinkins," 143–48.
104. Sanjek, *Future of Us All,* 154.
105. Felicia R. Lee, "Viewing a Verdict as Based on Race," *New York Times,* November 3, 1993.
106. Herbert D. Daughtry, Sr., *No Monopoly on Suffering: Blacks and Jews in Crown Heights (and Elsewhere)* (Trenton, N.J.: Africa World Press, 1997), 267.

5

CONFLICTING NARRATIVES

If loss of life and property damage is the standard by which riots are to be judged, the one in Crown Heights was not particularly momentous, although this was not the way those directly affected perceived it. Only one person died, fewer than two hundred people were arrested, property damage was not extensive, the geographical area affected was limited, life in Crown Heights went on much as it had before August 1991, and further riots did not ensue. This is not to say that the Crown Heights riot was not significant, but its importance lay in the response to it and not in the riot itself. It influenced relations between Jews and blacks, it challenged deeply held social and political beliefs, and it brought to the surface previously unstated assumptions and preconceptions.

One of the most important aspects of the riot's aftermath was the various efforts to make sense of what had occurred. Almost immediately a host of differing interpretations emerged seeking to explain its nature and origins. This effort at explanation, which continued throughout the 1990s, reflected the diverse political, religious, and social circumstances, the differing ideological assumptions, and the divergent understandings of the past by the journalists, sociologists, political activists, and historians who wrote about the riot. Such divergence was to be expected. As the literary historian Alan Mintz has said, all historical narratives, "from the personal story to complex novels, are not simply naive and faithful transcriptions of experience but are built around preexisting armatures or schemata or master plots. New narratives may add to, play with, and subvert these story lines, but an appreciation of their uniqueness must begin with an understanding of the preexisting models."[1]

Historians have distinguished between narratives of "memory" and narratives of "history." While memory is a product of folk remembrances, it is also shaped by contemporary concerns and is often an instrument of power. Historian David W. Blight pointed out that collective historical memories are often transformed into myths, "deeply encoded stories from history that acquire with time a symbolic power in a culture." History, by contrast, defers to professional standards and respects the integrity and complexity of the past. In his book *Imagining Russian Jewry: Memory, History, Identity,* the historian Steven J. Zipperstein argued that the historian's role has been to "implode collective memory, to juxtapose as starkly as possible the differences between history and myth, scholarship and error."[2]

This distinction between memory and history is important in understanding the various attempts to understand the Crown Heights riot. Blacks have a collective memory of racism and enslavement that has shaped their understanding of the past and contemporary events. Similarly, the collective memory of Jews, with its emphasis on anti-Semitism and the Holocaust, has influenced how they perceive reality. The conclusions of historian Hasia R. Diner regarding the study of American Jewish history are equally applicable to that of American black history. The study of American Jewish history, she wrote, has been complicated by a collective memory that provides "a series of linked images that have grown organically out of the contemporary cultural needs of the public, however diverse it may be, as it defines and justifies itself and its present condition." These images "provide the intertwined leitmotiv in American Jews' understanding of where they have been, where they are now, and possibly, even where they might be heading. This bundle of memories plays a crucial role in the creation of an American Jewish narrative." But, Diner concluded, these collective memories are often misleading, and "the right to interpret the experience" of American Jews must necessarily reside with historians because of their "emotional distance."[3]

The struggle over the interpretation of the Crown Heights riot was thus more than a conflict between history and memory. It was also a conflict between competing memories, most notably between those of Jews and African Americans. Their responses to the riot reminds one of Thucydides' statement in his *History of the Peloponnesian War,* written twenty-five hundred years ago, that "the People made their recollections fit in with their sufferings." For the Lubavitchers of Crown Heights, the riot was both enigmatic and intelligible. Accustomed to viewing themselves as victims, they denied any responsibility for the events of August 1991 and were mystified by its outbreak. They believed relations with their black and West Indian neighbors had been, if not close, at least cordial prior to the riot. "Today," wrote Edward Hoffman in *Despite All Odds,* a sympathetic study of Lubavitch Jewry written just before the riot and published in 1991, "Crown Heights is one of the few truly integrated sections of New York City, where black and Jewish homeowners co-exist as next-door neighbors, each determined to maintain the safety and viability of their community as a place for families to live peacefully. The contrast to other sections of Brooklyn could not be more striking: burned-out tenements and boarded-up storefronts dominate the rubble-strewn landscape."[4] The Lubavitchers claimed that the rioters could not have come from Crown Heights. Rather, they must have come from other parts of Brooklyn and been stirred up by outside agitators such as Alton Maddox, Sonny Carson, the Reverend Herbert Daughtry, and the Reverend Al Sharpton.

If blacks viewed the riot through the prism of race, the Lubavitchers viewed it through the prism of religion. For the Lubavitchers, the fault line in American society was between Jews and Gentiles; for blacks the fault line was between whites and blacks. The Lubavitchers saw themselves as an embattled Jewish island in a sea of Gentiles; they were viewed by blacks, however, as part of the American population privileged because of skin color. Nonetheless, the Lubavitchers did not see themselves primarily as whites but as Hasidic Jews. This vision shaped their understanding of the riot—which, they believed, had nothing to do with race and everything to do with the history of Gentile anti-Semitism stretching back to the confrontation between Jacob and Esau, the children of Isaac and Rebecca, recounted in the book of Genesis. Esau sold his birthright as the firstborn son to Jacob for a bowl of porridge, and then Jacob deceived his father into giving him the blessing intended for Esau. Esau vowed to kill Jacob, and Jacob was encouraged by Rebecca to flee to the land of her ancestors. According to Jewish teachings, the descendants of Jacob and Esau are joined in perpetual hatred and struggle. This was prophesied in God's warning to Rebecca: "Two nations are in your womb. Two separate peoples shall issue from your body."

On August 19, 1996, a memorial service took place in Crown Heights for Yankel Rosenbaum at the site where he had been murdered. Rabbi

Shmuel M. Butman, director of the Lubavitch Youth Organization and the only Lubavitch to speak at length, argued here that Rosenbaum's murder was symptomatic of the hatred that Gentiles have had toward Jews since the very beginnings of the Jewish people. Butman's analogy was helped by the fact that Rosenbaum's first name was Jacob, and his reference to the story of Jacob and Esau was readily understood by the Lubavitchers in the audience.[5] Jewish teachings clearly identified the descendants of Jacob with the Jews, but who were the anti-Semitic descendants of Esau? At various times in Jewish history they were identified as Edomites, Romans, Christians, and Gentiles in general; in 1991 Lubavitchers identified them with the blacks and West Indians of Crown Heights.

For a small number of the Lubavitchers of Crown Heights, the riot was a portent of the long-awaited messianic era. The belief in the coming of the messiah followed by the return of the Jews to the land of Israel and the coming of an era of peace and prosperity was a fundamental principle of traditional Judaism and was affirmed in the daily prayers of Jews. For Lubavitchers, it was not coincidental that the riot had been triggered by an accident involving a motorcade in which Rabbi Menachem Mendel Schneerson was a passenger. Messianism had assumed a more prominent view among the Lubavitch Hasidim in the 1980s when Schneerson declared that the coming of the messiah was imminent, and that it was the responsibility of Lubavitch Hasidim to prepare themselves accordingly. The often cryptic comments of Schneerson regarding messianism encouraged a minority of his followers to conclude that he, in fact, was the messiah.

This growing messianism took place at a time when earthshaking events could be interpreted as portents of the coming of the messianic era. In 1989 there was the death of the Ayatollah Khomeini in Iran, the student protests in Communist China, the breakup of the Soviet empire, the destruction of the Berlin Wall, and a mass exodus of Jews from Russia to Israel and the West. These were followed by the airlifting of Ethiopian Jews to Israel and America's war with Iraq in 1991 (which, despite the fears of Jews and the threats of Iraq, left Israel virtually unscathed). And then, almost simultaneous with the rioting in Crown Heights, there was Hurricane Bob and an unsuccessful coup in the Soviet Union. A full-page advertisement in the August 30–September 5, 1991 issue of the *Jewish Week* of New York, paid for by Joseph Gutnick, a wealthy Australian supporter of Lubavitch, put these events into an apocalyptic framework. "Any one of these phenomena by itself is enough to boggle the mind. Connect them all together, and a pattern emerges that cannot be ignored," it declared. "The Era of Moshiach is upon us. Learn about it. Be a part of it. All you have to do is open your eyes. Inevitably, you'll draw your own conclusion."[6]

But what conclusions could be drawn about the riot? On the one hand, most Lubavitch spokesmen downplayed any messianic significance of the riot as this would transform the rioters into the instruments of God. The rioters were simply anti-Semites. And yet the accident could not be merely accidental because Orthodox Judaism taught that everything that happened was part of God's plan. Schneerson's failure to speak directly about the riot fueled speculation that he believed it to be further confirmation of the impending arrival of the messiah.[7] The ambivalence of Rabbi Shmuel Butman, who delivered the keynote eulogy at Yankel Rosenbaum's funeral was characteristic of those Lubavitchers imbued with messianic fervor. For him the riot was both an attack on Jews everywhere and a sure sign that the messianic era was approaching.

WHO WAS YANKEL ROSENBAUM?

The conflict between memory and history appeared immediately after the riot as participants, onlookers, and scholars argued over its meaning. This conflict began with the description of Yankel Rosenbaum. In the wake of his murder, he was pictured in the press and by representatives of the Lubavitch community as a "religious scholar," "a "seminarian," a "talmudic scholar," a "Jewish theological student," and a "divinity student." More than a decade after his killing, a reporter for the *New York Times* was still portraying Rosenbaum as a "rabbinical student."[8] He was, in fact, neither a Lubavitcher (although his clothing and beard were typical of members of this community) nor was he a yeshiva student immersed in the study of sacred Jewish religious texts.

This characterization of Rosenbaum as a yeshiva student heightened his Jewishness and linked his death with the long and painful history of anti-Semitism. Many Jews in Crown Heights had experienced anti-Semitism personally in Europe, and both of Rosenbaum's parents were Holocaust survivors. It would have been incongruous to portray Rosenbaum as an academic; the Lubavitchers of Crown Heights did not, by and large, attend college, and they disdained the social and intellectual milieu of the university. Furthermore, picturing Rosenbaum as a budding academician who happened to be in the wrong place at the wrong time would also have detracted from the simplistic and dramatic imagery of blacks and Jews in conflict in Crown Heights. For those unfamiliar with Jewish history, it was natural to equate being Jewish with being religious, being religious with being an Orthodox Jew, and being an Orthodox Jew with being a yeshiva student. This distortion of Rosenbaum's background was pervasive, and it appeared in a variety of secular and Jewish newspapers and magazines.

This imagining of Rosenbaum was part of a more general view of the riot as a "pogrom" and the rioters as modern-day "Cossacks" and "Nazis." "Pogrom" was the most common word used by Lubavitchers to describe the riot, and it remains so to the present day. August 19, 1991, was, according to Rabbi Joseph Spielman, chairman of the Crown Heights Jewish Community Council, "the first pogrom here on America soil."[9] "Pogrom" provided a historical context for understanding the riot, and it linked what occurred in Crown Heights in 1991 to other attacks on Jews in such places as Kishinev, Baghdad, and Kielce. The still fresh memories of European anti-Semitism when combined with the actions of the rioters made it almost inescapable that Jews would place the riot within the context of Western anti-Semitism. Painful and often suppressed memories immediately surfaced as rioters marched through the streets of Crown Heights chanting "Heil Hitler" and singling out Jews in Hasidic garb for attack—and as self-styled black spokesmen declared that the targets of the black rioters were not undifferentiated whites but Jewish "diamond merchants."

Among the earliest and most important use of "pogrom" was by the *New York Times* columnist A. M. Rosenthal in his column of September 3, 1991, titled "Pogrom in Brooklyn." Rosenthal argued here that the anti-Semitism exhibited in the Crown Heights riot would spread to other neighborhoods and cities if Jews remained "blind to reality, deaf to history—and suicidal." The "black pogromists" of Crown Heights exhibited the classic symptoms of anti-Semites: the dehumanization and demonization of Jews, the call for violence, the exaggerating of grievances against a peaceful minority. Rosenthal was particularly disparaging of the news reporting of the riot that pictured it as "some kind of cultural clash between a poverty-ridden people fed up with life and a powerful, prosperous and peculiar bunch of stuck-up neighbors—very sad of course, but certainly understandable." Journalists unable to distinguish between political thugs and legitimate spokesmen for blacks, Rosenthal suggested, "are in the wrong business."[10]

Rosenthal's column was quite critical of the mayor and the police commissioner. Not only had David Dinkins and Lee Brown been remiss by failing to put down the riot immediately; they had compounded this failure by meeting with Al Sharpton, Alton Maddox, and other "hate peddlers," and according them the respectability they desperately craved. Rosenthal was also scornful of the indifference of establishment Jewish organizations to the suffering of the Jews of Crown Heights. "Their usually ferocious faxes were either silent or blurped out diplomatically balanced condolences to all concerned." Rosenthal's column was noteworthy as the *Times* had been generally supportive of the Dinkins administration.[11]

By contrast, the *New York Post* and Eric Breindel, the editor of its editorial page, had been strongly critical of the mayor long before August 1991, and the riot confirmed their opinion that he was simply out of his depth. The paper continually insisted during the remaining twenty-eight months of Dinkins's tenure that he had to go. It offered as evidence his performance during the riot, which Breindel, a child of Holocaust survivors, persistently referred to as a "pogrom." Former mayor Ed Koch, Mike McAlary, and Pete Hamill also described the riot in Crown Heights as a pogrom in their *New York Post* columns, and the paper called it the first pogrom in the West since the end of World War II.[12]

In his column of September 5, 1991, titled "Brooklyn Pogrom: Why the Silence," Breindel called the riot a "genuine pogrom" similar to those Jews had experienced in Europe. Breindel anticipated the major criticism of his use of "pogrom." He denied that a pogrom had to be sponsored by the government. A riot deserved to be called a pogrom if the government did not vigorously condemn the rioters and the police failed to put down the violence immediately. Breindel rejected any attempt to put a sociological gloss on the riot by portraying it as a natural response to economic and social deprivation. "This pogrom," he said, "was a case of the poor terrorizing the poor. Jews who read life in terms of class rather than race should bear this reality in mind." In any case, attempts to understand the thinking of the rioters were misguided, including the question, Why do so many black leaders dislike Jews? Jews should fight all manifestations of anti-Semitism and not be sidetracked into futile and undignified attempts to mollify anti-Semites.[13]

By September 1991 it had become routine within Jewish circles to describe the riot as a pogrom and remained so within the general Jewish community more than a decade later. While the city government did not incite the rioters, Jews explained, the failure of the police to protect Jewish lives and property warranted identifying it as a pogrom. On August 22, 1991, New York City Councilman Noach Dear, who represented the heavily Jewish neighborhood of Boro Park in Brooklyn, called the riot a "pogrom, just like we saw in Russia under the Czar, just like in Germany in 1939. This has to be stopped before the violence spreads." The *Jewish Week,* which had the highest circulation of any weekly Jewish newspaper in the city, declared in an editorial of August 30–September 5, 1991, "A Pogrom Grows in Brooklyn." The paper would run articles with titles such as "After the Pogrom—An Analysis and Proposal." Similarly, a press release of October 29, 1992, by Judah Gribetz, president of the Jewish Community Relations Council of New York, termed the riot a "pogrom." The *Jerusalem Post* also called it a pogrom and claimed it had been "fed by Arab propaganda and financed by Arab sources." The paper hoped the riot would encourage the Jews of Crown Heights to wonder whether "the time has not come to join their brethren in Kfar Habad in Israel." Nearly seven years after the riot, the *Forward,* a weekly national Jewish newspaper published in New York City, referred to the riot as a "pogrom," and on the riot's tenth anniversary the *Jewish Press,* a right-wing Orthodox weekly newspaper published in Brooklyn, carried an editorial by Rabbi Shmuel Butman titled "The Crown Heights Pogrom: Ten Years Later."[14]

Yet even the description of the Crown Heights riot as a pogrom was not enough for some residents of Crown Heights. They preferred "Kristallnacht," a reference to November 8, 1938, when Nazis destroyed synagogues and Jewish-owned stores throughout Germany. A group called the Crown Heights Emergency Fund placed a full-page advertisement in the *New York Times* of September 20, 1991, headlined "This year Kristallnacht took place on August 19th right here in Crown Heights." The statement warned that the Crown Heights riot was just the beginning and that Jews "everywhere" could expect attacks by "latter day Nazis." This neo-Nazism "does not distinguish between Hasidic and non-Hasidic, Orthodox and Reform, affiliated or non-affiliated." "The Jews of Crown Heights," it stated, "*are the first line of defense for all American Jews and for all law-abiding citizens of good will*—regardless of race, color or creed."[15]

Other Jews also compared the riot to Kristallnacht, ignoring the fact that Kristallnacht was not a spontaneous riot but was initiated and orchestrated from above. An article in the *Jewish Press* by Ronee Pollachek bewailed the reluctance of America's Jews to look realistically at the riot. "For some reason we are afraid to call it by name. It was America's Kristallnacht. Shame on us. Shame on all of us." A Jewish resident of Crown Heights who had survived the Holocaust agreed. "This has been like the pogroms," Hannah Popack said. "Or like Kristallnacht. It is almost as though Hitler has come to life again." Frequently the Jews of Crown Heights called upon both Jewish and American history to make sense of the riot. "What has happened to black people?" one Crown Heights Jew asked. "Why will no black leaders condemn these black Nazis, the black Ku Klux Klan?" (Some black leaders had, of course, condemned the rioters.) And when the accused murderer of Yankel Rosenbaum was acquitted in October 1992, one survivor of Kristallnacht said, "again, I heard the tinkling of the glass."[16]

While the Crown Heights riot did not rise to the level of a pogrom, much less the Holocaust, the rioters made no secret of their animus toward Jews. For the *New Republic*, the riot was "an anti-Semitic depravity." (The *New Republic* also said that the riot "looks more and more like the first pogrom in American history.")[17] The rioters' rhetoric was directed at Jews, and they only attacked Jews, those who looked like Jews, and the police who were protecting Jews. If recent history had taught Jews anything, it was to take very seriously the words of those seeking to do them harm. Jews were frightened even more by the failure of every black political and religious leader to promptly condemn the rioters and black anti-Semitic agitators. This silence indicated, they feared, that anti-Semitism within the black community was not restricted to a lunatic fringe.

"POGROM" AND POLITICS

The controversy over how to define the Crown Heights riot was not merely an issue of semantics. To discredit Dinkins and his administration, politicians, both past and present, resorted to words redolent of the bloodshed and mass devastation suffered by European Jews. Ed Koch, who had been defeated by Dinkins in the 1989 Democratic mayoralty primary and was a fierce critic of the mayor, continually used "pogrom" in characterizing the riot. It was, he said in 1993, "an ugly term, but it applies." Other political foes of Dinkins also used "pogrom" as it implied that he had been indifferent to an attack on Jews. Andrew Stein, a candidate in the 1993 Democratic mayoral primary, used it in his unsuccessful effort to oust Dinkins. The controversy over the word came to a head during the 1993 mayoral election. Rudolph Giuliani, the Republican-Liberal candidate, made Crown Heights a key issue in his campaign, and he used "pogrom" frequently in attacking the mayor. "You can use whatever word you want," he said in a Memorial Day weekend speech in the predominately white neighborhood of Bay Ridge in Brooklyn, "but in fact for three days people were beaten up, people were sent to the hospital because they were Jewish. There's no question that not enough was done about it by the city of New York. One definition of pogrom is violence where the state doesn't do enough to prevent it."[18]

Dinkins and his supporters realized the political potential of "pogrom," and they totally rejected its application to the Crown Heights situation. They argued that pogroms only applied to riots that were state-sanctioned, and no one could claim the Dinkins administration had fomented the Crown Heights riot. "To suggest that this is," Dinkins said, "is not to contribute to the resolution of the problem but to exacerbate tensions and problems that are there." Earl Caldwell, a black columnist for the *Daily News,* charged that Giuliani's use of "pogrom" was inaccurate, racially divisive, and politically driven. Giuliani's speech "does not bode well for a city that already has enough trouble." The *City Sun,* a Brooklyn-based black nationalist weekly, charged that Giuliani's use of "pogrom" resulted from a "quiet deal" he had made with the Crown Heights Jewish community. If any group was susceptible to a pogrom it was the city's blacks, as they faced the prospect of a police state led by Giuliani and supported by white right-wing Republicans and Crown Heights Hasidim. Al Sharpton said that Giuliani was engaged in "race-baiting" by using the word "pogrom."[19]

Dinkins refrained from such improbable conspiratorial notions. But he was personally offended by the use of "pogrom" because it insinuated that the riot was state-sanctioned and that he personally was an anti-Semite. "I am incensed by it," he told radio personality Don Imus. It is "patently untrue and unfair." Dinkins had many close Jewish friends, had appointed Jews to high positions within his administration, and had gone out of his way to support Jewish causes. To be called an anti-

Semite for political gain was, in his view, unconscionable, even in a city where the politics of personal destruction had become an art form. To make matters worse from his perspective, posters displayed at Jewish political rallies in Brooklyn during the campaign even charged Dinkins with responsibility for the murder of Yankel Rosenbaum. "Rarely has political discourse become so debased," wrote the journalist David Remnick, "and yet this language of rage is tremendously influential."[20]

But history, if not the memory of the Jews of Crown Heights, was on Dinkins's side. Michael Stanislawski, a Columbia University historian and a specialist in modern European Jewish history, noted that it was "historically inaccurate" to couple "pogrom" with Crown Heights, because the word denoted organized violence against Jews "having some sort of governmental involvement." Joyce Purnick, a writer for the *New York Times,* agreed. Giuliani's Bay Ridge speech, she said, was not only inflammatory and wrong, but "an insult to those who lived through the real thing." The city's police "didn't fail to protect the Jews of Crown Heights because they and David Dinkins wanted to see Jews killed. They weren't Cossacks in blue. Thousands of Jewish New Yorkers were not murdered."[21]

Liberal Jews who were emotionally committed to a black-Jewish political alliance were also loath to use "pogrom" and sought to deconstruct the call of the rioters to "kill the Jews." Henry Siegman, the executive director of the American Jewish Congress, warned against using such a loaded term as "pogrom." "It is strategically dumb and factually incorrect to insist that the violence in Crown Heights is essentially a black-Jewish problem," he said shortly after the riot. "It is not. It is essentially a black-white problem and . . . for Jews to insist that it is a black-Jewish problem is to take the monkey off the back of white Americans and to put it on our own back." Marc D. Stern, another official with the American Jewish Congress, agreed with Siegman. The riot, Stern said, was "in large part an anti-white riot, directed at the nearest available white community." But it also manifested "the frustration of an inner-city black population which is beset by familiar urban ills—unemployment, drug abuse, teen-age pregnancy, and most telling of all, utter despair and hopelessness."[22] Some blacks agreed. Cornel West, the black philosopher and political activist, echoed James Baldwin's famous piece in the *New York Times* four decades earlier that for blacks, Jews were not Jews but whites. "The particular interaction of Jews and blacks in the hierarchies of business and education cast Jews as the public face of oppression for the black community, and thus lend evidence to this mistaken view of Jews as any other white folk."[23]

If the Crown Heights riot was not a pogrom, then what was it? David Dinkins provided one analogy. As an African American with a different historical narrative, the answer was readily at hand, although it took Dinkins three weeks to voice it. Yankel Rosenbaum and the Jews of Crown Heights, the mayor said, had encountered precisely what blacks had known in the American South: racially motivated mob violence. Dinkins used the terms "bias crime" and "lynching"—words that resonated deeply within the historical consciousness of blacks—to describe the murder of Rosenbaum. He likened it to the "lynching" of Yusuf Hawkins, a black teenager killed by a mob of white youths in 1989 in Brooklyn while checking out a used car. "No question," Dinkins said. "Whatever term one gives to these kinds of vicious murders, that's what it is."[24]

By emphasizing the shared experience of victimization of blacks and Jews, Dinkins sought to repair the frayed political ties between the two groups, which were the basis of the city's liberal political culture, and to salvage his own political future, which depended upon strong support from both communities. Other blacks, however, strongly dissented from his use of "lynching" to characterize the killing of Rosenbaum. They also resented any comparison of Rosenbaum's murder with that of Hawkins. Just as Jews believed they had a proprietary interest in such words as "pogrom" and "Holocaust," so blacks argued that "bias crime" and "lynching" should be used only when describing the murders of blacks. "How could the murder of Yankel Rosenbaum be called a lynching?" asked Colin Moore, the black nationalist lawyer. "To even describe it in the same breath as Yusuf Hawkins is an abomination. It's pandering to the votes of a certain people." Moore and other like-minded persons hoped to use Dinkins's terminology as a weapon in their struggle against the black political establishment of New York City.[25]

Some black radicals also denied that American blacks could be guilty of racism, as Dinkins's statement claimed. Al Sharpton speculated that Rosenbaum was murdered while being robbed. It was common in the early 1990s to argue that racism consisted of two elements: prejudice and power. While blacks could be prejudiced, they could not be racists because they lacked the power to put their prejudices into effect. United States Senator Daniel P. Moynihan, an authority on American racial and ethnic relations, strongly disagreed. "The notion that there is any race that is immune to the failings and sins of other people is itself a racist idea."[26]

Moynihan drew upon a pastiche of American historical precedents to understand the Crown Heights rioting. He called the murder of Rosenbaum a "KKK-style lynching" and said that New York could use the South as a model. "We got rid of the lynching in the South by a process of . . . public abhorrence, so the people involved became ashamed, and law enforcement, which took a long time." In describing the riot itself, Moynihan called it a "race riot," one that "was as bad as what happened in Detroit in 1943 when black workers were dragged from streetcars and killed by white workers."[27] Moynihan's analogy at least put the Crown Heights riot within an American setting, although it is a stretch to equate the violence of the Crown Heights riot with that of the Detroit riot, which resulted in thirty-four deaths and required the military to restore order.

A STRUGGLE OVER TURF

Another interpretation of the Crown Heights riot argued that it was not directed at Jews per se but at the Lubavitchers and that it had not been caused by anti-Semitism but by the jostling of blacks, West Indians, and the Lubavitchers for housing, government funds, political power, and city space. A decade before the riot, Tim Robbins wrote in *City Limits*, a journal devoted to the study of New York City, that Crown Heights had seen "an ongoing tussle over turf and power between a large black and a West Indian population and an expanding community of Hasidic Jews." Historian Richard Wade agreed. Both groups were "locked into a unique historical struggle over a limited amount of space." From this perspective the riot was simply another chapter in the history of ethnic relationships and tensions in New York City—blacks versus Italians, Haitians versus Koreans, West Indians versus African Americans. The riot, sociologist Jonathan Rieder said, must be understood within "the totality of ethnic relations in Crown Heights."[28] This jostling, however, had been going on for years but without any large-scale violence and rioting. What caused this "unique historical struggle" to escalate into a full-scale riot?

The belief that the Crown Heights riot was an ethnic conflict helped explain to some why Jews living in other areas in the city were not so fearful regarding the future of ethnic and race relations in the city. According to Harriet Bogard, director of the New York regional office of the Anti-Defamation League, the circumstances in Crown Heights were unique and provided little instruction for understanding black-Jewish relations in general. The insular lifestyle of Lubavitchers was "culturally dissonant from what one assumes is normative for an American lifestyle" and made it difficult for them "to reach out beyond their own community." This resulted in a lack of contact with their neighbors that, in turn, led to a want of knowledge and understanding between the two groups.[29]

This "lack of contact" theory of prejudice became part of the conventional wisdom regarding the roots of the riot. But frequent contacts between groups do not necessarily further harmony. They can lead just as easily to hostility and contempt, as was the case in Crown Heights, where the contacts between blacks and Jews resulted from physical proximity and not from cultural interaction. The Lubavitchers rejected the "contact" theory. They noted that they were one of the few segments of the city's Jewish population living in close proximity to blacks and West Indians, and they believed they were sufficiently familiar with the lifestyles of their neighbors. By contrast, they pointed out, Jewish national organizations that espoused the contact theory were staffed by persons residing in the suburbs or in the city's white neighborhoods. Little wonder, then, that Crown Heights Jews became cynical about the advice proffered by mainstream Jewish organizations headquartered in Manhattan.

Those who argued that the riot was directed at the Lubavitch community and not at Jews were, by and large, generally unsympathetic to the Lubavitch way of life. Peter Noel, a reporter of Caribbean background for the *Village Voice*, claimed that the Lubavitchers were in large part responsible for the animosity of their black and West Indian neighbors. This resentment, Noel wrote, stemmed from the Lubavitchers' aggressive lobbying for funds from government poverty programs, their assertive search for housing for their growing population, and their forceful demands for preferential treatment by city agencies, particularly the police. In responding to a question regarding the sources of mutual distrust between blacks and Hasidim in Crown Heights, Monsignior John Powls, the white pastor of Saint Barbara's Catholic Church in the depressed Bushwick ghetto of Brooklyn, provided another answer. "The real problem," he said, is that "nobody understands how desperate inner-city communities like Crown Heights and Bushwick are right now. Young people there have absolutely nothing to live for. There are young adults 19 or 20 with nothing to do."[30] While this might have been true, it does not explain why only in Crown Heights did ethnic rivalry and conflict—a long-standing feature of New York City's history—escalate into a riot. Day-to-day relations between Italians and blacks were even worse than between Jews and West Indians and between Jews and blacks. But no anti-Italian riot occurred as a result of the killing of young blacks in the Italian neighborhoods of Howard Beach in Queens and Bensonhurst in Brooklyn in the late 1980s.

Mary Pinkett, who represented parts of Crown Heights in the New York City Council, also denied that the central story of the riot was anti-Semitism. "The incident," she said, "was the culmination of anger. The complaint the blacks have is the racism of American society." This complaint included the city's dealings with the blacks of Crown Heights. Black rage, Pinkett predicted, will continue "until the police and other agencies begin to do their jobs without fear or political favoritism."[31] This attempt to put a civil rights gloss on the rioting explained the use of the mantra "no justice, no peace" by blacks marching in Crown Heights. To them the symbolic event of the riot was not the murder of Yankel Rosenbaum but the death of Gavin Cato. While the Lubavitchers viewed the killing of young Cato as a tragic accident, blacks viewed his death, as well as the failure to prosecute Yosef Lifsh, as symptomatic of the racism permeating American society.

The Lubavitchers believed that characterizing the riot as anti-Lubavitch (or anti-white) rather than as anti-Semitic transformed them from victims into perpetrators. Even if the criticisms of the Lubavitch way of life were correct—which the Lubavitchers strongly rejected—did this justify violence against them? Were the Lubavitchers required to sit down at meals with their neighbors, to have their children play with non-Lubavitch children, to participate in interreligious and interethnic activities, and to educate others about the Lubavitch lifestyle in order not to be physically attacked? Lubavitchers feared that characterizing the riot as anti-Lubavitch diminished the culpability of the actual rioters.

The Yale sociologist Jonathan Rieder provided the most extensive "ethnic" explanation of the riot. He strongly argued in several articles that the roots of the riot were multifaceted, "defy[ing] neat and easy categorization." These roots included elements of racial, class, ethnic, economic, and generational conflict. In fact, Rieder said, while Jews were targeted by the rioters, "there was little evidence of coherent, formal anti-Semitic belief systems at work in Crown Heights," and the "mob's anti-Jewish rhetoric is hardly self-evident." (Southern lynch mobs also lacked a coherent, formal ideology of racism. This did not make them less malevolent.) Rather, Rieder argued, the riot resulted from the dysfunctional nature of ghetto culture, with its "repertoire of violent reprisals, collective allocation of blame, and communal vengeance" stemming from "alienation, antiwhite resentment, and retributive frustration." At various times this black rage was directed at whites in general, Korean grocery store owners, or Hasidic Jews.[32]

Crown Heights Jews disagreed with Rieder's attempt to fit the riot into a liberal academic framework. They questioned his claim that the racial and ethnic epithets expressed during the riot were ambiguous and murky, especially to "outside observers who may not understand the communicative routines and linguistic codes that shape both the usage and significance of vernacular denigration." Even the meaning of "Hitler should have finished the job!" was not so self-evident to this sociologist.[33] If, as Rieder believed, formal anti-Semitic belief systems were not present among the rioters (most of whom were young and poorly educated), certainly informal ones were. As even Rieder noted, the rioters baited Jews with shouts of "Hitler should have finished the job!" "Hitler was right!" "Sieg Heil!" and "Kill the Jew." Recent history had taught the Jews of Crown Heights, who certainly were not "outside observers," not to discount the words of those who said they wanted to kill Jews. Rieder's revisionism, by contrast, defied common sense. It also challenged the relevance of the Jews' own historical narrative.[34]

Rieder was one of many observers who stressed the social and economic roots of rioting in general and the Crown Heights riot in particular. Historian Robert Fogelson expressed the conventional liberal wisdom regarding the riots of the 1960s. They were, he said, "articulate protests against genuine grievances . . . [and] attempts to call the attention of white society to the blacks' widespread dissatisfaction with racial subordination and segregation."[35] Since the 1960s, liberals and radicals had frequently described rioters as "protesters," the riots as "insurrections" and "rebellions," and riotous behavior as "retaliatory violence." To their conservative critics, such explanations and terminology served to rationalize the violence of the rioters and to foster bizarre conspiratorial theories. For example, Richard Goldstein, a writer for the *Village Voice*, a left-wing weekly, said that the real culprit behind the

Crown Heights riot was a white power establishment that sought to funnel black rage onto poor Jews. This establishment hoped to divert black anger away from itself and to drive a wedge between progressive-minded blacks and Jews in the city.[36] There was, of course, no hard evidence of any such conspiracy.

More thoughtful observers emphasized the social and economic environment of the rioters. Their sociohistorical narrative underscored the role of material deprivation, alienation, and despair in determining the behavior of the poor, and was part of an emphasis on victimization and complaint that had become increasingly prominent in the nation since the 1960s. Taken to an extreme this explanation could lead to exculpating and even justifying the rioting. According to proponents of the sociohistorical narrative, the proper context for understanding the riot was the history of racism, both nationally and in New York City. Riots were, in effect, protests against racism and intolerable social and economic conditions. Thus the most important thing about the Crown Heights riot was the social and economic makeup of the rioters, not the ethnic and religious character of their targets. This emphasis on the rioters explains why reporters for New York newspapers could write stories about the riot without dwelling on the religious and ethnic nature of the victims.

One of these observers was *New York Times* columnist Anna Quindlen. Quindlen noted in her column of September 7, 1991, that while the anti-Semitic rhetoric of the rioters was "unforgivable and disgraceful," it was "also predictable." She believed the riot was, in essence, not a black-Jewish conflict but a racial clash between whites and blacks. "The misery that envelops the lives of poor black people in this country is so pervasive, so amorphous," she claimed, that "fixing blame" for the violence perpetrated by blacks in America "is often impossible." Quindlen's failure to mention Yankel Rosenbaum in her column was understandable as his death and the capture of his attackers was not relevant to what she believed to be the principal story of Crown Heights. She emphasized the struggle to better the lot of blacks. Quindlen concluded by saying that "the rage in Crown Heights is not about the death of one child," but about the daily racism experienced by blacks. "What must you feel," she asked her readers, "if your whole life is a slur, if you read the handwriting on the wall of your existence and the graffiti seems to say, 'Who cares?'"[37] Quindlen's critics charged that in her justified concern with the living conditions of the blacks of Crown Heights, she had ignored the pain of the Jews of Crown Heights. They had been the targets of a three-day riot, and one of them had been murdered and another had committed suicide. Weren't they also justified in feeling rage? Quindlen also failed to explain why most poor blacks did not riot, even though they were continually consumed by rage.

RACISM AS AN EXPLANATION

The urban rioting beginning in the 1960s had convinced many Americans that race was the key to understanding urban unrest. This view became an article of faith particularly within the American Left, and it was strongly affirmed by the Kerner Commission, established by the Johnson administration in the aftermath of the rioting in Los Angeles, Newark, Detroit, and other major cities between 1965 and 1967. The commission's mandate was to analyze the causes of the riots and then to suggest remedies. Its final report claimed that America was fast becoming two nations: one white, affluent, and suburban; the other black, poor, and urban (even though most poor people were white). Although this racial paradigm was hardly accurate even during the 1960s and was even more remote from reality during the following decades—by 1980 more than 23 percent of blacks and more than 50 percent of whites lived in suburbia—it was the most convenient and politically acceptable explanation for urban discontents.[38]

Race provided the context for the *New York Times*' reporting on the Crown Heights riot. Even when a *Times* article of August 21, 1991, noted that the antagonists were blacks and Hasidim, and not simply blacks and whites, the headline read "Two Deaths Ignite Racial Clash in Tense Brooklyn Neighborhood." The *Times* forced a conflict involving at least three groups—African Americans, Caribbeans, and Hasidim—into the pattern of a racial confrontation. "The antagonists of African descent," said the black political scientist Carole B. Conway, "belonged to ethnic groups that had very different histories and relationships with the Jewish community. An exclusively black/white or even black/Jewish frame misled readers when it referred to 'blacks and Jews' or 'blacks and Hasidim.'" Conway was particularly concerned with the effect of the *Times*' reporting on the image of blacks. "The inability to conceive of persons of African descent as having interaction more complex than racial conflicts with people whose skin color is white," she protested, "is symptomatic of a larger problem in American society itself—one that fails to define and understand individuals and communities of color as persons who have a complete range of humanity in their being, both for good and for evil."[39]

The *Times'* emphasis on race enabled it to bend over backward when describing the rioters, to narrow the moral differences between the rioters and their Hasidic victims by slighting the anti-Jewish animus of the rioters, and to stress that more had to be done in addressing the underlying causes of racial tensions. Hence the headline of one *Times* article on Crown Heights read "For Young Blacks, Alienation and a Growing Despair Turn into Rage," while another read "The Bitterness Flows in Two Directions." The *Times* continued well beyond 1991 to emphasize the racial nature of the riot. In an April 1992 article discussing the arrest of a suspect in the murder of Yankel Rosenbaum, the *Times* reporter noted that in Crown Heights the arrest had "served only to expose the scars left from the racial violence last summer." When Lemrick Nelson and Charles Price were convicted in February 1997 of violating the civil rights of Rosenbaum, the *Times* article claimed that the jury's decision had "laid bare once again New York's deep racial divide."[40] This emphasis on race ignored the fact that the victims of the Crown Heights riot, excluding the injured police, were not simply whites but Jews, or Gentiles mistaken for Jews.

The take of the *New York Times* on the Crown Heights riot reflected the political correctness of its ownership, editorial board, and reporters and was part of a pattern of reporting regarding racial issues. This pattern included the paper's account of a three-day riot fomented by illegal immigrant Dominican drug dealers, which it portrayed as justified community outrage prompted by the use of deadly force by the police; its coverage of the December 1995 arson slayings at a Jewish-owned clothing store on 125th Street in Harlem, in which the murderer was described as a soft-spoken man of principle and the store owner as an insular religious Jew; its description of the violence suffered by Asians at the hands of blacks, which downplayed the anti-Asian bias of the culprits; and a three-part series in March 1994 on Louis Farrakhan that suggested he was less extreme than commonly believed.[41]

Even those newspapers that did not share the politics of the *Times* used the racial paradigm to explain the riot. These included the *Daily News* and the *New York Post*, hardly paladins of racial political correctness. The *Daily News*, in two editorials in the week after the riot, called it a "racial explosion" and a "race riot." Neither mentioned anti-Semitism or dwelt on the religious and ethnic identity of the riot's victims. Reporter Mike McAlary titled one of his *New York Post* articles "Let's now seek justice in Yankel's lynching"; Eric Breindel, who had been among the first to depict the riot as a "pogrom," characterized it in 1993 as "New York's worst race riot in recent memory." In one piece for the *Wall Street Journal,* Breindel managed to call the riot an "anti-Semitic riot," an "urban race riot," and a "racial disturbance," and to state that Rosenbaum was "lynched." The two-volume report on the riot issued by Richard H. Girgenti, the New York State director of criminal justice, called it "the most extensive racial unrest New York City has experienced in over twenty years."[42]

The racial character of the Crown Heights riot came almost automatically to those who believed that race was the key to understanding the recent history of New York. These included *Newsday* columnist Jimmy Breslin, who had been attacked by blacks while covering the riot. "Blacks against whites is the fundamental story of the city in our time," he wrote in a July 1993 column. "Only now it is intensified to the point where the city rises or falls on the ability of whites to live with blacks." For him what made Crown Heights distinctive was not that it was the world center of the Lubavitch Hasidim or the center of the West Indian population in the United States. Rather, it was "the only place in the United States where you can find a group of whites in a neighborhood that is predominately of color." The Lubavitchers were distinctive not because of their Jewishness, but because they had not moved when blacks and West Indians settled in Crown Heights. The Lubavitch were less racist and "better than any other whites because they stayed and everybody else ran."[43]

The efforts of Breslin and others to put the Crown Heights riot within a racial context overlooked the sociological complexities of Crown Heights. The most numerous group in the area were not African Americans but first- and second-generation black West Indians. The West Indians could not be categorized simply in racial terms. Similarly, the whites of Crown Heights were not simply whites. They were also members of a hermetic religious community with its own traditions and values. These subtleties failed to affect the historical narrative of the riot propounded by some black politicians and black and white journalists for whom the major story was the deep-seated and ever-present racial oppression of blacks by whites.

A few blacks interpreted the Crown Heights riot within the matrix of black nationalism, racism, and Third World ideologies. For them the most salient characteristic of the Jews of Crown Heights was not their religion but their white skins, which provided them all the benefits accorded to the most privileged and oppressive sector of American society. From this perspective, the proper historical analogy was not between Crown Heights and Mississippi but between Crown Heights and Soweto or between Crown Heights and the Middle East, despite the fact that the Lubavitch lacked the political power and economic status associated with Western colonialists. Lubavitchers also were unable to exploit blacks economically, as they did not employ them in great numbers and had few blacks as tenants. Nevertheless, Al Sharpton described the Jews of Crown Heights as "diamond merchants," implying that the relationship between them and the blacks of Brooklyn was similar to that between white South African diamond mine owners and their black employees. "Talk about how Oppenheimer in South Africa sends diamonds straight to Tel Aviv and deals with the diamond merchants here in Crown Heights," he said in his eulogy at the funeral of Gavin Cato. "The issue is not anti-Semitism; the issue is apartheid." Sharpton also used his eulogy to encourage the young rioters to keep the pressure up. "Young people, don't apologize. Don't be ashamed and don't back up. You come from a great people. . . . In your body runs the blood of Malcolm X and Fannie Lou Hamer. Stand by; don't ever sit down. Forward ever, backward never! We will win because we're right."[44]

A few radical blacks also accused the Jews of Crown Heights of oppressing the blacks of Crown Heights in much the same way that the white "European" capitalist Israelis had suppressed the Palestinians, a people of color. As one radical black publication put it, Crown Heights was linked to South Africa and Palestine by "the common thread of racial and economic repression," while the international power of the "Zionist lobby" was indicated by David Dinkins's description of young blacks in Crown Heights as "hoodlums" rather than freedom fighters.[45] Critics of these black nationalist conspiracy theories responded that the Lubavitchers of Crown Heights were not wealthy, that few were involved in the diamond trade, that they had little influence over events in the Middle East, and that more than 50 percent of the Israelis came from Arab lands and were as much a "people of color" as the Arab Palestinians.

For black nationalists, Crown Heights was not a riot but a justified "rebellion" against racism and economic exploitation. This position was argued by a flyer advertising a rally on September 4, 1991, in Crown Heights to honor "The True Heroes of the Crown Heights Rebellion . . . Black Youth." It was distributed by a group calling itself the Black Consciousness Movement. The flyer described the young rioters as "the children of Malcolm X," and said that it was "better to fight on Utica and President Street than in Panama or the Persian Gulf, killing our own people of color." The headline of a 1994 *Crib News* article recounting the Crown Heights riot read "The Making of an Uprising." This claim that the violence of August 1991 was a "rebellion" or "uprising" was arguably the most important factor shaping the radical understanding of the Crown Heights riot.[46]

One example of such thinking was an article by Fred Goldstein in the far-left *Workers World* that appeared in the wake of the conviction of Lemrick Nelson in federal court for violating the civil rights of Yankel Rosenbaum. The trial and verdict, Goldstein said, was an example of "ruling-class retribution for an act of rebellion by an oppressed people." But the real villains were not the Lubavitchers of Crown Heights but the American ruling class, which had manipulated Crown Heights Jewry "for the purposes of oppression and division—in much the same way that the United States supports the Israeli state against the Palestinians and all the Arab people." Rebellion was inevitable under such conditions. "And in every rebellion there will be casualties."[47] Goldstein did not explain how the largely Protestant power elite used the Jews of Crown Heights or how they benefited from the poverty and high rate of unemployment of blacks in central Brooklyn and the "relatively privileged" status of the Lubavitch community.

Another radical attempt to justify the rioting was a 1998 article in *Revolutionary Worker,* an obscure radical publication, titled "Our Verdict Is: It's Right to Rebel!" The article was prompted by the sentencing of Lemrick Nelson and of Charles Price in federal court for depriving Yankel Rosenbaum of his civil rights and by Mayor Giuliani's apology to the Crown Heights Jewish community for the city's performance during the riot. These two events, the article claimed, reflected a view of what had occurred in August 1991 that "turns reality upside-down. It buries the real grievances that people have against police injustice and white supremacy in the Crown Heights community. It slanders a powerful and justified uprising among the people, and demonizes the Black and Caribbean youth of Crown Heights." The prosecution of Nelson and Price was part of the plan of the capitalist class and its lackeys in the government "to politically isolate the poorest sections of the population" and to carry out a policy of "divide-and-conquer." What occurred in August 1991 was not an anti-Jewish pogrom. Rather, "it was a justified rebellion protesting outrageous racist mistreatment, and it was overwhelmingly focused on driving the police out of the community." The "mass resistance" of the residents of Crown Heights was not directed at Jews, the *Revolutionary Worker* claimed, but at the police, the primary instrument for maintaining the "apartheid" of Crown Heights.[48] In fact, however, defenders of the rioters did not focus on the police. What complaints there were about the police came largely from Lubavitchers protesting the lack of protection. The police were criticized not for being oppressive but for being remiss in their duties.

Not all radicals, however, agreed with the black nationalists and their supporters. A group called the International Committee Against Racism published a statement that put the rioting within a nonnationalist Marxist framework. It favored uniting the working class against the "rich and powerful," irrespective of skin color. The events in Crown Heights, it said, were "only the tip of the iceberg; the rebellion is about many other things like police brutality, unemployment, rotten schools and health care, racist education, bad housing." It warned that attacking Jews and other whites because of their race and ethnicity divided the working class and furthered the capitalists' strategy of divide and rule. "We urge young people, who are in the leadership of this rebellion, not to be sucked into nationalist ideology. There are potentially thousands of white and other minority workers who would love to get involved in the struggle, if they felt they would be accepted as comrades-in-arms." Once all workers were involved, claimed the radicals, they could then move on to the overthrow of the "rotten system in a united, multi-racial, multi-cultural way."[49]

LIBERALS AND CONSERVATIVES

Liberals offered explanations of the Crown Heights riot that did not assume the racial balkanization of the city and the overthrow of capitalism. This judiciousness was particularly true of liberal Jews, for whom left-wing politics was a significant component of their Jewish identity and who rejected the idea that the riot signaled the end of the black-Jewish political alliance. One such individual was Victor A. Kovner, the chief corporation counsel during the Dinkins administration and a noted civil libertarian. In receiving the 1999 Stanley M. Isaacs Human Relations Award from the New York chapter of the American Jewish Committee, Kovner provided an interpretation of the riot that virtually ignored its anti-Semitic dimensions. He denied that the riot arose out of a basic conflict of interest between the city's Jewish and black communities. Rather, he argued, it had been triggered by "misunderstandings," particularly the widespread resentment among blacks regarding the special privileges accorded the Lubavitch by the city, including the police escort provided to Rabbi Schneerson on his frequent trips to the Lubavitch cemetery in Queens. Kovner was gratified that Jews dedicated to the civil rights movement had not been dissuaded by the riot. If anything, he said, their commitment had intensified.[50]

Rabbi Marshall Meyer of Temple B'nai Jeshurun on Manhattan's Upper West Side provided an alternative liberal explanation for the riot. Meyer had fled Argentina during the 1980s for political reasons, and his experience of living in a country dominated by an anti-Semitic military junta had shaped his understanding of the causes of anti-Semitism. These causes were to be found in economic and social injustices, whether in Argentina or in the United States. "It's no surprise that we might expect a problem with anti-Semitism after twelve years of Reagan and Bush in which social inequalities have grown," he said in 1993.[51]

Meyer's comments indicates the extent to which the Crown Heights riot had become a Rorschach inkblot in which people saw whatever they wanted. If the policies of Reagan and Bush had indeed caused an increase of anti-Semitism—a dubious proposition in view of public opinion surveys that showed that anti-Jewish sentiment continued to decline during the 1980s and early 1990s—one would expect an increase in anti-Semitic activity and in events similar to that which occurred in Crown Heights in August 1991. But there were none. The Crown Heights riot was sui generis and the result of unique local conditions.

Conservatives, by contrast, asserted that the sources of the Crown Heights riot were to be found in liberalism and multiculturalism. Richard Brookhiser of the right-wing magazine *National Review* claimed the riot had resulted from the attenuating of a common civic identity and the undermining of respect for authority brought about by multiculturalism. The riot had "exposed multiculturalism as an unworkable civic ideal, though whether anyone will come up with a workable one is another question."[52] But conservatives believed that multiculturalism was merely symptomatic of the deeper rot with which the Left had infected New York City. A contempt for a supposedly racist police force, a cult of victimization that excused violence when committed by those suffering from racial discrimination and economic deprivation, and a belief that social and economic conditions and not individual qualities determine one's fate—all of these ideas were key to the Leftist ideology and had seeped into the mind-set of the rioters. Conservatives also criticized explanations of the riot that emphasized its social and economic "root causes." These, conservatives believed, provided a patina of legitimacy and sociological exoneration for what was essentially lawlessness. For conservatives, it was not surprising that such rationalizations and the riot itself would occur in what was arguably America's quintessentially left-wing city.

Their criticisms of liberal "root causes" theories of the Crown Heights riot did not prevent conservatives from providing their own "root causes" for the riot, and these, not surprisingly, underscored the culpability of the Left. Amity Shlaes, in an op-ed piece in the *Wall Street Journal* published a week after the riot, delineated the social roots of the riot. It had primarily resulted from "thirty years of welfare culture in which fostering minorities' sense of entitlement has caused only greater rage." From Shlaes's perspective, rioting was rational for people embittered by society's indifference to their claims.[53]

The major problem with the conservative interpretation of the Crown Heights riot, as well as with the leftist claim that the riot was inevitable given the depressing social and economic conditions of the ghetto, is that there should have been additional riots in other parts of the city. The welfare culture and poverty among blacks and West Indians had existed before and after August 1991 and in other parts of the city (and country) besides Crown Heights. Neither conservatives nor the Left offered a credible explanation for the absence of other riots, showing the inherent weakness of any interpretation of the Crown Heights riot that ignores its ethnic dimensions.

While disagreeing as to the roots of the riot, liberals and conservatives agreed that the Crown Heights riot had a logic to it. In so doing they were in the tradition of sociologists as ideologically diverse as Gustave LeBon, Emile Durkheim, Max Weber, Vilfredo Pareto, Robert Park, Georg Simmel, Neil Smelser, and Talcott Parsons, all of whom had sought to fathom the sociological patterns of civil violence. In addition, historians such as Charles Tilly, E. P. Thompson, George Rude, and

Georges Lefebvre had asserted that rioting in France and England had not been aimless but purposeful. The urban riots of the 1960s strengthened the inclination to believe that rioting was rational. The riots in the depressed black ghettos of Los Angeles, Washington, Detroit, Chicago, Newark, and other American cities, it was argued, was an attempt by the poor and inarticulate to make themselves heard, to effect economic and social change. As Paul A. Gilje said in his history of American rioting, "riotous crowds do not act merely on impulse and are not fickle. There is a reason behind the actions of rioters, no matter how violent these actions may be. . . . In any given situation, rioters have an infinite number of options. But the activity selected by rioters is not capricious nor random."[54] But if the riots were purposeful, why were there not additional urban riots in the 1970s, particularly since the economic and social conditions of the inner city did not dramatically change from those of the 1960s?

Joe R. Feagin and Harlan Hahn's book *Ghetto Revolts* strongly argued that the riots of the 1960s could best be explained by examining the economic and social conditions of the cities and the pervasive racism of American society rather than by analyzing the psychological makeup of the rioters. The rioting, they argued, was "intimately related to the attempts of blacks to move out of the grip of the neocolonialism characteristic of the ghetto, to remove the control of modern-day white carpetbaggers over their lives." The riots were "politically disruptive acts in a continuing politically motivated struggle between competing vested interest groups," and collective violence was "one of the ultimate weapons of any people whose political aspirations remain significantly unfulfilled and other alternatives have been tried." Feagin and Hahn's use of the word "revolts" in the title of their book reflects their belief that the riots were essentially political events similar to the American, French, and Russian revolutions and not aimless violence. Other scholars preferred to call the riots "protests."[55]

Not everyone agreed. The McCone Commission, which investigated the Watts riot in Los Angeles in 1965, concluded that it had been irrational and purposeless. Many Americans blamed the urban riots on hostile lower-class youths, predatory hoodlums, and adolescents acting out their "animal spirits." The riots, they believed, were not provoked by legitimate economic, social, and political grievances, nor did the rioters have a program to alleviate the problems of the ghettos. The rioters were socially estranged and behaved outside the boundaries of acceptable social and political norms. Harvard political scientist Edward C. Banfield was the most prominent advocate of the apolitical character of the riots. He titled chapter nine of his controversial book *The Unheavenly City*, published in 1970, "Rioting Mainly for Fun and Profit."[56]

Some observers of the Crown Heights riot came to the same conclusion. They noted that the rioters did not articulate any social and economic goals, and their leaders did not advocate any collective political objectives. Columnist Murray Kempton argued that the ultimate cause of the 1991 riot was the existence of "a class of surplus persons, for whom no useful function is available and who are kept alive badly fed and warehoused and denied most means of expression beyond the angry shouts on the street." It was impossible to fathom a purpose behind the nihilistic actions of this *lumpenproletariat* besides assuaging their desperate and empty lives. If in 1991 this was to be achieved by attacks on Jews, in the future the underclass's aimless fury would have other targets.[57]

It was easier to claim that the riots of the 1960s, in contrast to the Crown Heights riot, were politically motivated because their targets included instruments of political power such as the police. But the economic and political grievances of the rioters against the Lubavitchers were less clear. The African Americans and West Indians of Crown Heights did not, by and large, shop at Lubavitch-owned stores in the neighborhood; and the rioters did not complain about price-gouging by the area's white merchants or of excessive rents of apartments owned by Lubavitchers. Nor did the rioters claim that the Lubavitch were "carpetbaggers" who did not belong in the area. It was also difficult to claim that the Lubavitchers were politically oppressing their neighbors. Crown Heights politics were controlled by African Americans and West Indians, and African Americans dominated the Democratic party of Brooklyn. Clearly, the Crown Heights riot differed dramatically from its predecessors of the 1960s.

This difference is clearly seen in the mandates of the Kerner Commission and the Girgenti Report on Crown Heights. In his executive order establishing the National Advisory Commission on Civil Disorders, President Johnson asked for it to discover, among other things, "What is the relative impact of the depressed conditions in the ghetto—joblessness, family instability, poor education, lack of motivation, poor health care—in stimulating people to riot? What Federal, State and local programs have been most helpful in relieving those depressed conditions?" Governor Mario Cuomo's charge to Richard H. Girgenti, the state's director of criminal justice, was more narrowly focused. He directed Girgenti to "review the response of law enforcement to the August, 1991 disturbance in Crown Heights and the facts and circumstances surrounding the criminal investigation and prosecution arising from the death of Yankel Rosenbaum."[58]

In contrast to the riots of the 1960s, there was little soul-searching among whites regarding the social and economic implications of the Crown Heights riot, nor were there calls for social and economic reforms. Politicians, including the governor and mayor, did not dwell on social and economic conditions in Crown Heights. Rioting, these officials said, was unjustified under any circumstances, and their major response to the Crown Heights riot involved improving police procedures in order to nip future riots in the bud. Thus the focus of attention in the two-volume Girgenti Report was on the failure of the police to preserve law and order; it said little regarding the social and economic conditions that might have been responsible for the riot in the first place.

The most popular interpretation of the riot among Crown Heights residents—Jews, blacks, and West Indians alike—was that the riot had been fomented by violent and alienated persons who did not live in Crown Heights, and that the riot conveyed too pessimistic a view of the race relations in the area. In Anna Deavere Smith's play *Fires in the Mirror,* Roslyn Malamud, a Lubavitcher living in Crown Heights, asked, "Do you know that the Blacks who came here to riot were not my neighbors? . . . The people who came to riot here were brought here by this famous Reverend Al Sharpton, which I'd like to know who ordained him? He brought in a bunch of kids who didn't have jobs in the summertime."[59]

Martin Markowitz, who represented Crown Heights in the New York State Senate, agreed. He described the riot as an "unfortunate incident" caused by outsiders "who see no hope for themselves and the future."[60] Markowitz and others emphasized the random and irrational nature of the Crown Heights riot in order to salvage what remained of the black-Jewish progressive political entente. Cornel West argued that the riot was an unorganized and "random act" brought on by the death of Gavin Cato. It was not proof of widespread anti-Semitism among blacks. In fact, West claimed, blacks "unequivocally" opposed anti-Semitism. Richard Goldstein of the *Village Voice,* the same person who argued that the riot had been fostered by the white power establishment, also emphasized the random nature of the riot. Its real lesson, he said, "is that Jews must learn to live in a more dangerous world, where hate goes unanswered and primitive passions are stoked as a safety valve for helpless rage."[61] But randomness and outside agitators do not explain a riot that lasted for some three days. Nor do they explain why Jews were the targets of the rioters, why violent, alienated, and hateful persons would riot only once, and why outsider agitators would select Crown Heights as the location for their one riot.

In *Zakhor: Jewish History and Jewish Memory,* his classic account of Jewish historiography, Yosef Hayim Yerushalmi noted that the historian aspires to do more than merely fill in the gaps in memory. "He constantly challenges even those memories that have survived intact."[62] The historian's task is particularly difficult regarding the Crown Heights riot because of intense historical memories involving ethnicity and political ideology. These memories were not only simplistic ways to understand the riot. They were also instrumental in the maintenance and acquisition of power, and they expressed deeply held group and individual identities involving what historian Michael Vorenberg has called the "contested nature of memory."[63]

Notes

1. Alan Mintz, *Popular Culture and the Shaping of Holocaust Memory in America* (Seattle: University of Washington Press, 2001), 72.
2. David W. Blight, *Race and Reunion: The Civil War in American History* (Cambridge, Mass.: Harvard University Press, 2001), 191; Steven J. Zipperstein, *Imagining Russian Jewry: Memory, History, Identity* (Seattle: University of Washington Press, 1999), 95.
3. Hasia R. Diner, *Lower East Side Memories: A Jewish Place in America* (Princeton, N.J.: Princeton University Press, 1999), 18–19.
4. Thucydides quoted in Blight, *Race and Reunion,* v; Edward Hoffman, *Despite All Odds: The Story of Lubavitch* (New York: Simon and Schuster, 1991), 148.
5. Henry Goldschmidt, "Peoples Apart: Race, Religion, and Other Jewish Differences in Crown Heights" (Ph.D. diss., University of California at Santa Cruz, 2000), 290–313.
6. Allan Nadler, "Last Exit to Brooklyn," *New Republic* 206 (May 4, 1992): 2; Jonathan Mark, "Crown Heights: 'Great Test' for Messianists," *Jewish Week,* August 30–September 5, 1991; David Remnick, "Waiting for the Apocalypse in Crown Heights," *New Yorker* 68 (December 21, 1992), 53; Binyamin Jolkovsky,

"Waiting for the King Messiah—and Wondering," *Forward*, November 19, 1994; Michael Specter, "Rabbi Menachem Schneerson: The Oracle of Crown Heights," *New York Times Magazine*, March 15, 1992, 35–38, 67–76. "Moshiach" is Hebrew for messiah. "In times of severe social dislocation, political change, and economic upheaval, individuals . . . may turn to apocalyptic millenarianism. They see the signs that their tradition has identified as portents of the end of time. The tribulation they experience is interpreted as the era of cataclysms that precede the eruption of a new order and God's reassertion of His beneficent rule." Daniel Benjamin and Steven Simon, *The Age of Sacred Terror* (New York: Random House, 2002), 424.

7. Alan Nadler, "Last Exit to Brooklyn," *New Republic* 206 (May 4, 1992): 28; Jonathan Mark, "Crown Heights."
8. Andy Newman, "Painstakingly, Picking a Jury for 3rd Trial in Race Killing," *New York Times*, April 26, 2003. An editorial in the New York *Daily News* of April 30, 2003 ("Crown Heights: The Defense Jests") described Rosenbaum as a "bearded, black-clad Hasid."
9. Goldschmidt, "Peoples Apart," 289.
10. A. M. Rosenthal, "Pogrom in Brooklyn," *New York Times*, September 3, 1991.
11. Ibid.
12. For an analysis of the *New York Post*'s coverage of the Crown Heights riot, see the unpublished paper by Professor Laurence Roth of Susquehanna University, "Tabloid Blacks and Jews: The *New York Post* Covers the Crown Heights Riots"; see also Richard Goldstein, "The Politics of Hate: Crown Heights and the Future of New York," *Village Voice* 37 (December 15, 1992), 12.
13. Eric Breindel, "Brooklyn Pogrom: Why the Silence?" *New York Post*, September 5, 1991. The editor of a collection of Breindel's writings retitled this column "Kristallnacht in Brooklyn." John Podhoretz, ed., *A Passion for Truth: The Selected Writings of Eric Breindel* (New York: HarperCollins, 1999), 108–111. In a *New York Post* editorial of June 10, 1993, that strongly defended the use of "pogrom," Breindel rejected the notion that a pogrom by definition must be state-sanctioned. Podhoretz, ed., *Passion for Truth*, 120–22. See also the editorial "An Ugly Word Grows in Brooklyn," *New York Post*, August 29, 1991.
14. Councilman Noach Dear News Release, "Dear Calls Upon Police Commissioner to Stop Pogrom," August 22, 1991, American Jewish Committee Papers, New York; Simon Schneebalg, "After the Pogrom—an Analysis and Proposal," *Jewish Week*, September 27–October 3, 1991; "Statement of Judah Gribetz, President, JCRC," October 29, 1992, Jewish Community Relations of New York Papers, New York; "Crown Heights Closure?" *Forward*, April 3, 1998; "The Brooklyn Pogrom," *Jerusalem Post*, August 26, 1991; Shmuel M. Butman, "The Crown Heights Pogrom: Ten Years Later," *Jewish Press*, August 17, 2001.

15. *New York Times*, September 20, 1991 (italics in original).
16. Jonathan Rieder, "Crown of Thorns," *New Republic* 205 (October 14, 1991): 28; Ellin Ronee Pollachek, "America's Kristallnacht: Anti-Semitism in Our Own Backyard," *Jewish Press*, October 11, 1991; Popack quoted in Dennis Duggan, "A Divide Uncrossed by Either Side," *New York Post*, August 22, 1991. George P. Fletcher, *With Justice for Some: Victims' Rights in Criminal Trials* (Reading, Mass.: Addison-Wesley, 1995), 69.
17. "Crown Depths," *New Republic* 209 (August 8, 1993): 7–8; Craig Horowitz, "The New Anti-Semitism," *New York* 26 (January 11, 1993): 23–24; Irving Greenberg, "Confronting Anti-Semitism: Steps for Blacks, Jews," *Jewish Week*, September 27–October 3, 1991; Richard Cohen, "Victims of Black Anti-semitism," *Washington Post*, October 4, 1991.
18. Ed Koch, "'Pogrom' Is an Ugly Term, But It Applies," *Daily News*, June 11, 1993; Guiliani quoted in *Daily News*, July 1, 1993. See also Koch, "City Silent in Face of a New Pogrom," *New York Post*, August 30, 1991. The August 26–September 2, 1996, issue of the *New York Observer* contained an editorial titled "The Pogrom in Crown Heights."
19. Dinkins and Sharpton quoted in Frank Lombardi, "Rev. Al: Rudy's Race Baiting," *Daily News*, June 2, 1993; Earl Caldwell, "Saying 'Pogrom' Does Violence to the City," *Daily News*, June 2, 1993; *City Sun*, June 2–8, 1993.
20. Dinkins quoted in Paul Schwartzman, "Angry Dinkins: Crown Hts. Wasn't a 'Pogrom,'" *New York Post*, December 8, 1992; Remnick, "Waiting for the Apocalypse in Crown Heights," 57.
21. Stanislawski quoted in Joel Siegel, "Dinkins Huffy at Wordplay," *Daily News*, December 8, 1992; Joyce Purnick, "Crown Heights Was Not Iasi," *New York Times*, June 3, 1993.
22. Siegman quoted in Jerome A. Chanes, "Intergroup Relations," in *American Jewish Year Book, 1993*, ed. David Singer (Philadelphia: American Jewish Committee, 1993), 93; Marc D. Stern, "The Problem of Crown Heights," *Congress Monthly* 60 (January 1993): 12.
23. Cornel West, *Race Matters* (New York: Random House, 1994), 111.
24. Dinkins quoted in *New York Times*, September 7, 1991. The *New York Post*, the mayor's leading journalistic foe, touched all the ethnic bases in describing the Crown Heights riot. On its first anniversary, it published an editorial titled "Anniversary of a Lynching." *New York Post*, August 19, 1992.
25. *New York Times*, September 10, 1991; Moore quoted in *Amsterdam News*, September 14, 1991.
26. Moynihan quoted in *New York Post*, September 7, 1991.
27. Ibid.
28. Tim Robbins, "Tales of Crown Heights: The Fruits of Harassment," *City Limits* 6 (December 1981): 12; Wade quoted in Goldstein, "Politics of Hate," 11; Jonathan Rieder, "The Tribes of Brooklyn: Race, Class, and Ethnicity in the

Crown Heights Riots," in *The Tribal Basis of American Life: Racial, Religious, and Ethnic Groups in Conflict*, ed. Murray Friedman and Nancy Isserman (Westport, Conn.: Praeger, 1998), 71.

29. Bogard quoted in *Newsday*, August 26, 1991.
30. Peter Noel, "Crown Heights Burning: Rage, Race, and the Politics of Resistance," *Village Voice* 36 (September 3, 1991), 37–40; Powls quoted in *Newsday*, August 26, 1991.
31. Mary Pinkett quoted in Jerome R. Mintz, *Hasidic People: A Place in the New World* (Cambridge, Mass.: Harvard University Press, 1994), 337; Pinkett quoted in Andrew W. Cooper, "The Two Nations of Crown Heights," *New York Times*, January 6, 1992.
32. Rieder, "Tribes of Brooklyn," 63–66; Rieder, "Reflections on Crown Heights: Interpretive Dilemmas and Black Jewish Conflict," in *Antisemitism in America Today: Outspoken Experts Explode the Myths*, ed. Jerome A. Chanes (New York: Birch Lane, 1995), 358–69; Rieder, "Crown of Thorns," *New Republic* 205 (October 14, 1991): 26–31.
33. Rieder, "Tribes of Brooklyn," 62, 64, 66.
34. Marvin Greisman, "Liberal Professor Engages in Crown Heights Revisionism," *Jewish Press*, April 12, 1998.
35. Robert Fogelson, "Violence as Protest," in *Riot, Rout, and Tumult: Readings in American Social and Political Violence*, ed. Roger Lane and John J. Turner (Westport, Conn.: Greenwood, 1978), 343.
36. Richard Goldstein, "The New Anti-Semitism: A Geshrei," *Village Voice* 36 (October 1, 1991), 34–36.
37. Anna Quindlen, "The Graffiti on the Wall," *New York Times*, September 7, 1991.
38. Kenneth T. Jackson, *Crabgrass Frontier: The Suburbanization of the United States* (New York: Oxford University Press, 1985), 301.
39. Carole B. Conway, "Crown Heights: Politics and Press Coverage of the Race War That Wasn't," *Polity* 32 (Fall 1999): 106, 118.
40. *New York Times*, August 23, 1991; ibid., April 9, 1992; ibid., February 11, 1997; Hilton Kramer, "What the *Times* Still Won't Say About the Crown Heights Riot," *New York Post*, April 2, 1996.
41. William McGowan, *Coloring the News: How Crusading for Diversity Has Corrupted American Journalism* (San Francisco, Calif.: Encounter Books, 2001), 26, 64–69. For a bitter criticism of the *Times'* reporting on Jewish issues, see Jonathan Silverman, "On the *New York Times* and Jews in Danger," *Jewsweek*, May 14, 2002, http.//jewsweek.com/editorial. For another hostile view of the *New York Times'* reporting on crime, race, and the police, see Heather Mac Donald, *Are Cops Racist?* (Chicago: Ivan R. Dee, 2003), 40–52, 57, 65–67, 100, 107–8, 123–28.
42. "Cooling Crown Heights Is a Long-Term Job," *Daily News*, August 22, 1991; "Crown Heights: The Vultures Descend," *Daily News*, August 23, 1991; *New*

York Post, September 9, 1991; Breindel, "The Lemrick Nelson Trial: Still No Valid Explanation," *New York Post*, July 29, 1993; Breindel, "Autopsy of a Riot," *Wall Street Journal*, July 22, 1993; Richard H. Girgenti, *A Report to the Governor on the Disturbances in Crown Heights*, vol. 1, *An Assessment of the City's Preparedness and Response to Civil Disorder* (Albany, N.Y.: New York State Division of Criminal Justice Services, 1993), iii.

43. Jimmy Breslin, "The Lubavitchers Will Never Run," *Newsday*, July 21, 1993.

44. Sharpton quoted in J. J. Goldberg, *Jewish Power: Inside the American Jewish Establishment* (Reading, Mass.: Addison-Wesley, 1996), 307–8.

45. *Arm the Masses* 1 (September 1991): 3. This magazine was published by the "December 12th Movement."

46. A copy of the flier is in the Crown Heights riot files in the archives of the Jewish Community Relations Council of New York; *Carib News*, August 23, 1994.

47. Fred Goldstein, "No Justice, No Peace: Behind the Crown Heights Verdict," *Workers World*, February 20, 1997.

48. "Our Verdict Is: It's Right to Rebel!," *Revolutionary Worker*, September 6, 1998 This article is available online at http://rwor.org.

49. The statement of the International Committee Against Racism is in the Crown Heights riot files in the archives of the Jewish Community Relations Council of New York.

50. Kovner quoted in Peter Noel, "Hillary's Crown Heights Problem," *Village Voice* 43 (August 24, 1999), 63. For a statement by the Brooklyn chapter of the left-wing New Jewish Agenda in the aftermath of the riot that denied that anti-Semitism was rife among blacks and called for strengthening the black-Jewish coalition, see the *Amsterdam News*, September 14, 1991.

51. Meyer's quote is from "Beyond Crown Heights: Strategies for Overcoming Anti-Semitism and Racism in New York," *Tikkun* 8 (January–February, 1993): 60. For an article that blames unemployment for the riot, see Sheryl McCarthy, "In Crown Heights, Jobless Numbers Tell the Story Behind the Violence," *Newsday*, August 26, 1991.

52. Richard Brookhiser, "On the Offensive," *National Review* 45 (February 2, 1993): 24; for a rejection of the"root causes" explanation of the riot, see the editorial "Failure in Crown Heights," *New York Post*, July 21, 1993.

53. Amity Shlaes, "In Brooklyn, Not Just Another Racial Incident," *Wall Street Journal*, August 26, 1991. The article on Crown Heights in the conservative monthly *Commentary* argued that the motivating force behind the riot was black anti-Semitism. Philip Gourevitch, "The Crown Heights Riot and Its Aftermath," *Commentary* 95 (January 1993): 30–31.

54. James B. Rule, *Theories of Civil Violence* (Berkeley and Los Angeles: University of California Press, 1988); Paul A. Gilje, *Rioting in America* (Bloomington: Indiana University Press, 1996), 6.

55. Joe R. Feagin and Harlan Hahn, *Ghetto Revolts: The Politics of Violence in American Cities* (New York: Macmillan, 1973), 47–54.
56. Edward C. Banfield, *The Unheavenly City: The Nature and Future of Our Urban Crisis* (Boston: Little, Brown, 1970).
57. Murray Kempton, "Blood and Anger and Indifference," *Newsday*, August 28, 1991. For other journalistic statements in this vein, see Felicia R. Lee, "For Many Young Blacks, Alienation and a Growing Despair Turn Into Rage," *New York Times*, October 25, 1991; Sam Roberts, "On the Mean Streets, A Greater Sense of Alienation," *New York Times*, September 8, 1991.
58. "Remarks of the President Upon Issuing an Executive Order Establishing a National Advisory Commission on Civil Disorders, July 29, 1967," in *Report of the National Advisory Commission on Civil Disorders* (New York: Bantam Books, 1968), 537; Governor Mario M. Cuomo, Executive Order 160, "Directing a Review of the Criminal Investigation and Prosecution Arising From the Murder of Yankel Rosenbaum," in *A Report to the Governor on the Disturbances in Crown Heights*, by Richard H. Girgenti, vol. 1, *An Assessment of the City's Preparedness and Response to Civil Disorder* (Albany, N.Y.: New York State Division of Criminal Justice Services, 1993), A-1.
59. Anna Deavere Smith, *Fires in the Mirror: Crown Heights, Brooklyn and Other Identities* (New York: Anchor Books, 1995), 123–24.
60. Markowitz quoted in *Newsday*, August 26, 1991.
61. Michael Lerner and Cornel West, *Blacks and Jews: Let the Healing Begin* (New York: Grosset/Putnam, 1995), 181; Richard Goldstein, "The New Anti-Semitism," 38.
62. Yosef Hayim Yerushalmi, *Zakhor: Jewish History and Jewish Memory* (Seattle: University of Washington Press, 1982), 94.
63. Michael Vorenberg, "Recovered Memory of the Civil War," *Reviews in American History* 29 (December 2001): 557.

6

JUDGES AND JURIES

No aspect of the post-1991 history of the Crown Heights riot attracted more public attention than the four trials resulting from the murder of Yankel Rosenbaum. These trials, which began in 1992 and ended in 2004, took place in state and federal courts and involved, among other matters, the Fifth and Fourteenth Amendments to the Constitution and the scope of federal civil rights legislation. The decisions in these trials inflamed rather than calmed a public unfamiliar with the subtleties of the law, and accusations of jury nullification, double jeopardy, and jury manipulation followed in their wake. For much of the public, these legal proceedings were as much political as legal events, and it is possible that David Dinkins would have been reelected mayor in 1993 had the jury not exonerated Lemrick Nelson on October 29, 1992.[1]

A guilty verdict would have dissipated much of the anger of Jews over the mayor's handling of the riot, would have obviated the need for a state investigation of the riot, and would have weakened the claims of incompetence directed at the mayor during the campaign. The mayor contributed to the political significance of the October 29 decision when he advised New Yorkers to respect the jury's decision. The mayor, however, did not believe jury decisions to be sacrosanct. He had previously criticized the jury in the Rodney King case in California that freed several white police officers accused of beating King. The mayor's critics charged that this demonstrated a double standard when it came to white and black defendants.

The response to the exoneration of Nelson was not surprising because the evidence of his guilt appeared to be overwhelming. Only a prejudiced jury, it was argued, could have come to such a bizarre conclusion. Lost in all this furor was that the racially diverse jurors—six blacks, four Hispanics, and two whites—had good reasons for their decision. Contrary to popular belief, the jurors did not act capriciously, did not have an inherent distrust of the police, and were not prejudiced against whites in general and Jews in particular. In fact, one of the jurors was married to a policeman and another said she was planning to attend the city's police academy.[2] The Girgenti Report concluded that the jury had little choice but to acquit in view of the incompetence of the police and bungling by the Brooklyn district attorney's office. "The reasonable doubts articulated by the jurors arose, to a great extent from the inconsistencies in the witnesses' testimony and deficiencies in the evidence. . . . Moreover, the jurors were not persuaded by the forensic evidence presented by the prosecution, because they did not understand its significance."[3]

Nelson had been indicted on two counts of murder in the second degree and one count of criminal possession of a weapon (the knife used to stab Yankel Rosenbaum) in the fourth degree. The two murder charges presented alternative theories of Nelson's responsibility for the killing of Rosenbaum, and this contradiction possibly confused the jurors. The first count charged that Nelson, acting in concert with others, intentionally caused Rosenbaum's death by stabbing him. The second count claimed that, even if Nelson did not intend to kill Rosenbaum, he was criminally responsible because, acting in concert with others and "under circumstances evincing a depraved indifference to human life," he had created a grave risk to Rosenbaum by inflicting wounds that ultimately caused his death.[4]

The government's case in all three counts rested largely on testimony from ten police officers regarding the events leading up to Nelson's arrest, his identification by Rosenbaum as the person who stabbed him, and his confession. The police named Nelson as one of the persons who had been crouching over Rosenbaum's body and then had fled when they approached the crime scene. Forensic witnesses for the prosecution testified that the blood on Nelson's pants, his knife, and a dollar bill found in his pants pocket was of the same blood type as Rosenbaum's and not Nelson's, and that only one percent of the population had Rosenbaum's blood subtype. The prosecution also introduced evidence indicating that the shape of Rosenbaum's wounds were consistent with the knife found on Nelson, and that these wounds caused Rosenbaum's death.[5]

Arthur Lewis, Nelson's attorney, called fifteen witnesses for the defense. He attempted to prove that the police were involved in an anti-Nelson conspiracy in order to cover up the "criminal and improper acts" they had committed at the scene of the Gavin Cato accident, that Rosenbaum somehow had provoked the attack on himself, that the police felt pressure to arrest someone, anyone, for the attack on Rosenbaum, and that Nelson's confession was coerced. There is no evidence that Lewis's provocative questioning of the prosecution's witnesses influenced the jury.[6] The witnesses he called were another matter. Mark Taff, a forensic pathologist from Long Island, testified that sloppy work by the Office of the Chief Medical Examiner of New York City made it impossible to determine whether Nelson's knife caused Rosenbaum's wounds. Two other defense witnesses testified that Nelson had not exhibited violent tendencies in the past, and that he was so mentally deficient that he could neither understand nor waive his *Miranda* rights when he confessed to the police without a lawyer being present.[7]

Although the prosecution seemed to have presented a far more convincing case than the defense, the jury, after four days of deliberation, cleared Nelson on all counts. The jury believed that he had been part of the group that assaulted Rosenbaum, but unanimously concluded that the prosecution had not proved he was guilty of murder or manslaughter "beyond a reasonable doubt." After the decision was announced, the city offered a $10,000 reward for information leading to the arrest and prosecution of those responsible for the death of Rosenbaum. A $10,000 reward offered in September 1991 by the Jewish Community Relations Council and the Crown Heights Jewish Community Council had not resulted in any additional arrests, and there was no reason to believe that any reward offered by the city would be more effective. The city's reward was criticized for being too little, too late, and cosmetic.[8]

Legal observers severely faulted the police investigation of Rosenbaum's murder. Even though Rosenbaum was alive for three hours after the initial attack and lucid during most of this period, he was never questioned by the police. This foreclosed any possibility that he could provide more information about Nelson and his other assailants. The police also failed to take a statement from Nelson immediately after his arrest. The statement provided by Nelson came three hours after he was arrested, and it was neither tape-recorded or video-recorded. While the police claimed Nelson had waived his *Miranda* rights against self-incrimination, he did not sign any document to that effect. Although Nelson supposedly confessed to police officers on two different occasions, there was only one officer present at each time, and neither one took contemporaneous notes of what Nelson said. Whether, in fact, Nelson ever admitted to stabbing Rosenbaum was unprovable as long as he continued to deny it. It was not until eight hours after the attack on Rosenbaum that an assistant district attorney even attempted to take a statement from Nelson, and by this time Nelson recognized that he was in serious trouble. He refused to waive his *Miranda* rights and to make any statement about the crime.[9] "No mode of interrogation could inspire less confidence," said Columbia University law professor George P. Fletcher.[10]

Sloppy police work also undermined the credibility of the prosecution's forensic evidence presented during the trial. From the jury's perspective, the bloodstained knife—potentially the prosecution's most important piece of physical evidence—had little probative value. It had been handled by too many people, mingled with other evidence, and not recorded in a timely manner. It was also impossible to prove that the DNA of the blood on the knife was Rosenbaum's. The jurors also wondered why the knife was found in his right pocket when Nelson was left-handed.[11]

Questions were also raised by the defense regarding Nelson's bloodstained pants. They were not properly tested to see whether the stains came from Rosenbaum's wounds or from Rosenbaum spitting at Nelson when he was presented to him for identification. While the blood on Nelson's pants was identical to the blood of Rosenbaum, it was also identical to the blood of 11 percent of the American population.[12] The jurors, the Girgenti Report concluded, "did not think that the forensic experts did everything that could have been done to ensure that the best possible evidence was discovered and analyzed. Also, the jurors said the value of the forensic evidence was discounted because they did not understand its significance."[13]

The jury was also not swayed by Rosenbaum's identification of Nelson as the person who stabbed him, one of the strongest elements in the prosecution's case. Although Rosenbaum was quite lucid before he was transported to the hospital, the jurors did not believe his identification of his assailant was reliable in light of the severity of his wounds. They also concluded that the police had been unduly suggestive when they showed Nelson's knife to the victim and then asked him whether Nelson was the person who had stabbed him. Furthermore, the jurors believed it was questionable whether Rosenbaum's statement "Why did you stab me?" even referred to Nelson. It was possible that "you" referred to all of his attackers and not merely to Nelson.[14]

The prosecution's case was also hampered by the conduct of the trial judge, Edward M. Rappaport.[15] The judge's frequent comments to the defense, his continuous interjecting of himself in the questioning of witnesses, and his skepticism regarding the testimony of several of the prosecution's witnesses probably influenced the jury and raised questions about his objectivity. At one point he ordered police officers to return to court in order to clarify their testimony. The jury got the impression that Rappaport believed that some of the prosecution's witnesses were lying. The Girgenti Report noted that the judge "did not remain an impartial arbitrator and instead conveyed to the jury his personal opinions about the evidence."[16] Rappaport's performance was certainly unusual by the standards of American jurisprudence. He "lacked a professional sense of decorum and restraint," said George Fletcher. "He often sucked candies during the trial. He took telephone calls while he was on the bench." But his most notable failing, Fletcher wrote, "was his inability to restrain his arrogance. He acted as though justice depended exclusively on him."[17]

The jurors believed Nelson was guilty of something even though the prosecution had not persuaded them that he had done the actual stabbing. Several said after the trial that they might have voted to convict if Nelson had been charged with a less serious offense such as assault in the first or second degree, manslaughter, or "depraved indifference to murder." A conviction of Nelson on a lesser charge would have partially pacified those convinced of his guilt and would have eliminated the pressure on Governor Cuomo to call for an investigation of the riot and the performance of the Brooklyn police and district attorney's office.[18]

THE BROOKLYN DISTRICT ATTORNEY RESPONDS

The office of the Brooklyn district attorney and its defenders were stung by the criticisms of the Girgenti Report. The Brooklyn district attorney, the ambitious Charles J. Hynes, was particularly embarrassed. He had hoped to use his position as a springboard to higher office, perhaps state attorney general. In a twenty-three-page rebuttal to the Girgenti

Report, Hynes defended his office's performance and its claim that Nelson was the only person who stabbed Rosenbaum. "I honestly would not have done anything any differently," Hynes said. "I picked out two of the finest prosecutors in the office, and they tried their hearts out." The two prosecuting attorneys were experienced trial lawyers and had handled nearly fifty homicide trials between them. The jury's decision, Hynes concluded, stemmed not from incompetence in the district attorney's office but from the jurors' distrust of the police, which caused them to disbelieve the cops' testimony.[19]

The day after Nelson was found not guilty, the Department of Justice announced that it would conduct an investigation to see whether civil rights violations had occurred during the Crown Heights riot, including whether Rosenbaum had been attacked because he was a Jew. The department's civil rights division had traditionally allowed local prosecutions to run their course before becoming involved. "Had he been convicted, we would stay out of such a thing," said Andrew Maloney, the United States Attorney for the Eastern District of New York. "We consider the assault on Yankel Rosenbaum a racial attack."[20] The New York Civil Liberties Union and the *New York Times* also favored a full and expeditious federal investigation.[21] Jewish politicians and leaders of Jewish organizations were particularly eager to have the federal government involved, and they pointed to the federal prosecution of four police officers involved in the beating of Rodney King as a precedent.

This eagerness to retry the case overlooked the sharp difference between the trial in Los Angeles and any federal trial in Brooklyn of Nelson. The four policemen were public officials who had been accused of violating the rights of citizens; as such, their actions clearly fell within the purview of the federal authorities as defined in the civil rights statutes. Any defendants in a federal trial in Brooklyn would be private individuals. This distinction partially accounted for the different responses of the Department of Justice to the two cases. The department produced criminal charges against the Los Angeles police officers three months after they were exonerated in their state trial in Simi Valley. Lemrick Nelson, by contrast, would not be indicted until nearly twenty-one months after his state trial.

Richard Girgenti, for one, believed that, due to jurisdictional and evidentiary problems, it would be very difficult for the federal government to convict Nelson or anyone else of violating Rosenbaum's civil rights. The jury in the Nelson case had good reasons for making its decision, and Girgenti believed it was doubtful that a federal jury would come to a different conclusion. He was also skeptical that Congress intended the various civil rights laws, including the most recent law of 1968, to be applied to an ordinary crime. Jewish groups and many New York politicians, both Republicans and Democrats, disagreed with Girgenti, and they urged the Department of Justice to become involved.

At first, Attorney General Janet Reno doubted whether the federal government had jurisdiction under the civil rights laws. Traditionally the federal government had stayed out of such cases unless there was evidence that local authorities had conspired to deprive persons of their civil liberties. But there was no evidence that such a conspiracy had occurred in Crown Heights in August 1991. Dinkins, his entourage, and the police might have been incompetent, but this was not grounds for bringing a civil rights case. It was also questionable whether there was sufficient evidence to convict Nelson of violating Rosenbaum's civil rights. The government would have to do more than merely show that Nelson had sought to injure and perhaps kill Rosenbaum. It would have to prove either that Nelson was part of a conspiracy that sought to "injure, oppress, threaten, or intimidate" Rosenbaum in the exercise of his constitutional rights, or that Nelson had stabbed Rosenbaum because he was Jewish. In attempting to show that Nelson's motivation in attacking Rosenbaum was anti-Semitism, the government would have to undertake the difficult task of reading his mind.[22]

The release of the Girgenti Report in July 1993 increased public pressure on the Department of Justice to launch a full-scale investigation of the riot. But Reno was still skeptical, and in the second week of September 1993, she was ready to announce that the Department of Justice would not be filing a civil rights case against any of Rosenbaum's attackers. She was prevailed upon to delay the announcement by Charles Hynes and Representative Charles E. Schumer. They asked that the Brooklyn district attorney be given more time to make the case for federal involvement. This delay, Reno made clear, would only be brief.[23] A few days later Hynes sent her a seventeen-page memo urging the Justice Department to take over the case. Here he proposed the novel theory that the use of a public street was included in the "benefit, service, privilege, program, facility or activity" protected under federal civil rights legislation. Whether this inclusion was Congress's intent, however, is questionable. Another issue raised by Hynes was whether Nelson and the rest of the mob that attacked Rosenbaum intended to deprive him of the use of public streets or whether they had other objectives in mind.

On September 29, 1993, the United States Senate by a vote of 97–0 approved a nonbinding sense of the Senate resolution offered by Alphonse D'Amato (New York) and Senate Republican Leader Bob Dole (Kansas) and cosponsored by Senators Daniel Patrick Moynihan (New York), Joseph Lieberman (Connecticut), Arlen Specter (Pennsylvania), and Jesse Helms (North Carolina), demanding that the Department of Justice launch a full-scale investigation into whether civil rights violations occurred during the Crown Heights riot and the murder of Yankel Rosenbaum. "The Justice Department's failure to investigate the horrors of what took place in Crown Heights is a national disgrace," D'Amato said. "The government's first and foremost role is to protect its citizens. When it fails in this responsibility, everything else is meaningless."[24]

Some legal scholars shared Reno's initial belief that retrying Nelson was a dubious use of the civil rights laws. If the federal government indicted Nelson, civil libertarians warned, it would be because of public emotions and political pressure. Civil rights laws were designed to rectify injustices when the local authorities refused to prosecute. In the Nelson case the Brooklyn district attorney's office had prosecuted, but the jury had refused to convict. For the federal government to second-guess juries when they appeared to have acted wrongly, critics warned, would undermine the jury system, involve the federal government in areas previously outside its traditional bailiwick, and distort the purpose of the civil rights laws. Furthermore, they argued, retrying Nelson came dangerously close to double jeopardy even though the Supreme Court had ruled in the 1920s that a defendant could face federal charges after being acquitted of state criminal charges because the federal and the state government were separate "sovereign" bodies.[25]

Despite these caveats, Reno on January 25, 1994, instructed Zachary W. Carter, the U.S. attorney for the Eastern District of New York, to seek an indictment of Lemrick Nelson. The Justice Department was not optimistic that it would succeed: it would have to prove that walking the streets of Brooklyn was a federally protected activity and that Nelson had assaulted Rosenbaum specifically because he was Jewish.[26] The *New York Times* praised Reno's belated decision. A federal grand jury investigation would reassure the public that the federal authorities had done everything possible to bring the killers of Rosenbaum to justice. "Nothing less can heal the festering outrage generated by that unpunished murder."[27] The *Times'* reasoning confirmed the fears of civil libertarians that public opinion and politics rather than the law would determine Nelson's fate. In fact, D'Amato and Moynihan had threatened to hold hearings if Reno failed to investigate Crown Heights.

A federal grand jury, assisted by a joint FBI–New York City police task force, was impaneled in March 1994 in Brooklyn, and on August 11, 1994, it indicted Nelson for violating Rosenbaum's civil rights. The grand jury accepted the government's novel reading of the civil rights laws. Its indictment charged that Nelson "did willfully injure, intimidate and interfere with, and attempt to injure, intimidate and interfere with, Yankel Rosenbaum, an Orthodox Jew, because of his religion and because he was enjoying facilities provided and administered by a subdivision of the state of New York, namely the public streets provided and administered by the city of New York, and bodily injury to and the death of Yankel Rosenbaum did result." "I can't believe this is happening again," Valerie Evans, Nelson's mother, said. "We already went through this and here we are, it's blown up again." Michael Warren, one of Nelson's attorneys, argued that the indictment was "illicit" because it subjected Nelson to double jeopardy; he accused Hynes of seeking to indict Nelson in order to polish his résumé prior to the Democratic Party's September 1994 primary for state attorney general. Hynes, Warren said, was "a political prostitute."[28]

In the meantime the police search for other suspects in the attack on Rosenbaum continued, and in 1996 Charles Price was arrested for violating Rosenbaum's civil rights. In August 1991, Price was a thirty-eight-year-old chronic petty thief, heroin addict, and resident of Crown Heights. He was well known to the neighborhood police. Minutes before the attack on Rosenbaum, a television news camera and a home video had recorded a bald black man inciting onlookers at the scene of the Cato accident. "Do y'all feel what I feel? Do y'all feel the pain?" A friend of Price's, who was also an informant for the FBI, recounted that Price was the man in the film. He remembered Price telling him, "There were so many people up there that motherfuckin' night . . . I thought I was in the '60s." According to a policeman who later testified at Price's trial, Price told the crowd at the scene of the accident, "We can't take this any more. The Jews get everything they want. They're killing our children. We get no justice, we get no respect." Another policeman who testified at Price's trial said that he then incited his listeners to accompany him to Kingston Avenue, the main Jewish shopping street in Crown

Heights, to "get the Jews!" Witnesses identified Price as the leader of the group that assaulted Rosenbaum. They claimed Price pointed to Rosenbaum, whose beard and skullcap marked him as an Orthodox Jew, and exhorted his followers, "Let's go get a Jew," and "There's one: Let's go get him!"[29]

On August 6, 1996, Price was indicted for violating Rosenbaum's civil rights, and Nelson was reindicted for the same crime. The indictment charged that Price and Nelson "by force and threat of force, did willfully injure, intimidate and interfere with, Yankel Rosenbaum, an Orthodox Jew, because of his religion." Federal prosecutors believed that linking the two men strengthened their case. They hoped to demonstrate that Price's incendiary rhetoric "aided," "abetted," "incited," and "instigated" Nelson's attack on Rosenbaum, and that Price was therefore as guilty as Nelson.[30] For Price to be found guilty, the government would have to prove that his words directly contributed to Rosenbaum's death, and this need raised several questions. Did Price mean for his words to be taken literally? Did Nelson hear Price's speech? Did Nelson act directly because of what Price had said? The two defendants faced a maximum penalty of life in prison and a $250,000 fine.[31]

The timing of the indictment was suspect to some. It came two weeks before the fifth anniversary of the death of Rosenbaum and the expiration of the five-year statute of limitations on most federal crimes. Law enforcement officials denied that there was anything untoward about the timing of Price's arrest. A conspiracy of silence by blacks in Crown Heights had made it difficult to find evidence incriminating Price, they said, and it was only in 1995 that a suspect in another crime had implicated him. These claims did not convince everyone. A few blacks, including the Reverend Herbert Daughtry, charged the indictment of Price was a "rush to judgment," a political "lynching," and a result of the power of the "Jewish lobby."[32]

THE TRIAL OF NELSON AND PRICE

In the months leading up to the 1997 trial of Nelson and Price, David G. Trager, the trial judge, bent over backward to be fair to Nelson. But Nelson's defense, in an attempt to lay the groundwork for an appeal, accused the judge of a conflict of interest. Its major argument was that Judah Gribetz, the president of the Jewish Community Relations Council of New York in 1992, had chaired the selection committee that had recommended Trager's appointment to the federal bench, and that same year, after Nelson was exonerated for Rosenbaum's murder, the council had called for a federal investigation of the Crown Heights riot.[33] This relationship between Trager and Gribetz, however, was too tenuous, as even Nelson's attorneys later admitted, and Trager correctly refused to recuse himself.[34]

One of the reasons for the interval of two and a half years between Nelson's original indictment in August 1994 and the 1997 trial was legal wrangling over whether Nelson should be tried as a juvenile or an adult. Nelson had been sixteen in August 1991, and federal law provided that defendants who were older than fifteen could be tried as adults for felonies. But granting adult status was at the discretion of the presiding judge, who presumably would do so only if he believed it was in the interest of justice. The judge would have to take into consideration the seriousness of the defendant's alleged offense, his age, his social background, his intellectual and psychological development prior to the crime, his prior delinquency record, his response to previous psychological treatment, the likelihood that he would commit additional acts of violence, and the availability of programs to treat his behavioral problems. Whether Nelson was tried as a juvenile or an adult would affect his sentence. The longest sentence for a juvenile was five years in prison; for an adult, it was life imprisonment.[35]

On April 12, 1995, Judge Trager agreed with Nelson's attorneys that he should be tried as a juvenile. He argued it was unlikely that Nelson had committed premeditated murder, and there was a "glimmer of hope" he could be rehabilitated in a juvenile institution. Trager noted that Nelson did not have a record of serious delinquent behavior prior to August 19, 1991, and did not "suffer from significant psychopathology or have strong antisocial tendencies" that indicated a clear tendency for future violence. Federal juvenile facilities would also be able to treat his psychological problems.[36] Nelson's attorneys and family were pleased by Trager's ruling. By contrast, the Jewish Community Relations Council of New York, the Anti-Defamation League of B'nai B'rith, Mayor Giuliani, Governor Pataki, Senator D'Amato, Congressman Schumer, and other political figures strongly urged the government to appeal Trager's decision.[37]

The government did appeal. In October 1995, a three-judge panel from the United States Court of Appeals for the Second Circuit released a nineteen-page decision questioning Trager's reasoning and ordering him to reconsider his ruling. The judge had erred, the panel said, in not considering whether Nelson's current age made juvenile-type rehabilitation programs inappropriate for him. The panel also rejected Trager's "glimmer of hope" as a legal standard for determining whether a juvenile defendant should be tried as a juvenile.[38] In March 1996, Trager reversed his earlier decision and said that Nelson would be tried as an adult. Trager continued to maintain that there was a "reasonable probability" that Nelson could be rehabilitated, but this did not meet the standard for a juvenile court trial enunciated by the appeals court's panel.[39]

The federal trial of Nelson and Price began on January 16, 1997, in the federal courthouse in Brooklyn. The trial lasted for four weeks and was extensively covered in the New York press. The jury differed from that of Nelson's previous trial. The jury in the 1992 state trial had no Jews, six blacks, four Hispanics, and two whites, all of whom lived in Brooklyn. The 1997 jury consisted of five whites, two of whom were Jewish, three blacks, and four Hispanics, and came from Brooklyn, Queens, Staten Island, and Long Island.[40]

The prosecution was determined not to repeat the mistakes made by the state prosecution in the 1992 trial, and it benefited from the Girgenti Report's criticisms of the performance of the Brooklyn district attorney's office. For example, it did more extensive testing of the bloodstains on the pants Nelson was wearing on August 19, 1991. The federal prosecutors' task was also easier because Nelson and Price were not being charged with the murder of Yankel Rosenbaum but with violating his civil rights. The prosecution had merely to prove that Rosenbaum was attacked because he was Jewish and using the public streets.[41]

The federal prosecutors methodically went over the same points stressed by the prosecutors in the 1992 trial. They also introduced additional witnesses who claimed that Nelson had confessed to them that he had killed Rosenbaum, and presented witnesses who testified that it was Price's incendiary language that prompted the attack on Rosenbaum. The defense countered that the evidence was as ambiguous in 1997 as it had been in 1992, that the testimony of the police remained unreliable, and that Price's words did not influence the actions of the gang that attacked Rosenbaum. In his instructions to the jury, Trager emphasized that Nelson and Price could only be found guilty if the jurors were convinced that Rosenbaum was attacked because he was Jewish and while using a public street. It was not necessary for the jurors to conclude that the defendants' actions were responsible for his death, only that they caused him "bodily injury." After deliberating for more than four days, the jury on February 10 declared Nelson and Price guilty, Nelson for wielding the knife that killed Rosenbaum and Price for inciting the crowd to attack the victim. Public officials, including Giuliani, Hynes, D'Amato, and Pataki, welcomed the decision, as did the city's newspapers. The *Times* claimed the verdict was a "reasoned legal ending to a long ordeal" for the city.[42]

At a news conference immediately after the guilty decision was handed down, Zachary Carter said it was unlikely that his office could secure other indictments, because of lack of evidence and because the five-year statute of limitations for civil rights violations had run out. "This is it," he concluded. "Period. End."[43] Carter also said something that five years later would come back to haunt him. "The verdict should have credibility because it came from a conscientious jury drawn from a broad cross-section of the community."[44]

On March 31, 1998, Judge Trager sentenced Nelson to a maximum term of nineteen and a half years in prison and five years of probation. The judge also forbade Nelson from ever possessing a weapon. Nelson, Trager said, was "prone to violence and the use of weapons," was "a danger to the community," and had shown no remorse. Because there was no parole in federal crimes, the earliest date Nelson could be freed was 2012, when he would be thirty-six. At his sentencing, Nelson continued to deny involvement in the killing of Rosenbaum. "What about my civil rights?" Nelson asked the court. "You violated my civil rights."[45]

Three months later Trager sentenced Price to twenty-one years and ten months in prison. His sentence was longer than Nelson's because of his lengthy criminal record, which included pleading guilty ten times to drug and larceny charges. Price could have received an even longer sentence, but Trager did not believe that he had intended that the mob kill Rosenbaum. Nonetheless, "the bottom line is he is morally and legally responsible for the events he set off." Trager also noted that Price also did not exhibit any remorse.[46]

According to an editorial in the *Jewish Week* of April 3, the sentencing of Nelson had brought "Closure in Crown Heights."[47] A poignant incident at the conclusion of sentencing indicated how difficult achieving closure actually would be. Fay and Max Rosenbaum, Yankel's parents, had traveled from Australia in order to present a victim's statement to the court, to appeal for a lengthy sentence for Nelson, and to be present for the sentencing. Shortly before Nelson was sentenced, Valerie Evans, a devout Christian, approached Fay Rosenbaum to offer condolences. "I understand your pain and loss," Evans said, and the two women briefly held hands. But Evans also stated that her son was innocent. Fay Rosenbaum responded, "Before he lost consciousness my son identified your son." She pulled her hand away from Evans's and ended the conversation.[48]

SUING THE CITY

The sentencing of Nelson occurred two days before the Giuliani administration agreed to settle a federal class-action civil suit brought against the city and the police department by twenty-seven individuals, the estate of Yankel Rosenbaum, a Crown Heights yeshiva, a Crown Heights synagogue, and the Crown Heights Jewish Community on behalf of "all those who suffered injury to their person or their property as a result of the anti-Semitic violence." The plaintiffs claimed the city and the police had "discriminatorily and selectively withheld police protective and investigative services from the Crown Heights Jewish community," had allowed blacks to rampage through Crown Heights without fear of punishment, had denied the Jews of Crown Heights equal protection under the law, had refused to conduct a "meaningful investigation" of the "pogrom," had "failed to identify, apprehend and charge those responsible for it, and have destroyed evidence of their own wrongful behavior."[49] The plaintiffs asked for unspecified monetary compensation for their ordeal.

The original suit, originally filed in November 1992, had included the mayor and his police commissioner as defendants, but a federal court in August 1997 severed them from the case, thus removing any liability for financial damages. Judge Frederic Block ruled that the plaintiffs had not shown that the mayor and police commissioner conspired to deny the Jews of Crown Heights police protection. In fact, their actions during the riot were "objectively reasonable" in the midst of "chaotic conditions," and they were entitled to the "qualified immunity" from prosecution that courts grant government officials for actions performed while they are carrying out their public functions.[50]

This suit was as much an attempt to embarrass Dinkins and Brown politically as it was an attempt to provide compensation to the victims of the riot. The fact that it had been filed less than a year before the mayoral election of 1993 was noted by the mayor's supporters. The mayor himself claimed the suit's allegations to be "simply preposterous," and he accused those behind it of escalating racial and ethnic tensions within the city and of seeking his political downfall.[51] Dinkins and Brown continuously denied they had ever told the police to show restraint toward the rioters, and police officials adamantly disavowed the claim that they had received instructions from city hall or Brown telling them to refrain from vigorously enforcing the law. But the police had not received orders from the mayor or police commissioner to crack down, either.[52] The Dinkins administration, noted Wayne Barrett of the *Village Voice,* had "bumbled its way to catastrophe, preferring to hope a brutal race war would just go away, rather than affirmatively acting to end it."[53]

Dinkins assumed that the city and the police department would win the case if it ever came to trial. He opposed settling with the plaintiffs, a possibility that had been mentioned frequently in the New York press during early 1998. In January the city had settled with Isaac and Yechiel Bitton for $200,000. The Bittons had been among the original plaintiffs in the suit against the city, but they decided to settle separately.[54] With the Bittons' suit out of the way, a settlement with the other plaintiffs became more likely. The major stumbling blocks were the size of the financial indemnity and whether Giuliani would apologize in the name of the city for the failure to protect the Lubavitchers during the riot. The city was also concerned that any settlement could become a precedent for future costly suits against the city. Any settlement, particularly one that included an apology, would be a rebuke to the Dinkins administration and would be resented by the former mayor and his supporters.

With the approval of Judge Block, Giuliani announced a settlement on April 2. The announcement occurred in Gracie Mansion, the mayor's official home, in the presence of Yankel Rosenbaum's parents and brother. Dinkins had been correct to fear a settlement. Giuliani noted that "the Jews of Crown Heights had been sacrificed for political correctness," and that the response of his predecessor to the riot was "clearly inadequate." The riot was "one of the saddest chapters in the history of the city." An accompanying statement issued by the mayor's office said that "the City of New York accepts responsibility for the mistakes that were made in August 1991, and apologizes to the residents of Crown Heights." After the announcement of the settlement, Fay Rosenbaum briefly spoke outside Gracie Mansion. Had Giuliani been mayor in August 1991 instead of Dinkins, she declared, "Yankel would be alive today." Left unsaid was how anyone could have predicted the random attack on her son.[55]

The city got off cheap. It agreed to pay the claimants $1,100,000 plus $250,000 to cover part of their legal expenses. The settlement prevented a possibly lengthy trial that could have rekindled the passions resulting from the riot and resulted in a larger financial award. The plaintiffs received what they claimed had always been their major objective: an apology from the city acknowledging the culpability of Dinkins and Brown. Jewish organizations welcomed the settlement and hoped that it could bring closure to the controversy surrounding the riot.[56]

According to public opinion polls, more than 60 percent of white New Yorkers but less than one-third of black New Yorkers approved the settlement. Dinkins and Brown were outraged and saw the settlement as an effort to humiliate them. Dinkins accused the mayor of risking the city's fiscal future in order to win political points in the Lubavitch community. Instead of apologizing and thereby "sending a message that anyone with enough political clout can profit at the city's expense," the city should have fought these "false and irresponsible accusations" against city leaders and police officials who had acted in good faith.[57] Mainstream blacks also condemned the settlement as unfair to the city and demeaning to Dinkins and Brown. U.S. Congressman Charles B. Rangel of Harlem claimed that Giuliani's apology had further polarized the city along racial lines, and the Ministerial Alliance of the African Methodist Episcopal Church charged that the settlement was a political tactic to court the Jewish vote.[58]

The mayor responded in kind. The reason the city had to agree to the settlement was because Dinkins "didn't know how to be mayor and allowed a riot to go on under a set of circumstances that I can't imagine anybody else allowing to happen." Dinkins, Giuliani said, "was half asleep most of the time he was mayor of New York."[59] The city's press played up the conflict between Giuliani and Dinkins. Not since the election of 1993, noted a *Newsday* reporter, "has the language between them been so venomous."[60]

In what he said was an attempt to build bridges "in the spirit of faith and hope of this Easter and Passover week," Dinkins publicly invited Giuliani and his wife to dinner at his residence. "As much as we disagree, I extend to him my hand in brotherhood. I ask him to take my hand." It is unlikely that Dinkins believed that Giuliani would accept his invitation, which was initially tendered on April 7 in a Dinkins press conference. Some viewed it as a publicity stunt. Such offers, political journalist Michael Tomasky noted, played to the crowd and were "designed to be turned down."[61] Nor was it likely that Giuliani would show up for dinner with his estranged wife, Donna Hanover, with whom he rarely appeared in public. Shortly after Dinkins's press conference, Giuliani declined the invitation. Such a meeting, the mayor said, "would only serve as a major press event or media circus rather than aiding in the healing."[62]

Blacks interpreted Giuliani's response as another attempt to humiliate his predecessor. Wilbert Tatum, the publisher of the *Amsterdam News*, compared it to Hitler's supposed refusal to shake the hand of Jesse Owens during the 1936 Berlin Olympics. Dinkins, Tatum said, was misguided to invite Giuliani, "a polarizing bigot, racist and fool into his home with his wife, Joyce. We can only ask David, 'Don't you understand anything? Yet? Why did you have to compromise your dignity and ours by rolling over?'"[63]

CONVICTIONS OVERTURNED

The sentencing of Nelson and Price along with the settlement of the suit against the city seemed at the time to be the closing chapter in the story of the Crown Heights riot. New Yorkers were relieved that finally—after nearly seven years—closure had finally come. But this sense of relief overlooked the vagaries of the federal courts. On January 7, 2002, a surprising turn in the Crown Heights saga occurred when the convictions of Nelson and Price were overturned by a three-judge appellate panel of the United States Court of Appeals for the Second Circuit.

During the appellate hearing of May 3, 2000, the attorneys for Nelson and Price charged that Judge Trager had erred in seeking a racially and ethnically balanced jury. The attorneys rejected the government's argument that its prosecution of Nelson and Price was a valid exercise of federal authority under the commerce clause of the Constitution; they claimed that the murder of Yankel Rosenbaum was a matter for the local police and not for the federal government. They also noted that the Fourteenth Amendment, which the prosecution had used as a basis for trying Nelson and Price, had been passed during the Reconstruction era in order to combat racial discrimination. Hence its provisions did not apply to Jews, who constitute a religious and not a racial group.

Finally the defense attorneys asserted the alleged deeds of Nelson and Price were not covered by the civil rights legislation of the 1960s. This legislation criminalized actions that stem from racial, religious, and anti-immigrant bias and that seek to prevent individuals from "participating in or enjoying any benefit, service, privilege, program, facility or activity provided by or administered by any State or subdivision thereof." But there is no mention of streets in this legislation. Instead, Congress had in mind voting booths, schools, and libraries. Had Congress intended the legislation to cover streets it would have specifically said so.[64]

The most persuasive of the defense attorney's arguments concerned Judge Trager's manipulation of the jury selection process. Trager had seated a Jew as a juror even though the juror had doubted his own objectivity, and the judge had selected a Jew and a black out of order from the alternate jury pool to serve on the regular jury. Everyone agreed that Trager's objective of having a racially and ethnically jury was laudable in order that its decision, in his words, have "moral validity" and be accepted by the public. But Trager's actions raised questions whether in abandoning the principle of racial neutrality in the jury selection process, he had deprived Nelson and Price of a fair trial—even though their attorneys had assented to Trager's machinations at the time. Even the federal prosecutors admitted that Trager had acted in an "unorthodox" manner, although they also argued that this had not deprived the defendants of a fair trial, and their petition for a new trial should be denied.[65]

The appellate panel thought otherwise. Its 109-page ruling of January 7, 2002, severely chastised Trager's "race conscious" rulings. "The significance of a jury in our polity as a body chosen apart from racial and religious manipulations is too great to permit categorization by race or religion even from the best of intentions." Trager's "jurymandering" violated "even the most minimal standards of due process" under the Fifth Amendment, and it denied Nelson and Price the right to an impartial jury under the Sixth Amendment. Not even the defendants' attorneys can waive these rights. By a vote of 2–1, the panel ordered Nelson and Price to be retried "before a properly chosen jury."[66]

Although based on sound constitutional reasoning, the decision came as a surprise. The headlines on the front page of both the *New York Post* and the *Daily News* of January 8 used the word "shocker" to describe the ruling. Although agreeing with the decision, a *New York Times* editorial called it "startling." "Judge Trager's violation of rules designed to preserve the randomness essential to the integrity of the jury system," the *Times* said, "is hard to dismiss as harmless error. His troubling behavior left the appellate court with an unpalatable choice between fudging on basic constitutional principles, much as he did, or ordering a new trial."[67]

Jeffrey Abramson, a Brandeis University authority on juries, also concurred with the panel's "sensible" decision. The Supreme Court in 1986 and 1992 had ruled that prosecutors and defense lawyers could not exclude jurors simply because of their race. If the parties to a case could not act in a race-conscious manner, Abramson declared, then neither could the judge. "When judges select jurors as if they are there simply to deliver the Jewish vote or the African-American vote, the noble ideal of representative juries collapses into a vulgar invitation for jurors to be loyal to their own groups, and ultimately undermines all confidence in the jury system."[68] Stephen Gillers, a professor of legal ethics at New York University Law School, agreed. Randomness, Gillers noted, is "the first principle of jury selection."[69]

The appellate panel's ruling, however, was hardly an unmitigated defeat for those who wished Nelson and Price to remain in prison. The panel rejected the defendants' argument that the federal government lacked jurisdiction and took an expansive view of the Constitution's protection of civil rights. Jews welcomed the panel's inclusion of religious groups as among those protected by the guarantees of the Fourteenth Amendment. The panel concluded that the evidence presented at the 1997 trial was sufficient to support the conviction of the defendants and that they should be retried.

The Department of Justice decided not to appeal the panel's decision and to seek a new trial for Nelson and Price. The attorneys for Price feared a new trial, and they negotiated an agreement with the government. Price's sentence was reduced to eleven years and eight months, and with time off for good behavior, his release from prison was expected in 2006. In exchange, Price at an April hearing apologized for inciting attacks on Jews on August 19, 1991. "In my heart, I have never been racist, and I have no hatred to any group of people," he read from a prepared statement. "I feel very sorry for all the people who were hurt or died in Crown Heights that night." But Price also attempted to justify his actions. "[O]n that night I felt that black people in Crown Heights were treated unfairly and that Jewish people were treated much better and that revenge was appropriate."[70]

Nelson's defense adopted a different strategy. Initially it had considered a plea agreement similar to Price's, but then decided to appeal the appellate panel's ruling to the Supreme Court. Several recent decisions of the court had taken a more restrictive view of federal power, and Nelson's attorneys believed there was a possibility the court might rule that Nelson should never have been tried in federal court in the first place.[71] In October 2002, however, the Supreme Court refused to consider Nelson's appeal, and the Department of Justice then filed charges against him.

Nelson's second federal trial began on April 28, 2003, Judge Frederic Block presiding. The jury consisted of eight blacks, two whites, and two men of Guyanese ancestry, one of whom appeared to be African and the other East Indian. No Jews were on the jury.[72] The highlight of the week-long trial came when Nelson's attorney in his opening statement admitted that his client had stabbed Yankel Rosenbaum, but not because the victim was Jewish; rather, because Nelson was drunk from drinking beer and got caught up in the excitement of the moment. This strategy was ingenious. If the jury accepted this contention, then Nelson could not be found guilty of violating Rosenbaum's civil rights because he was a Jew, the charge for which he was on trial. And because Nelson had already been acquitted for murder in the state trial in 1992, the principle of double jeopardy precluded him from being tried again for murder.[73]

The strategy was, however, risky, and it reflected the desperation of Nelson's defense team. Because Nelson's lawyers had denied at his two previous trials that he had stabbed Rosenbaum, the government could argue before the jury that, as Nelson's attorneys had lied earlier, it could be assumed they would not be reluctant to do so again. It was thus imperative for the defense, in order to retain its credibility, to prevent the prosecution from introducing any information about the 1992 and 1997 trials. They were unsuccessful in this regard. The defense would also have to prove that Nelson, in fact, was drunk on the night of August 19, 1991, and this was the reason he stabbed Rosenbaum, not because Rosenbaum was a Jew. This approach would prove difficult. The defense presented no witnesses who testified to Nelson's mental state. In fact, the defense called no witnesses at all. In effect, it was asking the jury, without any evidence, to accept its interpretation of Nelson's motivations for stabbing Rosenbaum.

The prosecution's task was easier. It had simply to prove to the jury that Nelson had killed Rosenbaum because he was a Jew and not because he was drunk. Two police officers testified that Nelson did not appear drunk when he was taken into custody, and the defense did not refute their testimony.[74] The jury began deliberating on May 7, and a week later it reached a decision. The verdict had something for everyone. On the one hand it said that Nelson had violated Rosenbaum's civil rights; on the other hand it asserted that the government had not proved beyond a reasonable doubt that Nelson was directly responsible for Rosenbaum's death. Evidently the jury was swayed by the defense's cross-examination of a medical examiner who testified that botched medical care and not the stabbing was directly responsible for Rosenbaum's death. This testimony saved Nelson from a life sentence. The maximum sentence for Nelson's crime was ten years. With time already served and time off for good behavior, he faced only another half a year in prison.[75]

The Crown Heights Jewish Community Council welcomed the verdict. "Now everyone knows that Yankel's blood is on Nelson's hands," said a statement issued by the council. "It is regrettable that it has taken twelve painful years to reach this decision."[76] Norman Rosenbaum was more critical. The jury, he said, "didn't want to acquit a guilty man, but the price they had to pay was a disgrace to the criminal justice system."[77] Jewish organizations also criticized the verdict. A statement from the Anti-Defamation League said it was "saddened and disappointed by this compromise verdict that did not recognize what the evidence in the case sustained: That Mr. Nelson's actions led to Mr. Rosenbaum's death."[78]

On August 20, 2003, twelve years to the day that Yankel Rosenbaum had died, Judge Block sentenced Nelson to the maximum of ten years. Block regretted that he could not impose a longer sentence on Nelson for his "horrendous and pathetic act of racial and religious bigotry," but he was restricted by federal sentencing guidelines.[79] The sentencing of Nelson, Adam Dickter of the *Jewish Week* noted, was "the last chapter in what arguably was the most resilient case of racial strife in New York City history."[80]

At the sentencing hearing, attended by Yankel Rosenbaum's parents and brother, Nelson apologized for the first time for stabbing Rosenbaum. "If there was anything I could do to bring him back, I'd do it in a heartbeat. . . . Now I would like to move on and put the past behind me and become a better man, rather than a belligerent young boy." The

Rosenbaums were skeptical that Nelson was truly remorseful, and they were angry that he would be soon released from prison. "It's a black day for American justice," Norman Rosenbaum said.[81] "For the Rosenbaum family," remarked Rabbi Shea Hecht, "as much time as they need to bring closure and as many legal actions as they need to bring closure, let peace be upon them. But for Jews in Crown Heights and even beyond Crown Heights we have to move on."[82]

Nelson remained in a federal prison in Texas until June 2, 2004, when he was transferred to the Kintock halfway house in Newark, New Jersey, for nine months of supervised care and vocational counseling. When released from prison, he was twenty-nine, the same age of Yankel Rosenbaum when he died.[83] By this time a degree of closure also had come to the Cato family. On January 9, 2002, a financial settlement between New York City and the Cato family was announced. The city agreed to pay the family $400,000, and the family agreed to drop its lawsuit against the city's Emergency Medical Service alleging negligence in treating Gavin Cato's wounds.[84]

This left only the Rosenbaum family's civil suit against the city's Health and Hospitals Corporation for medical malpractice to be resolved. This trial had been put off until after the fate of Lemrick Nelson and Charles Price had been determined. On June 17, 2005, while a jury was being selected in state Supreme Court in Brooklyn to hear the case, an agreement was suddenly announced between the city and the Rosenbaum family. The original Rosenbaum suit had asked for $10,000,000 in damages; the family now agreed to accept $1,250,000, most of which went to pay legal expenses.

The family had previously rejected a one million dollar offer from the HHC because it did not include an admission of guilt. An apology should not have been difficult for the HHC since investigations by the state and city shortly after Yankel Rosenbaum's death had stated that he "was not provided care that meets generally accepted standards of professional practice." An apology was part of the 2005 agreement: "Kings County Hospital recognizes that diagnostic and treatment errors made during the emergency room care provided to Yankel Rosenbaum in the hours after his stabbing played a role in his death. Recognition of these errors played an important part in significant reforms that have enhanced and improved patient care at the hospital over the ensuing years," a spokeswoman for the HHC said. "We extend our condolences to the Rosenbaum family."[85]

The settlement was a financial bargain for the city, as was its 1998 settlement with the residents of Crown Heights. The Rosenbaum family claimed that the amount of monetary compensation was not important, and that they were more concerned that the HHC admit culpability. "It's an important development today that they accepted responsibility," Norman Rosenbaum said. "The loss is in no way diminished. The pain remains." He vowed to explore other legal options, including bringing legal actions against Yankel's emergency room doctors and tracking down the other members of the group who had attacked his brother. His chance of success was, however, slight. The doctors who treated his brother were covered by the agreement of June 17, and the statute of limitations had run out on all crimes committed in August 1991 except for murder.[86]

Notes

1. Court TV produced a documentary hosted by Fred Graham on the Nelson trial. Titled "A Community Torn: Murder in Brooklyn," it contains forty-five minutes of footage from the trial.
2. Patricia Hurtado, "Crown Heights Jury: It Didn't Add Up," *Newsday,* November 8, 1992. Jews wondered why there was no Jew on the jury even though Jews composed one-sixth of the population of Kings County (Brooklyn) and twenty percent of those eligible for jury duty. In fact, several potential Jewish jurors asked to be excused from serving. Jean Herschaft, "Jews in Jury Pool Refused to Serve in Rosenbaum Murder Case," *Algemeiner Journal,* November 13, 1992.
3. Richard H. Girgenti, *A Report to the Governor on the Disturbances in Crown Heights,* vol. 2, *A Review of the Circumstances Surrounding the Death of Yankel Rosenbaum and the Resulting Prosecution* (Albany, N.Y.: New York State Division of Criminal Services, 1993), 133; Adam Dickter, "Report: Rosenbaum Case Bungled," *Jewish Week,* July 23–29, 1993.
4. Girgenti Report, 2:23.
5. Nelson denied that the knife was found in his pocket. Donatella Lorch, "Youth Denies He Killed Man in Crown Hts.," *New York Times,* September 11, 1992.
6. Donatella Lorch, "Sparring at the Bench Disrupts Crown Hts. Trial," *New York Times,* October 17, 1992.
7. Girgenti Report, 2:34–47.
8. Ibid., 2:63–65.
9. Ibid., 2:73.

10. George P. Fletcher, *With Justice for Some: Victims' Rights in Criminal Trials* (Reading, Mass.: Addison-Wesley, 1995), 90.
11. Girgenti Report, 2:74–76, 105–109; Donatella Lorch, "Arrest Procedures in Stabbing Questioned," *New York Times*, September 26, 1992.
12. Girgenti Report, 2:109–114.
13. Ibid., 2:10.
14. Ibid., 2:96–99.
15. Shortly before the trial commenced, Rappaport was named by the *Village Voice* as one of the city's ten worst judges. Shaun Assael and J. A. Lobbia, "New York's 10 Worst Judges," *Village Voice* 37 (September 15, 1992), 32–41.
16. Girgenti Report, 2:10–11, 95, 142.
17. Fletcher, *With Justice for Some*, 95, 195, 238.
18. Girgenti Report, 2:114–16.
19. Bill Farrell and Tom Robbins, "Hynes on the Defense: Says Prober Reached Wrong Conclusions," *Daily News*, July 22, 1993; Charles J. Hynes, letter to the editor, *New York Post*, September 4, 1995; Dan Janison, "Hynes: Yankel May Still Get Justice," *New York Post*, July 26, 1993; Joseph P. Fried, "Brooklyn District Attorney Defends Handling of Crown Heights Prosecution," *New York Times*, July 22, 1993.
20. Frances McMorris, "Feds Launch Probe in Crown Hgts. Slay," *Daily News*, October 31, 1992.
21. Norman Siegel, Robert Levy, and Arthur Eisenberg to Janet Reno, August 6, 1993, Miller Papers; *New York Times* editorial "Justice for Yankel Rosenbaum," April 26, 1993.
22. Fletcher, *With Justice for Some*, 104–105.
23. Stephen Labaton, "U.S. Attorney General Delays Closing Inquiry on Crown Hts.," *New York Times*, September 10, 1993.
24. "Senate Passes D'Amato Resolution on Crown Heights Probe," September 29, 1993, press release, Robert A. Bush Papers, Brooklyn, New York; Bob Dole to Janet Reno, September 27, 1993, Anti-Defamation League Archives, New York; Clifford Krauss, "Senate Urges Federal Inquiry on Crown Heights," *New York Times*, September 30, 1993. In a telephone conversation of February 7, 2004, with the author, Reno said she was aware of these political pressures but denied that they influenced her. Zachary W. Carter, the United States Attorney for the Eastern District of New York, also denied that political pressure played any role in his office's prosecution of Lemrick Nelson or Charles Price. Stewart Ain, "U.S. Attorney: Pressure Didn't Sway Us to Retry," *Jewish Week*, February 14, 1997.
25. "In Jeopardy," *New Republic* 209 (November 15, 1993): 9.
26. Stephen Labaton, "Reno to Take Over Inquiry in Slaying in Crown Heights," *New York Times*, January 26, 1994; Joseph P. Fried, "Crown Heights Case 'Very Difficult,'" *New York Times*, January 30, 1994.

27. *New York Times* editorial "Better Late Than Never," January 27, 1994.
28. Alison Mitchell, "U.S. Indicts Teen-Ager Acquitted in Stabbing Death in Crown Hts.," *New York Times,* August 12, 1994; Joe Sexton, "Not Guilty Plea in Crown Heights Killing: U.S. Charges Man in a Hasidic Death," *New York Times,* August 18, 1994; Patricia Hurtado, "Son in a Spot: Court Scene Is Familiar," and Pete Bowles and Patricia Hurtado, "Nelson Enters Plea of Innocent," both in *Newsday,* August 8, 1994; Joan Shepard, "Hasidim Gunning for Lemrick Nelson," *City Sun,* August 24–30, 1994
29. Henry Goldschmidt, "Peoples Apart: Race, Religion and Other Jewish Differences in Crown Heights" (Ph.D. diss., University of California at Santa Cruz, 2000), 58–60, 71, 93, 229; Adam Nossiter, "Official Says Man Told Mob to 'Get a Jew': U.S. Details Rights Case in Crown Heights Killing," *New York Times,* August 22, 1996; Joseph P. Fried, "Prosecutors Say Videotaped Meetings Back Their Evidence That Suspect Incited Crowd," *New York Times,* December 8, 1996.
30. Al Guart, "Crown Hts. 'Instigator' Charged—After 5 Yrs.," *New York Post,* August 15, 1996.
31. Dan Morrison and Patricia Hurtado, "Tale of the Tape: Man Accused of Inciting Crowd in Crown Heights Riot," *Newsday,* August 18, 1996; Jan Hoffman, "Proving Incitement Is Complicated Task," *New York Times,* August 15, 1996.
32. Peter Noel, "Marking a Milestone in Crown Heights: Rev. Daughtry on Hasidim: 'They've Got the Power Because We Give It to Them,'" *Daily Challenge,* August 20, 1996. See also Noel, "In Crown Heights, Rejoicing in Hasidic Sector," *Daily Challenge,* August 15, 1996; Noel, "Is It Justice They're After or Is It Just Us?" *Daily Challenge,* August 18–19, 1996; Charles Baillou, "Attorney Claims Arrest of his Client in Crown Heights Case Politically Driven," *Amsterdam News,* August 24, 1996.
33. Joseph P. Fried, "Tough Tactics on Crown Hts. Are Typical for Defense Lawyer," *New York Times,* September 11, 1994.
34. *New York Post,* October 13, 1994; Joseph P. Fried, "Crown Hts. Defense Team to Ask Judge to Step Down: Conflict of Interest Charged by Lawyers," *New York Times,* September 8, 1994; Fried, "Judge's Ties to Jewish Leader Stir Debate in Crown Hts. Case," *New York Times,* September 20, 1994.
35. Alison Mitchell, "Adult Court to Be Sought in Crown Heights Trial: No Decision by Judge on Unsealing Records," *New York Times,* August 13, 1994.
36. Joe Sexton, "Trial as Juvenile Ordered for Crown Hts. Defendant: Rights Charges in Killing of Hasidic Student," *New York Times,* April 13, 1995.
37. "Mayor Rudolph Giuliani Urges Federal Judge Trager to Try Lemrick Nelson as an Adult for the Murder of Yankel Rosenbaum" press release, August 12, 1995; "D'Amato Calls on Justice Dept. to Appeal Crown Heights Ruling," press release, August 13, 1995; "Statement of Michael S. Miller, Execu-

tive Director, Jewish Community Relations Council," press release, August 13, 1995, all in Jewish Community Relations Council Papers, New York.

38. United States of America v. Lemrick Nelson, Jr., 68 F.3d 583 (United States Court of Appeals, Second Circuit, October 17, 1995).
39. United States of America v. Lemrick Nelson, Jr., 921 F. Supp. 105 (United States District Court, Eastern District of New York, March 21, 1996); Joseph P. Fried, "Suspect in '91 Crown Heights Death Faces Trial as an Adult," *New York Times,* March 23, 1996.
40. Joseph P. Fried, "This Time, Diversity in Crown Heights Jury," *New York Times,* February 3, 1997.
41. Jan Hoffman, "Learning from a Loss: Federal Prosecutors Win a Guilty Verdict by Avoiding Mistakes Made in First Trial," *New York Times,* February 11, 1997.
42. "A Second Crown Heights Verdict," *New York Times* editorial, February 11, 1997.
43. "Statement by Martin S. Begun, President, Michael S. Miller, Executive Director, on Crown Heights Verdict," press release of Jewish Community Relations Council of New York, February 10, 1997, JCRC Papers; "American Jewish Committee Deeply Gratified Over Verdict in Yankel Rosenbaum Trial," press release, n.d., ibid.; Paul Starick, "Yankel's Brother: 'They Should Rot in Hell!'" *New York Post,* February 11, 1997; Paul Starick and Eric Stirgus, "Yankel Kin's Quest Continues," *New York Post,* February 17, 1997; Adam Dickter, "New Push for Crown Heights Arrests: Jewish Leaders, Victim's Brother Calling on Federal Prosecutor to Bargain for More Suspects from Convicted Pair," *Jewish Week,* February 21, 1997.
44. Maria Puente, "Federal Jury Convicts 2 in Crown Heights Killing," *USA Today,* February 11, 1997.
45. Mark Kriegel, "Not Man Enough to Say He's Sorry," *Daily News,* April 1, 1998; Joseph P. Fried, "19½-Year Term Set in Fatal Stabbing in Crown Heights," *New York Times,* April 1, 1998.
46. John Sullivan, "21-Year Term for a Death in Crown Hts.: Man Sentenced for Role in Stirring Up a Crowd," *New York Times,* July 10, 1998.
47. *Jewish Week,* April 3, 1998. "Closure" became a buzzword. See, for example, the *Forward* editorial "Crown Heights Closure?" April 3, 1998.
48. Adam Dickter, "Closure on Crown Heights?: Even with the Lemrick Nelson Sentencing and Impending Civil Suit Settlement, Tensions Suggest 6-Year-Old Crown Heights Saga Will Linger," *Jewish Week,* April 3, 1998.
49. Eli B. Silverman, *NYPD Battles Crime: Innovative Strategies in Policing* (Boston: Northeastern University Press, 1999), 77; Chapin Wright, "Suit: Dinkins Stopped Cops from Stepping In," *New York Newsday,* November 18, 1992.
50. For Block's decision, see Estate of Yankel Rosenbaum et al. v. City of New York, David N. Dinkins, and Lee Brown, 975 F. Supp. 206 (U.S. District Court, E. D., NY), August 22, 1997.

51. "Statement by Mayor Dinkins on Federal Class-Action Lawsuit Charging the City with Civil and Constitutional Violations," press release, November 17, 1992, JCRC Papers.
52. Joseph P. Fried, "Police File Affidavits on Melee: Tactics Inadequate in Crown Heights," *New York Times,* February 2, 1993.
53. Wayne Barrett, "Dinkins's Do-Nothing Defense: The Crown Heights Conspiracy Case Gets Hot," *Village Voice* 38 (March 16, 1993), 14.
54. David W. Chen, "Hasidic Family Hurt in Unrest Settles Lawsuit," *New York Times,* January 26, 1998; *Algemeiner Journal,* January 23, 1998.
55. "Statement by Mayor Rudolph W. Giuliani Regarding the Settlement of the Crown Heights Lawsuit," press release, April 2, 1998, JCRC Papers; Craig Barrett, "The Cape Man of Crown Heights," *Village Voice* 43 (April 14, 1998), 45–46. Joseph P. Fried, "Mayor Apologies for City Response to Crown Heights: $1.1 Million Payment Set," *New York Times,* April 3, 1998.
56. "ADL Hopes NYC Apology and Settlement Brings Closure for the Crown Heights Hasidic Community," press release by the Anti-Defamation League of B'nai B'rith, April 2, 1998, JCRC Papers; "Orthodox Union Applauds Giuliani Settlement of Crown Heights Suit," press release by the Institute for Public Affairs of the Union of Orthodox Jewish Congregations of America, April 2, 1998, ibid.; "Statement of Michael S. Miller, Executive Vice President, Jewish Community Relations Council of New York," press release by the JCRC, April 2, 1998, ibid.
57. "Statement by David N. Dinkins Regarding Crown Heights Lawsuit," press release, March 27, 1998, JCRC papers; Andy Newman, "Pataki and D'Amato Meet Kin of Crown Heights Victim," *New York Times,* March 30, 1998; Goldschmidt, "Peoples Apart," 89; Michael Finnegan, "Dinkins Blasts Riot Deal: Sez Rudy's Wasting City Cash," *Daily News,* March 28, 1998; *New York Times,* April 3, 1998.
58. Browne, "Rangel and Sharpton Cannot Fathom Giuliani's 'Immoral' Apology," *New York Amsterdam News,* April 9–15, 1998. Browne, "Ministers Condemn Giuliani Over Apology," *New York Amsterdam News,* April 23–29, 1998; Liz Willen and Merle English, "Rudy's Barbs at Dinkins Keep Coming," *Newsday,* April 4, 1998.
59. Dan Barry, "Giuliani and Dinkins: A War of Words Still Rages," *New York Times,* April 4, 1998; David Seifman, "Hizzoner Won't Let 'Sleeping Dave' Lie," *New York Post,* April 4, 1998.
60. Leonard Greene, "Mayor, Dinkins Makes Politics Personal Battle," *Newsday,* April 6, 1998.
61. Norimitsu Onishi, "In Crown Heights Mayoral Fight, an Invitation is Rebuffed," *New York Times,* April 8, 1998; Michael Tomasky, "Slam Dink," *New York* 31 (April 20, 1998): 22.

62. "Statement by Mayor Rudolph W. Giuliani," press release, April 7, 1998, JCRC papers; *Daily News* editorial, "Guess Who's Not Coming to Dinner," April 8, 1998; Leonard Greene, "Giuliani Won't Bite: Rejects Dinkins' Crown Heights Peace-Talks Offer," *Newsday*, April 8, 1998.
63. Wilbert A. Tatum, "Who Speaks for the Jews? Rudolph Giuliani?" *Amsterdam News*, April 9–15, 1998.
64. Mark Hamblett, "New Trial Sought Over Crown Heights Jury Pool," *New York Law Journal* 223 (May 4, 2000): 1–2; *New York Post* editorial, "A Judge's Jurymandering," May 6, 2000.
65. Hamblett, "New Trial Sought Over Crown Heights Jury Pool," 1–2; Greg B. Smith, "Eye Jury Juggle in Lemrick Trial," *Daily News*, May 4, 2000.
66. Sherry F. Colb, "The Second Circuit's Recent Reversal of Two Guilty Verdicts in the Yankel Rosenbaum Killing, and the Difficult Issue of Race-Conscious Jury Selection," http.//writ.news.findlaw.cm/colb/2002016.html, January 16, 2002.
67. Jane Fritsch, "2 Win New Trial in Killing During Brooklyn Unrest: Jury Selection Faulted in Crown Hts. Case," *New York Times*, January 8, 2002; *New York Times* editorial, "The Crown Heights Saga, Cont'd.," January 12, 2002.
68. Jeffrey Abramson, "What Makes a Jury Fair," *New York Times*, January 9, 2002.
69. Joyce Purnick, "Reaching for Justice, Maybe Too Far," *New York Times*, January 10, 2002.
70. William Glaberson, "Judge Accepts a Guilty Plea in '91 Crown Heights Unrest," *New York Times*, April 13, 2002.
71. William Glaberson, "Talks In a Crown Hts. Plea Deal Have Failed, the Defense Says," *New York Times*, April 20, 2002.
72. Andy Newman, "Painstakingly, Picking a Jury for 3rd Trial in Race Killing," *New York Times*, April 26, 2003.
73. Andy Newman, "In Twist, Defendant Admits to Stabbing in '91 Racial Unrest," *New York Times*, April 29, 2003; *Daily News* editorial, "Crown Heights: The Defense Jests," April 20, 2003; Stewart Ain, "Attorneys Analyze Strategy," *Jewish Week*, May 2, 2003. Because Nelson had not testified at his two previous trials, he could not be prosecuted for perjury for now admitting that he had murdered Rosenbaum. He also did not testify at the 2003 trial.
74. Andy Newman, "Suspect in Crown Heights Case Seemed Sober, Officers Testify," *New York Times*, April 30, 2003; Kati Cornell Smith, "'Drunk' Lemrick a Crock: Cop Duo," *New York Post*, April 30, 2003.
75. Anthony M. DeStefano, "Nelson Celebrates: Guilty in Stabbing But Not in Death of Man in '91 Riot," *Newsday*, May 15, 2003. One interesting sidelight of the trial was the presence in the courtroom of Carmel Cato, who came to show support for Norman Rosenbaum. The two men sat together during

parts of the trial. John Marzulli, "Jury Out on Lemrick: Defense Says Victim Slain by 'Scared Little Boy,'" *Daily News,* May 8, 2003.

76. nyNewsday.com, May 14, 2003.
77. John Marzulli, "Lemrick Convicted in Yankel's Stabbing," *Daily News,* May 15, 2003.
78. Adam Dickter, "Nelson Found Guilty in Retrial: Yankel's Killer Spared Life Sentence," *Jewish Week,* May 16, 2003.
79. Andy Newman, "Penalty in Crown Hts. Case Means a Little More Jail Time," *New York Times,* August 21, 2003; Herbert Lowe, "One and Done: Nelson May Leave Prison Within a Year; Victim's Family Seethes," *Newsday,* August 21, 2003.
80. Adam Dickter, "Is Crown Heights Over? 'We Have to Move On,' Neighborhood's Jews Say After Last Week's Sentencing," *Jewish Week,* August 29, 2003.
81. Kati Cornell Smith and Cynthia R. Fagen, "Lemrick Gets Max: But He'll Be Free in Under a Year," *New York Post,* August 21, 2003; Jacob Gershman, "Nelson Receives 10-Year Sentence for Crown Heights Murder," *New York Sun,* August 21, 2003.
82. Dickter, "Is Crown Heights Over?"
83. John Marzulli and David Goldiner, "Crown Hts. Lemrick Out of Jail," *Daily News,* June 3, 2004.
84. Tim Kelley, "City and Crown Hts. Family Reach $400,000 Settlement," *New York Times,* January 10, 2002.
85. Jennifer Lee, "City Settles with Family of '91 Victim," *New York Times* June 18, 2005.
86. Nancie L. Katz, Maggie Haberman, and Monique El-Faizy, "Yankel's Kin to get $1.25M," *Daily News,* June 18, 2005; Nasncie L. Katz, "Yankel Kin Target Hosp," *ibid.,* April 10, 2005; Adam Dickter, "Yankel's Brother: It's Not Over," *Jewish Week,* June 23, 2005.

7

EFFORTS AT HEALING

Although the population of Crown Heights was mostly of Caribbean background, the press and other observers described the tensions before and after the riot as mainly involving Jews and African Americans. Similarly, those involved in the post-riot healing process virtually ignored the Caribbeans. Jews saw the riot as one aspect of a degeneration in black-Jewish relations that had reached crisis proportions. This rift needed to be mended, Jews believed, in order to preserve the fabled liberal black-Jewish political alliance and to protect the security of Jews living and working in the inner city.

The Crown Heights riot was the latest in a series of recent incidents pitting blacks against Jews. Two of these had occurred in 1991 prior to the riot, and, together with the riot, seemed to indicate that relations between Jews and blacks were worsening. The first was the publication of the first volume of the Nation of Islam's book *The Secret Relationship Between Blacks and Jews.* This work purported to show the involvement of Jews in the slave trade and slavery. Professional historians dismissed *The Secret Relationship* as an anti-Semitic screed.[1] Jews, however, took *The Secret Relationship* seriously enough to write several books in refutation.

The second incident was a much-discussed speech in Albany, New York, by Leonard Jeffries, chairman of the black studies department at City College and a proponent of a bizarre distinction between black "sun-people" and white "mud-people." Jeffries also claimed that Jews had subjected blacks to derogatory stereotyping through their control of the mass media, particularly Hollywood. Jews were outraged by Jeffries's speech and demanded that he be disciplined by the City College administration. He was ultimately deprived of his department chairmanship, although he retained his tenured academic position.

The Secret Relationship and Jeffries's address called into question one of the fundamental principles of the political liberalism to which most Jews adhered: the commonality of interest between Jews and blacks that had been forged in a shared experience of victimization and in what the rabbi-historian Arthur Hertzberg termed a "comradeship of excluded peoples." This belief in the black-Jewish entente was particularly strong during the 1950s and 1960s, the golden decades of black-Jewish cooperation, when Jewish lobbying and funding had helped dismantle the structure of court decisions and state laws supporting racial segregation. At no other time, wrote the historian Howard M. Sachar, "did Jews identify themselves more forthrightly with the liberal avant-garde." Jews and blacks saw the events of 1991 as aberrations that should not be allowed to detract from the underlying oneness of the two groups. "The relation between Jews and blacks does not allow divorce," the political commentator Paul Berman wrote two and a half years after the riot in Crown Heights. "It was the past that made the blacks and the Jews almost the same, and the past has the singular inconvenience of never going away." Blacks also spoke in this vein. "The truth is that there is a kinship between our two communities," said the Reverend Patricia Reeberg, pastor of Saint Paul's Baptist Church in Harlem. "It's based on past histories and a feeling that there is a gut understanding of what oppression is about."[2]

This identification of Jews with the cause of civil rights and black uplift was not completely disinterested. Under the pressure of the civil rights movement, universities, corporations, housing projects, and social clubs had opened their doors to Jews as well as to blacks. But Jews preferred to think that they had acted solely out of a generous regard for the welfare of blacks. "The myth of this involvement," wrote two Jewish sociologists, "enhances the self-image of the Jews as a caring, sensitive minority, selflessly contributing to improve the lot of other minorities."[3] As proof of their concern for the welfare of blacks, Jews pointed to the deaths of Andrew Goodman and Michael Schwerner in Mississippi in 1964 and to the many Jews who worked in the Magnolia State during the "freedom summer" of 1964. Blacks, however, while appreciative of Jewish support, were more realistic about its motivation and did not share the romanticism that Jews infused into black-Jewish relations.

Jews reacted to the events of 1991 with dismay, as they impugned the idealistic concern that Jews believed they had for the welfare of blacks. By contrast, Jews responded enthusiastically to *Liberators: Fighting on Two Fronts in World War II*, a 90-minute documentary film sponsored by the Public Broadcasting System. The film and an accompanying book purported to tell the story of two black military units, the 761st Tank Battalion and the 183rd Combat Engineers, which supposedly liberated Jews from the Buchenwald, Dachau, and Lambach concentration camps in Germany in April 1945. Appropriately enough, the movie's two producers were a black and a Jew.

The film's original purpose was to help rectify the amnesia regarding the contribution of blacks to the American military victory in World War II. Nina Rosenblum, one of the producers of the film, claimed that a racist conspiracy had obliterated evidence of the role of blacks in World War II. "Army photographers went by the black troops and didn't photograph them," she claimed.[4] By the time the film was completed in 1992, however, it had become enmeshed in the aftermath of the Crown Heights riot and the tangled history of recent black-Jewish relations. The press and viewers of the documentary were less interested in its recounting of the contribution of black soldiers to the war effort than in its significance for black-Jewish relations. The black-Jewish theme was stressed at the very beginning of the film with the showing of a logo of a Star of David and the 761st's Black Panther emblem joined together. The book, which appeared simultaneously with the movie and had the same title, made the identical point in its introduction. "In our rather tragic present, when black and Jewish Americans indulge in conflict that . . . gives joy and comfort only to those racists and anti-Semites who are their common enemies, there is reason to remember a period in the not too terribly distant past . . . when those of both groups who were progressively inclined attempted with some success to collectively comprehend their horrific historical experiences."[5]

Liberators opened at a special showing on November 9, 1992, the fifty-fourth anniversary of Kristallnacht, to a capacity audience at Alice Tully Hall in New York City's Lincoln Center. Two days later, Veterans Day, it was shown on the PBS series *The American Experience*. The film's opening, coming ten days after the acquittal of Lemrick Nelson in state court for the murder of Yankel Rosenbaum, could not have been more fortuitous. The movie provided a counterimage to that of black-Jewish hostility and hearkened back to an era of black-Jewish comity. The film's emotional power came from the recollections of Jewish inmates of the concentration camps and their black liberators, now allies in the struggle against racism and persecution. In one scene two blacks have their arms around a Jew as he views Buchenwald, where he had been imprisoned. "An image of black American and Jew embracing through the pain of their memories," wrote John J. O'Connor in the *New York Times,* "is all the more moving in the current context of scattered tensions between the two groups."[6]

A month later on December 17, *Liberators* was shown at the Apollo Theatre, Harlem's most famous center of black culture and entertainment. The politically ambitious Jesse Jackson had suggested the showing. Jackson was eager to mend political fences with Jews still smarting over his 1984 anti-Semitic description of New York as "Hymietown." The event, which was called "Neighbor to Neighbor," was sponsored by a group calling itself the "Liberators" Commemoration Committee. It was cohosted by Congressman Charles B. Rangel of Harlem and Peggy Tishman, a member of a prominent New York City Jewish real estate family and a past president of New York UJA–Federation and of the Jewish Community Relations Council of New York, and was underwritten by the Time-Warner Corporation. There was a reception after the showing of the film that featured a politically correct menu of grits, gefilte fish, catfish fritters, collard greens, kishkes, and kasha varnishkas. Among the twelve hundred people at the screening and the reception were black and Jewish community leaders, city officials, black veterans of World War II, and Holocaust survivors. Four persons spoke—Mayor David Dinkins, Jesse Jackson, Manhattan District Attorney Robert Morgenthau, and Elie Wiesel—two blacks and two Jews. As the program for the evening made clear, the memories of Crown Heights were never far away. The city's residents, it said, "hope that by learning about an important piece of our collective history of both discrimination and collaboration we can identify new ways to confront and move beyond what divides us as New Yorkers." Their common history of suffering and persecution, the audience was frequently told, made blacks and Jews natural allies.[7]

The contrast with August 1991 was clear. Jews and blacks at the Harlem event vowed to put aside their differences and work for a better New York. Jesse Jackson led the audience in singing "We Shall Overcome," and told them that "the walls that came down in Dachau and Buchenwald must not be resurrected in Crown Heights or any place." "The pain and violence surrounding Crown Heights," he said, "is a challenge to come together, not to fall apart." Spotting Hertz Frankel and Leib Glanz, two bearded rabbis in the crowd, and perhaps believing that they were from Crown Heights, Jackson asked them to join him on the stage. He embraced them and, enthused by the evening's ecumenical euphoria, asked whether he could preach in their synagogue. They politely declined the offer. Jackson did, however, prevail on a reluctant Glanz to offer a prayer. With Crown Heights in mind, Glanz prayed for "peace and tranquility between all human beings, no matter their color, their race, or where they came from." While Glanz's prayer might have earned him points with the crowd at the Apollo, it was not popular with his fellow Hasidim in the Williamsburg section of Brooklyn, who opposed any consorting with the likes of Jackson. Ironically, Frankel and Glanz were actually Satmar Hasidim, bitter enemies of the Lubavitchers of Crown Heights. It had been fear of violence by Satmars that had initially convinced the New York City police in the 1970s to provide an escort for the Lubavitcher rebbe during his frequent trips to the cemetery in Queens.[8]

Absent from the Harlem event were representatives from the Lubavitch community of Crown Heights, who failed to recognize its public relations importance. Rabbi Shmuel M. Butman of Crown Heights mocked the idea of traveling from Brooklyn to Harlem to see a documentary about black soldiers. This event, he said, was strictly "cosmetic" and diverted attention from more substantive issues such as the increasing crime rate in Crown Heights caused by blacks. "We're not big on going to movies," he scoffed. "We wanted to send a message by not going. That this is not the way to solve the issues of Crown Heights." The Lubavitchers were also loath to participate in a media event that would inevitably benefit Dinkins, who they believed had failed to protect them during the riot.[9]

Dinkins and other city politicians hoped that *Liberators* could lessen the rift between blacks and Jews and help keep the city peaceful. Dinkins had another reason to be pleased by *Liberators.* He faced a tough reelection campaign in 1993 in which his conduct during the Crown Heights riot would inevitably be a significant issue. Anything that could bring blacks and Jews—the two most important Democratic voting blocs—together would redound to his political advantage. He used the screening of *Liberators* to help cement the political ties between the two groups. How sad it was, Dinkins told a cheering audience at the Alice Tully Hall showing, when "the hand of an African-American—which once placed food in the mouths of starving Jewish concentration-camp victims—plunges a knife into the breast of an innocent Jewish divinity student." He repeated these sentiments a month later at the Apollo Theatre. "The bond between African-Americans and Jews have [*sic*] frayed because of the actions of a minority, but the children of light far outnumber the children of darkness in New York."[10]

The liberation of the Nazi concentration camps was actually a secondary topic in the *Liberators* book. It did not get around to discussing the liberation story until the last quarter of the book, and then the topic occupied only a few pages. The "two fronts" mentioned in the subtitles of the book and film referred not to the liberation of the concentration camps but to the simultaneous struggle against racial discrimination in America and the war against Germany overseas. The evidence presented in the book that blacks had liberated any concentration camps was sparse and anecdotal, owing largely to the fact that the liberation story was mere conjecture. The motivation for discussing the role of blacks in liberating the concentration camps was not to strengthen black-Jewish relations, but rather to refute the racist notion that blacks had contributed little to the war effort. Thus black historian Clement A. Price praised the film because it countered "white hegemonic history that blacks could not fight heroically in battle"—and not because it showed blacks liberating Jews from the camps.[11]

Blacks and liberals emphasized that the film's importance was what it said about American race relations, not what it said about the Holocaust. In defending *Liberators,* Richard Cohen of the *Washington Post* emphasized that the film's significance had little to do with black-Jewish relations. The controversy surrounding the documentary's historical accuracy was unfortunate because it undermined the struggle against racism. "In terms of contemporary race relations," he said, "it hardly matters whether several black soldiers or an entire all-black unit liberated two of the most famous concentration camps. . . . For the bulk of the film deals with the African-American experience here in the United States and has a power independent of any connection—purported or real—to the Holocaust."[12]

But for New Yorkers, particularly Jews concerned with combating anti-Semitism and politicians wishing to preserve the liberal black-Jewish coalition, the importance of *Liberators* was precisely the connection it made between blacks and Jewish survivors. The New York City Board of Education believed the film could lessen tensions between blacks and Jews, and it proposed distributing copies of the documentary to all of the city's public junior and senior high schools. Jewish philanthropists competed for the privilege of underwriting this work. The film's producers also hoped to raise sufficient funds to provide copies to all of America's seventy thousand junior and senior high schools.[13]

The New York press also emphasized the potential of the *Liberators* in healing the rift between blacks and Jews. The headline of a Jack Newfield column in the *New York Post* was "New film could help heal wounds of race hate." Newfield claimed the documentary had the potential of helping rescue New York from its recent violent obsession with race. *Liberators,* he wrote, "should be shown not just to schoolchildren, but to everyone. All who aspire to run for mayor in this time and place must see it. If they don't shed a tear, they lack the soul to govern this vibrant volcano of a city." New Yorkers, he continued, should celebrate the movie's producers "for creating a healing work of art that makes people more informed, more tolerant, more spiritual."[14]

THE *LIBERATORS* CONTROVERSY

Liberators won the International Documentary Association award and received an Academy Award nomination for best documentary, even though doubts regarding its historical accuracy had been raised almost immediately after its initial showing by black veterans, Holocaust survivors, and historians. The Academy Award nomination came after PBS on February 12, 1993, had already withdrawn the film from circulation because of these doubts. It was soon revealed that the research that had gone into the film and book was slipshod. The film's producers had never researched any American military records or documents at the United States Holocaust Museum. They preferred instead to rely on the type of oral history pioneered by the journalist Studs Terkel. "In eschewing scholarship and embracing sentiment," the film historian Thomas Doherty asserted, "*Liberators* belied its name. Ironically, the ethnically correct/ethically suspect documentary has become a watchword not for liberation but for deception." The journalist Stephen J. Dubner agreed. "Invention," he wrote, "does indeed seem to have played its part in this sad scenario of good intentions gone wrong."[15]

It was clear even before the Apollo Theatre event that PBS and the producers of *Liberators* were in serious trouble. Veterans, both blacks and whites, almost immediately denied that either the 761st or the 183rd had liberated Buchenwald or Dachau, and their denials were picked up by the city's press.[16] The *New York Post* waged a two-month campaign against *Liberators* and its producers. Eric Breindel, the paper's editorial page editor, argued that "intergroup harmony can't be built on a false foundation. . . . [S]ervice records ought not to be misrepresented to serve the ideological goals of contemporary filmmakers."[17]

The *Forward,* a New York–based Jewish weekly that had criticized the Dinkins administration's handling of the Crown Heights riot, also criticized *Liberators.* The film's producers, it charged, "want to portray blacks as liberators, Jews as victims so as to reinterest blacks and Jews in their famous partnership during the civil rights struggle. That proposition will not become clearer if it is based on a historical lie." Jeffrey Goldberg, the *Forward*'s New York bureau chief, brought the *Liberators* controversy to national attention when his appropriately titled article, "The Exaggerators," appeared in the *New Republic* in February 1993. Goldberg noted that black veterans were particularly angry at the film's subordination of truth to politics. They feared their accomplishments during the war would be tarnished by the easily disproved fantasies of *Liberators.* "We had been stripped of our history in our slavery," E. G. McConnell, a black soldier with the 761st and a Purple Heart winner, said. "But apparently some other people didn't mind a few lies."[18]

The American Jewish Committee produced the most detailed examination of the *Liberators* controversy. This was "*Liberators:* A Background Report," a fourteen-page, single-spaced document written by Kenneth S. Stern, an AJC program specialist. Stern noted that the film "has become a tool for building bridges between blacks and Jews, reinforcing the common interest of both groups in fighting prejudice and discrimination." The documentary, however, had "serious factual flaws" and made claims that were "negligently sloppy." On February 13, 1993, the day after the release of the Stern report, WNET, the public broadcasting station in New York City, withdrew *Liberators* from circulation pending the release of its own investigation.[19]

The WNET report, "Findings of the Review Team: An Examination of 'Liberators: Fighting on Two Fronts in World War II,'" declared that *Liberators* "was diminished by an initial paucity of basic research and an almost exclusive reliance on oral history. Apparently little effort was made to seek corroboration of this oral history, either from the military or from primary or secondary sources." The report's conclusion was damning: "the research for this documentary was not as diligent and comprehensive as basic documentary practice would require." PBS refused to show *Liberators* until it was revised, and the station demanded that its name be removed from the credits on the video prints. The *Amsterdam News* strongly protested and claimed that PBS had backed down as a result of Jewish pressure. There were forces in the city, the paper warned, that after Crown Heights did not wish to see a rapprochement between blacks and Jews.[20]

In 1995 the publisher of *Liberators,* while refusing to recall the book, admitted that "it is now clear that certain facts are in dispute in *Liberators,* for which Harcourt Brace and Company must take at least partial responsibility and which we deeply regret." Throughout the controversy, the film's producers refused to back down, despite incontrovertible proof that the two black military units were nowhere near Buchenwald and Dachau when they were liberated. The producers attacked the WNET report as biased, argued that those who questioned their conclusions, including black veterans, were motivated by racism, and claimed that they were the victims of censorship.[21] "The key thing is to understand we've been lied to, that the sins of omission in our history have given us a warped and a skewed perspective," Nina Rosenblum said. "We have to look at our past so that we can honestly and justly act now and in the future." In fact, the future and not the past had always been her major concern, particularly a future in which American Jews would be allied once again with blacks.[22]

TRUTH OR FALSITY

For some Jews, the truth or falsity of *Liberators* was irrelevant. More significant was the film's role in mending the breach between blacks and Jews. "Why would anybody want to exploit the idea that this is a fraud?" Peggy Tishman asked rhetorically. "What we're trying to do is make New York a better place for you and me to live." She seemed unembarrassed by the liberties that the film's producers had taken with the truth. More important was healing the wounds inflicted by Crown Heights. "We are a very troubled city," she told the *Jewish Week* of New York. "The purpose of that evening [at the Apollo] was to bring us together. I felt that the film had done that. The most important issue at this particular time was to bring the communities together." If the film was not factually true, so much the worse for truth. "There are a lot of truths that are very necessary," she said. But the criticisms of *Liberators* "is not a truth that's necessary."[23]

Letty Cottin Pogrebin, writing in the radical bimonthly Jewish magazine *Tikkun*, warned that criticisms of the film played into the hands of those seeking to capitalize on black-Jewish hostility. She admitted that the inaccuracies in *Liberators* were "artistically unnecessary, ethically wrong, and historically indefensible," and that the film "presents us with a problem of ethical slippage and well-intentioned embellishment." But its "fact-checking" critics were wrong in describing it as a hoax. More important than fidelity to historical details was the documentary's "search for truth at a level deeper than facts." Literal truth must be defended, she concluded, "but so must the liberal vision of Black advancement and the struggle for Black-Jewish harmony." If blacks and Jews were to advance beyond the dead end symbolized by Crown Heights, it could only be on the basis of reciprocity and equality. This basis required that Jews rethink their relations with blacks. "Any such reshuffling of the power balance between our two peoples," she concluded, "disturbs the well-burnished narrative that for decades has reflected the Jewish self-image in warm, flattering tones." Critics of *Liberators,* by contrast, hoped to preserve this conventional understanding of the subordinate relationship of blacks to Jews and to impede black economic advancement.[24]

A VALENTINE FOR THE CITY

While the *Liberators* story was coming to an end, another attempt at black-Jewish healing occurred. This involved the cover of the Valentine's Day issue (February 15, 1993) of the *New Yorker.* The cover was drawn by the Pulitzer Prize–winning cartoonist Art Spiegelman, the author of *Maus: A Survivor's Tale,* a two-volume comic book based on his parents' experiences in Nazi-occupied Poland during World War II. It showed a Hasid and a black woman embracing and kissing. The woman was scantily dressed and appeared to be of Caribbean descent. For Spiegelman, a resident of New York City, the *New Yorker* cover was his contribution to black-Jewish harmony so necessary now in the wake of the riot and the acquittal of Lemrick Nelson. "This metaphoric embrace is my Valentine card to New York, a wish for the reconciliation of seemingly unbridgeable differences in the form of a symbolic kiss," he explained. He recognized that kissing was hardly a substitute for programmatic solutions to the problems afflicting black-Jewish relations and the social and economic problems facing blacks in New York City. "But once a year, perhaps, it's permissible to close one's eyes, see beyond the tragic complexities of modern life, and imagine that it might really be true that 'All you need is love.'"[25]

The *New Yorker* had high hopes for Spiegelman's cover. "In the context for which it was intended and in which it is embedded—that of Valentine's Day with its momentary suspensions, its sweet hopes and fond wishes," declared Tina Brown, the magazine's editor, "it seems to us conducive beyond its surface impact, to profound reflection and discussion." The cover did provoke discussion, but it is doubtful that it aroused profound reflection. Crown Heights needed more than romantic platitudes. The core of the problem, as the novelist Cynthia Ozick pointed out, was the mistaken assumption that the opposites of hatred and violence were love and sex. The obverse of violence was not love but peace. The problems of Crown Heights, Ozick concluded, could not be solved by the trivialization of black-Hasidic differences.[26]

Both blacks and Jews deplored Spiegelman's cover. "Never," quipped one Orthodox Jew, "has there been a more egregious case of bussing to achieve integration." For blacks, the cover brought back memories of the sexual exploitation of black women by white men during slavery. It also reinforced the stereotype of the black female as temptress. "Disrespect of the Black Woman" was the headline of one article published in the *City Sun*, a black newspaper in New York City. The article was written by Carroll Carey Howard, a black woman who had been a member of the editorial staff of the *New Yorker.* Howard claimed Hasidic men viewed black women as whores and subjected them to constant sexual harassment. The cover by Spiegelman reflected this "despicable attitude," and the *New Yorker* owed black women "a profound apology." Black women, she claimed, did not find Hasidic men attractive, and they certainly did not desire to have intimate relations with them. The clash of interests between blacks and Jews in Crown Heights, Howard concluded, could not be resolved by "provocative magazine covers" and additional public relations ploys. Other blacks also criticized the cover. "Would the *New Yorker* have published a cover that showed an African-American man kissing a Hasidic woman?" the Reverend Herbert Daughtry asked rhetorically. In fact, Spiegelman said that this had been his original intention, but aesthetic concerns had dissuaded him.[27]

Jews had their own reasons for being offended by Spiegelman's drawing. Orthodox Jewish men are forbidden by Jewish law to touch women who are not family members, much less kiss them. Even showing physical affection to a spouse in public is frowned upon. Spiegelman anticipated that some Jews might be offended by the cover, and he was not to be disappointed. The *Jewish Press*, a Brooklyn-based weekly popular among the right-wing Orthodox, called the cover "the ultimate in bad taste." Rabbi Joseph Spielman, chairman of the Crown Heights Jewish Community Council, agreed. "Rather than healing, this just makes everything ludicrous. I don't think it has any relevance with what's going on in Crown Heights. We need to find solutions, but this is a shame." Even non-Orthodox Jews were irritated by the *New Yorker* cover, as it appeared at a time when an increasing intermarriage rate threatened American Jewish continuity. The cover seemed implicitly to sanction intermarriage; to make things worse, it appeared on the occasion of a holiday rooted in Christianity and paganism.[28]

Spiegelman was unrepentant. "The main problem," he said, "is we live in a world with no sense of humor or irony, and it requires . . . some sophistication not to take this [i.e., his cover] literally." He suggested that if blacks and Jews would get together to discuss what they found in his drawing so mutually offensive, then it would serve its purpose. Blacks and Jews, however, were not appeased by Spiegelman's soothing words. The cover, said Rabbi Abraham Flint of Crown Heights, "is a tasteless publicity stunt. I don't see how anyone could say that it would advance harmony. It's insulting." The controversy left a bad taste in everyone's mouth.[29]

A COMMON QUEST

In his report on the *Liberators* controversy, Kenneth Stern of the American Jewish Committee proposed the creation of a publication that would "speak of and to, by and for, blacks and Jews—a publication that treats the stories of individual people, so the humanness that poke like a laser in the LIBERATORS can speak of our current concerns." This proposal occasioned the appearance in the spring of 1996 of *CommonQuest: The Magazine of Black Jewish Relations.* The magazine was jointly sponsored by the American Jewish Committee and Howard University, America's most illustrious black university. A grant from the Harry and Jeanette

Weinberg Foundation of Baltimore helped to get it off the ground. *CommonQuest* appeared three times a year until it folded in 2000 after the American Jewish Committee discontinued its annual subsidy of $25,000. At that time, the AJC said it was investigating other ways to explore the issue of relations between blacks and Jews, including conferences, the subsidizing of books, a newsletter, a Web site, and even a new magazine. Evidently the AJC was disappointed that after five years of publication the circulation of *CommonQuest* had only reached twenty thousand.[30]

The title *CommonQuest* reflected the belief of the magazine's founders that blacks and Jews, despite their recent disagreements, had similar interests and were natural allies. "We will ask our contributors to illuminate the real conflicts that exist," said Robert S. Rifkind, president of the AJC, "but also to identify fruitful fields for cooperation between blacks and Jews in advancing a common agenda." The magazine's editorial advisory board included U.S. Congressional Representatives Howard Berman, Barney Frank, John Lewis, Nita Lowey, Kweise Mfume, and Major Owens; U.S. Senators Joseph Lieberman and Paul Wellstone; community activists Hyman Bookbinder, Johnetta Cole, Murray Friedman, Rabbi Irving Greenberg, Rabbi David Saperstein, Rabbi Harold Schulweis, Albert Vorspan, and the Reverend Johnny Ray Youngblood; and academicians Clayborne Carson, Hasia Diner, Gerald Early, Henry Louis Gates, Jr., Paula Hyman, Randall Kennedy, Julius Lester, Deborah Dash Moore, Anna Deavere Smith, Cornel West, William Julius Wilson, and Alan Wolfe.[31]

The coeditors of the magazine were a black and a Jew: Russell Adams, the chairman of the Department of African American Studies at Howard University, and Jonathan Rieder, a Barnard College sociologist, who had written extensively on black-Jewish relations in general and on the Crown Heights riot in particular. The periodical's initial issue portended the type of material *CommonQuest* would feature. It contained a symposium on the Million Man March of 1995; an essay by Gerald Early, a professor of Afro-American studies at Washington University in Saint Louis, titled "Who is the Jew? A Question of African-American Identity"; an article by Samuel G. Freedman on the Reverend Johnny Ray Youngblood and Saint Paul Community Baptist Church in Brooklyn; an excerpt from Melissa Fay Greene's book *The Temple Bombing* on the 1958 bombing of an Atlanta synagogue whose rabbi, Jacob Rothschild, was a fervent advocate of civil rights; and a review by Philip

Kasinitz, a sociologist and authority on the West Indians of New York City, of Murray Friedman's book *What Went Wrong: The Creation and Collapse of the Black-Jewish Alliance.* Future issues contained articles on Jews and blacks in the music business ("Rhythm-and-Jews"), Jews and blacks in Hollywood, Paul Robeson and Yiddish culture, George Gershwin's *Porgy and Bess,* black Jews, marriages between blacks and Jews, blacks and Jews on campus, and multiculturalism.

In its first issue the magazine's two editors laid out its rationale. Adams's "As the Twig is Bent" and Rieder's "Beyond Frenzy and Accusation" argued that blacks and Jews were bound together by a shared history of victimization, "mutual need as well as principled commitment to do the 'right thing'" (Adams), and "mutual stakes in a just and civil society" (Rieder). A publication such as *CommonQuest* could help restore that "vision of humanistic universalism" and "coalition of conscience" (Rieder) on which the black-Jewish entente of the 1950s and early 1960s was based. "At the most elemental level," Rieder concluded, "the quest we share is for the clarity of truth." This quest for truth and black-Jewish reconciliation also characterized the most important literary work resulting from the Crown Heights riot: Anna Deavere Smith's play *Fires in the Mirror.*[32]

CROWN HEIGHTS ONSTAGE

Fires in the Mirror was one in a series of plays Smith planned to write and to title "On the Road: A Search for American Character." Smith, an actress and a professor of drama at Stanford University, dedicated *Fires in the Mirror* "to the residents of Crown Heights, Brooklyn, and to the memory of Gavin Cato and Yankel Rosenbaum." The play opened in New York City in May 1992 at the Joseph Papp Public Theater and ran for three months. The play was highly acclaimed. It was a finalist for the Pulitzer Prize in drama and won the 1993 Kesselring Prize for the best new American play.[33]

Smith recalled that when she initially visited Crown Heights for research she was a typical liberal dreaming about "the possibility of unity among the culturally disenfranchised—so this would even include . . . collaborations between blacks and Jews." Such illusions soon disappeared. "The good thing that's happened to me in these three years is I forgot all that," she recalled in 1994. "Coming to Crown Heights was like being *thrown* off of that cloud." The result was a work of artistic merit rather than of political cant. The play was not, Smith emphasized, a "wonderful, healing thing."[34]

In his foreword to the published version of *Fires in the Mirror,* Cornel West declared it to be "the most significant artistic exploration of Black-Jewish relations in our time." It shows how art "can take us beyond ourselves as we examine ourselves even in an ugly moment of xenophobic frenzy," and reveals what must be done if we are "to overcome the xenophobic cancer that threatens to devour the soul of the precious yet precarious democratic experiment called America." Melanie Kirkpatrick's review in the *Wall Street Journal* described *Fires in the Mirror* as an "extraordinary play" and "an unsparing rendering of the myriad emotions of the incident—not just the rage that hit the headlines but also the bitterness, grief and bewilderment that touched the community." Frank Rich, the drama critic of the *New York Times,* called the play a "compelling and sophisticated view of urban racial and class conflict," with Smith's skillful interviewing rivaling that of Studs Terkel. The play's "moving and provocative" analysis of race relations, so free of platitudes and polemics, stemmed from Smith's "objective grasp of the troubling big picture." Here Rich mirrored the politically correct slant of his employer that the "troubling big picture" of the Crown Heights riot involved "race and poverty," not anti-Semitism.[35]

In this one-woman play, Smith played twenty-six different characters, and the dialogue consisted in large part of verbatim excerpts from interviews she had conducted earlier with her subjects, including Sonny Carson, Carmel Cato, Angela Davis, Richard Green, Rabbi Shea Hecht, Leonard Jeffries, Michael S. Miller (executive director of the New York Jewish Community Relations Council), Minister Conrad Mohammed of Louis Farrakhan's Black Muslim sect, Letty Cottin Pogrebin, Norman Rosenbaum, the Reverend Heron Sam, the Reverend Al Sharpton, Rabbi Joseph Spielman, and several anonymous black and Jewish residents of Crown Heights. The one exception to using dialogue derived from interviews was a section when she used words from a speech given by Norman Rosenbaum at a political rally. John J. O'Connor of the *New York Times* said that Smith's skillful use of interviews reminded him of John Dos Passos's use of interviews in his famous trilogy *USA.*[36]

Smith tried not to interject her own feelings into *Fires in the Mirror,* preferring that the play's characters speak for themselves. Several of those interviewed had had no direct involvement in the riot and spoke not about Crown Heights but about more general topics such as racism, anti-Semitism, and what it means to be a black or a Hasid in contemporary America. Smith's main objective was not to provide an etiology of the riot. Rather, *Fires in the Mirror* was a meditation on the deaths of Gavin Cato and Yankel Rosenbaum and on how African Americans, West Indians, and Jews negotiated their distinctive identities and differences. It was also an attempt to get blacks and Jews to see and hear each other. "There's something very deep in all of us," she said, "that is taught to us when we are very, very little. Which is the disrespect and fear of the other." The play ends with Carmel Cato's recollections of August 19, 1991. "I am a special person," he says. "I was born different. I am a man born by my foot. I born by my foot. Anytime a baby comin' by the foot they either cut the mother or the baby dies. But I as born with my foot. I'm one of the special." For Smith, all the people in *Fires in the Mirror* are special.[37]

In November 1998, *Crown Heights,* another play about the riot, began a three-week Off-Broadway run at the Castillo Theatre in Lower Manhattan. Alex Garfield, a Jewish businessman, was so moved by the play that he contributed $25,000 so that it could be staged in local schools. *Crown Heights* starred five young blacks from All Stars Talent Network, one of the city's leading nonprofit antiviolence programs, and several young Jews. The actors were unpaid. *Crown Heights* was an amateurish production and lacked the dramatic power of *Fires in the Mirror.*

Crown Heights was written by Dan Friedman, Jacqueline Salit, and Fred Newman. Newman, a psychotherapist, was the founder of ASTN and the artistic director at the Castillo Theatre. But he was better known for his shady political past. Newman, along with Lenora Fulani, had founded the New Alliance Party in 1979, a local political party that, despite his own Jewish background, often trafficked in anti-Semitism and anti-Zionism. *Crown Heights* centered on the murder of an Orthodox Jew during the Crown Heights riot and the subsequent trial of the accused black murderer. In the play's final act, the accused proposes marriage to a Jewish social worker and she matter-of-factly accepts. "This is a theater of questions, not answers," said Roger Grunwald, the publicity director of the Castillo Theatre. "We play scripts even in real life. Life is a performance, too, and we have to change it to make a new life."[38]

Answers and not questions dominated a revised version of *Crown Heights,* coauthored by Friedman and Newman, which opened for a brief run in New York in January 2004. This new version presents a bizarre account of the riot. It blames Jews for initiating the riot, and it depicts blacks acting defensively in response to the rocks and bottles hurled at them by Jews. The rabbi's car strikes a black child, and it, along with a Jewish ambulance, immediately leave the accident scene, allowing the injured youth to die. A rabbinical student runs into a knife that a pacifist black youth is holding for a friend during a fight begun by a Jew. The writer Thane Rosenbaum rightly called the play "a desecration to the memory of Yankel Rosenbaum."[39] The play's prologue claimed it to be "probably closer to the truth than what is sometimes labeled New York reality." Fred Newman, however, said it better: "I don't believe in the truth."[40]

The Crown Heights riot also made itself felt in music. The Mighty Sparrow, the stage name for a West Indian singer, released an album in 1991 titled *Crown Heights Justice,* which presented a black perspective on the riot. Not to be outdone, Ira Heller, a young Jewish singer from Long Island popular within Orthodox circles, released a recording of "One Dark Day" in August 1993, on the second anniversary of the riot. The song had been written by Cecelia Margules, a child of Holocaust survivors, who had previously written songs about the Holocaust, Rabbi Meir Kahane, and Jonathan Pollard. "One Dark Day" was her way of dealing with family memories of the Holocaust that had surfaced as a result of the murder of Rosenbaum, and with her fears about an America indifferent to the killing of a Jew.

> One dark day in history
> A single voice cries out.
> One dark day of bigotry
> A single light dies out.
> No one really seemed to care,
> No one shed a tear.
> No one questioned why or who
> About this fallen Jew.

Margules claimed the message of "One Dark Day" was universal, a protest against all forms of bigotry. But clearly her major concern, as was Heller's, was the security of America's Jews in the wake of the Crown Heights riot.[41]

REEL STORIES

There were several cinematic attempts to make sense of the Crown Heights riot. Perhaps the most important of these was the 1997 film *Blacks and Jews.* Three years in the making, this eighty-five-minute documentary was produced by Deborah Kaufman and Bari Scott, a Jew and a black, was directed by Kaufman and Alan Snitow, two Jews, and appeared in the PBS documentary series *P.O.V.* (Point Of View). The film opens with politically correct footage describing the relationship between blacks and Jews "defined by a public ritual of mutual blame." It then discusses the Crown Heights riot, the black-Jewish coalition during the 1950s and 1960s, the conflict over the movement of blacks into the Jewish neighborhood of Lawndale in Chicago during the 1960s, the Million Man March, and the negative reaction of a group of black students in East Oakland, California, during a showing of the film *Schindler's List.* All three of the film's makers were veterans of the civil rights era and pined for a return to the days when blacks and Jews marched arm in arm. They realized, however, that this era was gone. "The film is definitely not about affirmation," Snitow noted. But neither was it completely somber. "In America, African-Americans have been the principal movers and shakers of social improvement and in the white community it's been the Jews," Scott said. "So if those people can't find common ground, then the society is lost."[42]

Two commercial movies released in the early twenty-first century also emphasized the need for black-Jewish healing. *Brooklyn Babylon,* a low-budget feature film, was released in August 2001. The movie begins with an automobile accident on Eastern Parkway in Crown Heights between two cars carrying Orthodox Jews and West Indians. One of the passengers in the Jewish car is Judah, a hotheaded racist Orthodox Jew and head of a neighborhood watch group that targets blacks. Judah believes Crown Heights Jews must take up arms to protect themselves against violent blacks, while his father urges peace and tolerance. Also in this car is Judah's fiancée, Sara. Sara is only eighteen and dreading marriage to Judah, which had been arranged by her family. She wants to leave behind her cloistered religious environment and go to college. One of the passengers in the other car is Solomon, a West Indian musician with dreadlocks. Sara and Solomon exchange glances, and their brief encounter leads to a passionate affair.

Sara is broad-minded, at one point asking her father why they never have had non-Jews in their house. He responds that brotherhood is fine, but it is necessary to maintain boundaries between the Jewish and Gentile worlds. Sara is unconvinced. She tells Solomon, "I was brought up to fear anything that is different from me." This rebelliousness attracts her to Solomon, and he introduces her to rap music, marijuana, and sex. She becomes pregnant, and the film ends by asking whether what was acceptable in the time of King Solomon is permissible in contemporary Crown Heights.

The movie is ambivalent as to whether love can conquer all. On the one hand, there are frequent references to the erotic Song of Songs and to the romance between King Solomon and the black Queen of Sheba ("Sheba was black, Solomon was white / Their hearts saw no color, only love at first sight"). On the other hand, there is also mention of *Romeo and Juliet* and *West Side Story*, in which lovestruck characters meet tragic ends. If Solomon's name refers back to the lover of the black Sheba, Sara's name harks back to the Sarah of the Bible, the mother of the Jewish people. But will her biracial child be accepted as a Jew? *Brooklyn Babylon* ends with Sara walking alone on a Crown Heights street pushing a pram while the sun sinks behind the Brooklyn skyline.

The good intentions of the makers of *Brooklyn Babylon* were insufficient to make the film a commercial success. The film's plot is improbable, its direction amateurish, its dialogue stilted, and its message that sex and music can transcend social, racial, and religious barriers unreflective of the realities of Crown Heights. The film's stay in the theaters was mercifully short. It played in one Brooklyn theater, and then hardly longer than the riot itself. Lubavitchers do not go to the movies or watch television; few ever heard of the film, much less saw it. They would have been flabbergasted at its picture of a betrothed girl from their community attracted to the world of Rastafarian rappers. They would also have been turned off by the film's ignorance of Orthodox beliefs and practices. Black moviegoers, in turn, would not have welcomed the film's stereotypical view of the young black male as stud and of black and West Indian culture as primitive and vulgar.[43]

Crown Heights, another film on the Crown Heights riot, debuted on the cable television channel Showtime on February 16, 2004.[44] The movie focuses on the efforts of Yudi, a yeshiva student, and T.J., a black teenager, to become friends despite the cultural gap separating them. Yudi complains at one point that T.J. is making him "do stuff that I don't want to do," things alien to Hasidic ways, such as dancing with a black girl at a club. They do achieve a limited rapport, partially through a common interest in break dancing and rap music: "Can we find a different way / cuz we was all slaves back in the day / we're all trying to get by / one borough to share / we can all survive." The cultural pluralism espoused in both *Crown Heights* and *Brooklyn Babylon*, however, is strictly one-way. Jews are attracted to break dancing and rap music, but there is no corresponding efforts by blacks to appreciate klezmer music and Hasidic dances.

Crown Heights resembles *Brooklyn Babylon* in its ambivalence as to whether good intentions can overcome the cultural and social differences between blacks and Hasidic Jews. As Nacha Cattan noted in the *Forward*, "though the characters are based on real people, they often appear to be one-dimensional vehicles for advancing the movie's agenda of showing both the difficulties and ultimate benefits of interracial dialogue."[45] In the film, Jews complain about the criminal behavior of blacks, and blacks murmur about the wealth and power of the Hasidim. *Crown Heights* ends on a somber note with Yudi and T.J. standing on opposite platforms in a Brooklyn subway station doing a break dance while waiting for their trains to take them in different directions. When T.J.'s train leaves, Yudi is left alone, looking at the empty platform across the tracks.

LOCAL EFFORTS

There were also local efforts in Crown Heights to bridge the gulf between Jews and blacks and Caribbeans. These efforts included visits to Jewish homes during the Jewish holiday of Sukkoth, joint picnics and barbecues, art shows, museum exhibitions, concerts, marches, and athletic events. In 1998 the city government established the Crown Heights Community Mediation Center to help keep the peace. During the 1990s the local police sponsored a "Crown Heights Family Day Parade and Picnic" at a local public park. Here thousands of local residents—Jews, blacks, and West Indians—heard speeches, listened to music, rode carnival rides, and munched on food provided free by local merchants. The food served on this day reflected the theme of coming together. Dishes that reflected the ethnic diversity of Crown Heights, such as jerk chicken and pickled herring, were avoided. Instead, American food, such as hot dogs and hamburgers, was served. This effort at culinary integration was limited, however, by the need to separate the kosher from the non-kosher foods. One observer argued that this division in food reflected the immutable social divide present in Crown Heights. Instead of one meal, the picnic offered "two separate meals in close proximity—just as Blacks and Jews in Crown Heights live apart in close proximity the rest of the year."[46]

Brooklyn's cultural institutions also attempted to bridge the social divisions of Crown Heights. The Brooklyn Children's Museum held an exhibit in 1992 titled "My Culture, Our City," which portrayed the contributions of blacks and Jews to New York City. A year later the museum joined with the Brooklyn Historical Society and the Society for the Preservation of Weeksville and Bedford-Stuyvesant History on a project titled "Bridging Eastern Parkway," funded by the New York Tolerance Committee (which had been established as a result of the riot). The three cultural institutions proposed an ambitious program of oral history interviews, walking tours, museum exhibits, community forums, and lectures tracing the diverse histories of the African Americans, Caribbean-Americans, and Lubavitchers of Crown Heights. The ultimate goal of these activities was to produce material that could be incorporated into the curriculum of the city's schools. It was hoped this material would break down the distrust and ignorance that, it was believed, had caused the riot. "We hope that by aiming many of our programs at young people, we can be part of the process of creating a generation that grows up without the misunderstandings that previous generations experienced," said Joan Maynard, the executive director of the Weeksville Society.[47]

The most famous of the local healing efforts was a series of basketball games among young blacks and Lubavitchers. These resulted from conversations between blacks and Jews of the neighborhood shortly after the riot. The fundamental assumption of these conversations and the resulting basketball games was that one of the causes of the riot was the lack of contact between the two groups. The most publicized of these games was a brief scrimmage in January 1993 during halftime of a New York Knicks–Philadelphia 76ers game. The Knicks billed the evening's program "Racial Harmony Night" and provided awards for the participants. The scrimmage was sponsored by Project CURE, whose slogan was "Increase the Peace."[48]

Project CURE, which stood for Communication-Understanding-Respect-Education, had been established after the riot by Richard Green, the black head of the Crown Heights Youth Collective, a local city agency working with black youths, and David Lazerson, a charismatic Crown Heights Lubavitcher who had rapport with blacks. Lazerson had played piano in black music clubs in his hometown of Buffalo and had written *Skullcaps 'n' Switch Blades* about his experiences as a learning disabilities teacher in largely black schools in Buffalo during the 1970s. Rabbi Menachem Mendel Schneerson encouraged Lazerson to work with Green to bridge the gulf between young blacks and Jews. Their efforts resulted in conflict resolution seminars, bilingual T-shirts, concerts, joint Hanukkah-Kwanzaa celebrations, and the basketball games.[49]

Lazerson and Green believed that basketball could help alleviate the tensions in Crown Heights, and had initiated the games in 1991. Each team included blacks and Jews. Players held hands and prayed after each game, and then they sat down to discuss the issues facing the neighborhood. These games marked the first time that many of these blacks and Lubavitchers had had more than a perfunctory contact with one another. "We have to start the young people talking, and little by little we'll be able to chip away" at the mutual fear and resentment, Green said. Score was not kept at the games. Lazerson explained: "when one team wins, the other team loses. . . . Everybody's a winner at this ball game."[50]

Other Crown Heights efforts at healing were more limited in scope. A week after the riot, Hatzolah, a volunteer Jewish ambulance service, helped paint and refurbish an ambulance owned by the Tri-Community Volunteer Ambulance Corps, a black-owned ambulance service. This work was funded by a gift from an anonymous Jewish donor. "I think this is an excellent idea," said Harold Jacobs, president of Hatzolah. "What happened in Crown Heights was most unfortunate. All we were doing was trying to save the lives of the people there." Hatzolah hoped its assistance to Tri-Community would dispel the rumor that it had refused to tend to the injured Cato children.[51]

In April 1992 the Brooklyn Borough President sponsored a "seder of reconciliation" in Crown Heights. Ten blacks and ten Lubavitchers participated. The next year blacks and Jews put on a free concert in Crown Heights. Titled "The League of Neighbors Unity Concert," it featured the black folksinger Richie Havens and the Hasidic singer and songwriter Rabbi Shlomo Carlebach. It was funded by the Coca-Cola Company and the *Daily News*. Also performing were Crown Heights–based blues, jazz, and reggae ensembles, and a group of Crown Heights black and Jewish rap singers called Dr. Laz and the Cure, named for David Lazerson and the CURE organization.[52]

Of these local efforts, the most poignant was the meetings of Mothers-to-Mothers, which were based on the gatherings between Roman Catholic and Protestant mothers in Northern Ireland. Mothers-to-Mothers comprised approximately twenty African American, Caribbean-American, and Lubavitcher mothers from Crown Heights. One was Jean Griffith Sandiford, whose son Michael Griffith was killed in a 1986 racial attack in Howard Beach in Queens. The group began meeting monthly in early 1992 in a conference room at the Brooklyn district attorney's office. When they became comfortable with one another they moved their meetings to members' homes.[53]

During these meetings the Crown Heights mothers discussed their diverse backgrounds and mutual concerns, listened to speakers, and planned how to convey their experience in tolerance and understanding to others. Mothers-to-Mothers also sponsored a backyard barbecue for its participants featuring kosher food. David Lazerson had Mothers-to-Mothers in mind when he suggested that face-to-face contacts between blacks and Jews was the best way to counter prejudice. Hatred, he claimed, "is largely based on misunderstanding and myths about each other, and this can be dispelled, and is being dispelled right now in Crown Heights, through people actually sitting down with each other and talking to each other."[54]

A degree of closure came to Crown Heights on August 19, 2001, the tenth anniversary of the riot. A street fair for children was held in Crown Heights in memory of Gavin Cato and Yankel Rosenbaum and to celebrate a decade of healing. The residents feasted on kosher and Caribbean dishes and mingled with politicians mindful of the upcoming elections for mayor and city council. The Borough of Brooklyn commemorated the anniversary with a banquet at the Brooklyn Museum of Art titled "The Future is Now." The highlight of the anniversary celebration was the first meeting between Carmel Cato and Norman Rosenbaum. The meeting was initiated by Cato, and it took place on Monday, August 20, at a kosher delicatessen in Brooklyn. Richard Green and several representatives from the Giuliani administration also were present at the lunch.[55]

After lunch the group proceeded to city hall where the mayor, a fervent New York Yankees fan, presented each with a Yankees baseball bat. At city hall, Rosenbaum gave Cato a letter from his mother that emphasized the symbolic importance of their meeting. "This is, unfortunately, a very special time for our respective families," the letter said, and "no words can fully express our feelings . . . at this time. We hope and pray that you can also draw on the good memories of your son to give you, with God's help, the strength and courage to carry on, as we try to do." Cato, in turn, gave Rosenbaum a plaque from the Crown Heights Youth Collective commending Rosenbaum for his "strength and courage." Rosenbaum said he had turned down many plaques in the past, but he was very happy to accept this one because it came from the Cato family and the collective. The next day, Cato stated that he had come to terms with the fact that no one would be indicted for the killing of his son, and that it was time to move on.[56]

The New York press was ecstatic over the Cato-Rosenbaum meeting. "Crown Hts. Peacemakers" was the headline on the front page of the *New York Post* of August 20, 2001.[57] A few discordant notes were struck, however. Malcolm Honlein, the executive vice chairman of the Conference of Presidents of Major American Jewish Organizations, praised the efforts of blacks and Jews in Crown Heights to improve relations. But he also warned against equating the killings of Gavin Cato and Yankel Rosenbaum. One was an accident, the other a murder.[58] The *Jewish Press* agreed. It protested against "the revising of history" by those who likened the deaths of Cato and Rosenbaum and described the Crown Heights riot as a clash between Jews and blacks and not as an anti-Semitic attack against defenseless Jews.[59]

REMAINING TENSIONS

Street fairs and other such events in which blacks and Jews participated were not universally popular within the Lubavitch population. For these skeptics, the problem lay in not understanding the very real differences in values and interests. They opposed close contacts between their children and children of other groups, including blacks, not because they were racially bigoted, but because they feared such relationships could estrange their children from the Lubavitch community and undermine the insular Lubavitch way of life. "We don't want in any way that someone should substitute a cosmetic remedy for real solutions," Rabbi Shmuel Butman said. "Jewish children should be playing games with Jewish children. Black children should be playing games with black children. Just leave each other alone." Rabbi Shea Hecht agreed. Hasidic children should focus on education. "Being that that is their primary goal, neighborhood relations and community relations are only a hindrance to their progress." The insularity the Lubavitch prized was seen by outsiders as part of the problem, particularly when it was expressed in an insensitive and exclusionary manner. But whose problem was it? As one Lubavitcher said, "We're just insular. You don't like my being insular, that's your problem. It's not my problem."[60]

Such sentiments, which undoubtedly reflected the true feelings of many Jews in Crown Heights, were articulated in a speech Butman gave at an October 13, 1991, event sponsored by the New York Jewish Community Relations Council. His comments could not have been more maladroit and divisive. They enraged his black listeners, particularly Michael Meyers, the head of the New York Civil Rights Coalition. Butman implied that blacks devalued education and were prone to a host of pathologies, including crime, arson, drug usage, welfare dependency, rape, and illegitimacy. The Lubavitch, by contrast, constituted a model population, "a community of taxpayers, not welfare dependents."[61]

Meyers, an "honored guest" of the JCRL at the rally, walked off the podium in disgust, dismayed that no Jewish speaker had rebuked Butman. A week later he wrote a six-page, single-spaced response to Butman that made the rounds of Jewish organizations. Meyers's statement accused Butman of stigmatizing blacks, sabotaging efforts at reconciliation between blacks and Jews, and encouraging ethnic and religious tribalism. Jewish community relations officials were dismayed by Butman's words and Meyers's letter, which threatened to ruin any attempt at healing and reconciliation. Not only had Butman made a serious public relations blunder by his racist remarks, he had also angered one of the staunchest foes of anti-Semitism and black nationalism within the black community.[62]

The healing process so dear to Jewish professionals had limited impact, but this did not mean that blacks and Jews were at each others' throats. Two recent automobile accidents indicate that the events of August 1991 were a unique occurrence. The first took place on August 28, 2000. An Hatzolah ambulance driven by Shamai Goldstein, an Orthodox Jew, collided in Flatbush with a motorcycle carrying Alberto Curtis and his son Alberto, Jr. Both of the Curtises, who were black, were killed. Those who remembered Crown Heights anticipated difficulties because of the accident, but there were no protests, marches, and rioting. This absence of violence was due in part because the city and police were better prepared, because it was more difficult for demagogues to capitalize on an accident involving an ambulance than a car in a Lubavitch motorcade, and because black-Jewish relations were different in Flatbush from those of Crown Heights. "There isn't the general hostility," Rabbi Yechezkel Pikus, executive director of the Council of Jewish Organizations of Flatbush, said. "You don't have that militancy." Pikus also noted that blacks and Jews did not live together in Flatbush as they did in Crown Heights; as a result, there was less competition for housing and other community resources.[63]

The second accident occurred in Crown Heights in the late afternoon of August 20, 2002. It was eerily reminiscent of the crash involving Gavin Cato almost exactly eleven years earlier. Tiamani Gittens, a three-year-old black girl, was critically injured when hit by a car at the intersection of Lincoln Place and Washington Avenue, less than a mile from where Cato had been struck. The car's driver, Solomon Stern, was a Hasid from the Williamsburg section of Brooklyn. A potentially very dangerous situation was prevented when several blacks stepped forward to protect Stern from an increasingly angry crowd. Black leaders immediately came to the accident scene and urged restraint, and the police blanketed the area. Accounts of the accident differed. The police and friends of Stern claimed the girl had run between two parked cars into the street. The Gittens family said that she was walking hand in hand with her mother, and residents claimed that one policeman made racist remarks and others joked about the accident. Although objects were thrown at the police, there were no other repercussions. In contrast to 1991, a Lubavitch leader immediately went to Kings County Hospital to offer condolences to the Gittens family.[64]

The less than apocalyptic status of black-Jewish relations in New York City was also manifest in the events surrounding the torching of Freddy's Fashion Mart in Harlem on December 8, 1995. A black man named Roland Smith entered the store, located down the block on 125th Street from the famous Apollo Theatre, in the heart of Harlem's shopping district. Smith started shooting at those inside and set fire to the building. Seven of the employees—six Hispanics and one black—died in the flames, and three whites and a Guyanese Indian were wounded by gunshots. Smith then committed suicide. Smith's actions stemmed from a controversy over the terms of the lease between the landlord, the United House of Prayer for All People, a church founded by C. M.

"Sweet Daddy" Grace, and Fred Harari, a Syrian Jew from Brooklyn. The lease allowed Freddy's to take over the space occupied by the Record Shack, a black-owned store selling gospel, Caribbean, and rhythm and blues records.

When news of the agreement became public in the summer of 1995, Al Sharpton and other blacks instigated protests in front of Freddy's. Signs carried by picketers described Harari as a "bloodsucking Jew" and threatened to "burn the Jew store" and kill Harari. Evidently Smith became convinced that Freddy's was about to commit a heinous affront to the black community even though the decision to evict the record store was made by a black church for economic reasons. "The fact that Harari was Jewish," Philip Kasinitz and Bruce Haynes noted, "encouraged a simplifying set of narratives among outside observers, especially the media, that guided the framing of the event as a conflict between blacks and whites, more particularly between blacks and Jews, elucidating some aspects of the story while obscuring others."[65]

As was true in 1991, the *New York Times,* in contrast to the *Daily News* and the *New York Post,* downplayed the anti-Semitic aspects of the event and ignored Sharpton's highly charged appeals to racial solidarity. A week after the arson the *Times* ran a profile titled "Sharpton Buoyant in a Storm" in which the Brooklyn firebrand was described as a "consoler" and a "conciliator." The *Times* preferred to see the Harlem incident as the product of a solitary "madman" bent on committing suicide to protest white racism rather than of an ardent black nationalist and anti-Semite. *Times* reporter Matthew Purdy even wrote a profile of Harari emphasizing that he was partially responsible for the fire. Harari, according to Purdy, had an "unvarnished" and "blunt" personality and lived in an "insular world" of Syrian Orthodox Jews in Brooklyn, far from the Harlem neighborhood of his store.[66]

Just as they had done in 1992 after the acquittal of Lemrick Nelson, Jr., in state court, the *Jewish Press* and Beth Gilinsky's Jewish Action Alliance called for a civil rights investigation by the Department of Justice into those supposedly responsible for Smith's actions, including Al Sharpton and radio station WLIB.[67] For Jews, the torching of Freddy's was the latest in a disturbing pattern of anti-Semitic acts committed by blacks and was an exemplar of the inability or refusal of city officials to protect Jews and their property.

There were no other torchings of Jewish-owned property in Harlem, indicating that the fire at Freddy's was the work of an isolated and deranged individual and not the result of any anti-Jewish conspiracy. The *Amsterdam News,* nevertheless, feared that the fire would be used by Mayor Rudy Giuliani to enhance his bid for reelection in 1997, just as he had used the Girgenti Report to win the 1993 election. Neither the fire at Freddy's or the Crown Heights riot, however, were important issues in the 1997 election.[68]

By 1997, David Dinkins had been out of office for four years; Lee Brown, his police commissioner, lived in Houston; and the city was prospering. Neither Giuliani or his liberal Jewish Democratic challenger, Ruth W. Messinger, dwelled on the riot during the campaign.[69] The riot also was not an important issue in Senator Al D'Amato's reelection campaign in 1998. The 1992 election had occurred days after the acquittal of Lemrick Nelson in state court, and D'Amato's attacks on the Dinkins administration's handling of the riot had resonated among Jewish voters. D'Amato had even carried the heavily Jewish congressional district of Charles E. Schumer in Brooklyn, which encompassed Flatbush and Boro Park. Elizabeth Kadetsky, writing in the *Nation* magazine, had argued that the 1992 vote illustrated "the endurance of a politics that favors special-interest ethnic enclaves like the Hasidim—even . . . if it means exacerbating racial tension."[70]

In 1998, however, D'Amato's efforts to play the Crown Heights card failed. As in 1992, he campaigned with Fay and Norman Rosenbaum. "He's always been there for us," Fay Rosenbaum said. "I feel it's the least I can do."[71] D'Amato's opponent was Congressman Schumer, a Jew and a strong backer of Jewish causes. When a D'Amato radio advertisement accused the congressman of being AWOL during the riot, the Schumer camp responded that the congressman had, in fact, lobbied Janet Reno to launch a Department of Justice investigation of the riot.[72] Despite initial predictions of a close election, Schumer won easily. He captured 54 percent of the votes, and ran much better among Jewish voters than the 1992 Democratic candidate, State Attorney General Robert F. Abrams. This falloff in his Jewish support, said Adam Nagourney of the *New York Times,* "explains why D'Amato spent so many hours at the end of the campaign in Orthodox Jewish communities, appealing to voters who historically were solidly in his camp."[73]

The fading memory of Crown Heights was also evident in the 2000 New York senatorial race in which the Democratic candidate was Hillary Rodham Clinton. When Clinton announced she would run for the Senate seat held by the retiring Daniel Patrick Moynihan, concern was voiced by Jews in Crown Heights and elsewhere regarding her close ties with Dinkins and the role the former mayor would play in her campaign. Another problem was Clinton's seemingly close relationship with Al Sharpton.[74] Clinton was facing a Catch-22: she risked losing support among Jews if she did not distance herself from Dinkins and Sharpton; and she risked losing support among black voters if she displayed a lack of respect for New York's only black mayor and Sharpton. In fact, by 2000 Crown Heights mattered to few voters, and Clinton's opponent, Congressman Rick A. Lazio, did not make it an issue during the campaign. Clinton soundly defeated Lazio by twelve percentage points.[75]

Although city officials and community leaders bragged about the improvement of black-Jewish relations in Crown Heights and in the city generally after 1991, polling data emphasized continuity rather than dramatic change. Only a third of the five hundred black and Jewish respondents to a 2001 survey by the Foundation for Ethnic Understanding believed relations between the two groups had improved since the riot. A majority in both groups thought they had, in fact, worsened or were unchanged. The results were hardly definitive in light of the small number of those polled. Still, they give pause to those who assumed black-Jewish relations had fundamentally changed for the better since August 1991. Rabbi Marc Schneir, the president and cofounder of the Foundation for Ethnic Understanding, said that he was disappointed by the findings. While black and Jewish leaders had "wonderful relationships and general friendships," this had not seeped down to the masses.[76] Journalist Uriel Heilman believed "irrelevance" best characterized black-Jewish relations in New York. There were no "grand causes compelling them to join forces . . . [and] neither community is sufficiently monolithic to buttress the notion of a single African-American community or a single Jewish community."[77]

The calm in Crown Heights after 1991 was not due to any striking change in race relations. Blacks and Jews continued to view each other warily and to live in parallel worlds with little social interaction. But both groups were eager to leave the riot behind and to move on. And the city was determined to prevent a repetition of the riot. Once Mayor Giuliani "re-established the rule of law, the norms and expectations about violence were changed," Fred Siegel, a history professor at Cooper Union wrote. "Violent racial confrontation seemed to be ending."[78] Different ethnic and religious groups don't have to love one another in order to live peacefully.

Since 1991, Crown Heights has prospered along with the rest of the city. Here as well as elsewhere crime is down and property values are up. Crown Heights homeowners have discovered to their pleasant surprise that they are now affluent, at least on paper, and Crown Heights is again viewed as a desirable area by Brooklyn residents aspiring to middle-class status. Small numbers of Koreans, West Africans, and Arabs have settled recently in the neighborhood. These new residents, as well as those recently arrived from the West Indies, do not have the resentments and memories of those who lived in Crown Heights at the time of the riot.

The Lubavitch community has also flourished. Their population has increased by perhaps 20 to 25 percent since the riot, and they have established new institutions to meet the needs of their growing numbers. The influx of Jewish families into the neighborhood combined with a high birthrate have expanded the area of Jewish settlement in Crown Heights. Lubavitchers have moved north of Eastern Parkway, which had been the unofficial line of demarcation separating Jewish and black Crown Heights.

The post-riot calm in Crown Heights surprised those who had predicted additional racial confrontations in neighborhoods where blacks and Jews lived in close proximity and who had urged the Lubavitch to leave the area.[79] The riot, Diane Steinman of the American Jewish Committee said, "was a watershed event. . . . It's almost like we've reached the mountaintop and it's a blizzard up there, and we'd better find a way to get down, because it's dangerous."[80] In fact, the Crown Heights riot was not a watershed. The neighborhood did not fundamentally change and the Jews did not flee.

The process of healing had limited appeal to the blacks and Jews of Crown Heights. Most blacks in Crown Heights were not concerned with any "commonquest" and had more immediate economic and social matters. To the majority of Lubavitch, the healing process was a public relations maneuver concocted by politicians and liberal Jewish organizations. They had not marched on behalf of civil rights and were skeptical that Jews and blacks had that much in common. The iconic black-Jewish entente had never been an important part of their Jewish identity as it had been for liberal Jews. They wanted to live in peace with, but at arm's length from, their black Christian neighbors in Crown Heights.

Three decades before the riot, Brandeis University professor Ben Halpern had warned Jews against mythologizing the black-Jewish relationship. By seeing only the similarities between themselves and blacks, they elided "the equally, if not more, important fact that there are many significant ways in which they do not belong together at all; and may indeed have conflicting interests."[81] The Lubavitch of Crown Heights would have agreed.

Notes

1. Ralph A. Austen, "The Uncomfortable Relationship: African Enslavement in the Common History of Blacks and Jews," in *Strangers and Neighbors: Relations Between Blacks and Jews in the United States*, ed. Maurianne Adams and John Bracey (Amherst: University of Massachusetts Press, 1999), 133.
2. Arthur Hertzberg, *The Jews in America: Four Centuries of an Uneasy Encounter: A History* (New York: Simon and Schuster, 1989), 335–41; Howard M. Sachar, *A History of the Jews in America* (New York: Knopf, 1992), 801–808; Paul Berman, "The Other and the Almost the Same," *New Yorker* 70 (February 20, 1994): 71; Reeberg quoted in J. J. Goldberg, *Jewish Power: Inside the American Jewish Establishment* (Reading, Mass.: Addison-Wesley, 1996), 35–36; Charles S. Liebman and Steven M. Cohen, *Two Worlds of Judaism: The Israeli and American Experiences* (New Haven, Conn.: Yale University Press, 1990), 16, 44, 103–104.
3. Liebman and Cohen *Two Worlds of Judaism*, 16; For black-Jewish relations, see, among many works, Robert G. Weisbord and Arthur Stein, *Bittersweet Encounter: The Afro-American and the American Jew* (Westport, Conn.: Negro Universities Press, 1970); Hasia R. Diner, *In the Almost Promised Land: American Jews and Blacks, 1915–1935* (Westport, Conn.: Greenwood, 1977); Jonathan Kaufman, *Broken Alliance: The Turbulent Times Between Blacks and Jews* (New York: Scribner, 1995); Jim Sleeper, *The Closest of Strangers: Liberalism and the Politics of Race in New York* (New York: Norton, 1990); Milton D. Morris and Gary E. Rubin, "The Turbulent Friendship: Black-Jewish Relations in the 1990s," *Annals* of the American Academy of Political and Social Science 539 (November 1993): 42–60; Murray Friedman, *What Went Wrong? The Creation and Collapse of the Black-Jewish Alliance* (New York: Free Press, 1995); Jack Salzman and Cornel West, eds., *Struggles in the Promised Land: Toward a History of Black-Jewish Relations in the United States* (New York: Oxford University Press, 1997); and V. P. Franklin et al., eds., *African Americans and Jews in the Twentieth Century: Studies in Convergence and Conflict* (Columbia: University of Missouri Press, 1998).
4. Nina Rosenblum quoted in Charles Baillou, "PBS Documentary, 'Liberators,' Portrays History of Blacks in WWII," *Amsterdam News*, November 14, 1992;
5. Lou Potter with William Miles and Nina Rosenblum, *Liberators: Fighting on Two Fronts in World War II* (New York: Harcourt Brace Jovanovich, 1992), xiv.
6. John J. O'Connor, "America's Black Army and a Dual War Front," *New York Times*, November 11, 1992; Jack Newfield, "New Film Could Help Heal Wounds of Race Hate," *New York Post*, December 1, 1992; Renee Graham, "Revealing the Black 'Liberators' of WWII," *Boston Globe*, November 11, 1992;

Rick Kogan review of *Liberators* in *Chicago Tribune,* November 10, 1992; Tony Scott review of *Liberators* in *Variety,* November 9, 1992.

7. There is a copy of the Apollo Theatre program in the *Liberators* file in the archives of the Jewish Community Relations Council of New York. See also Stephen J. Dubner, "Massaging History: How Presumably Good Intentions Turned a Poignant World War II Documentary Into a Fantasy of Black-Jewish Healing," *New York* 26 (March 8, 1993): 47–48.
8. Jackson quoted in Thomas Doherty, "The Strange Case of *Liberators: Fighting on Two Fronts in World War II*" (unpublished essay in possession of author), 2; Ari L. Goldman, "Blacks and Jews Join Hands for a Brighter Future," *New York Times,* December 18, 1992; Letty Cottin Pogrebin, "Truth or Consequences: 'The Liberators' Controversy," *Tikkun* 8 (May–June 1993): 57; Glanz quoted in Alisa Solomon, "Showtime at the Apollo: Why Collard Greens and Kasha Are Not Enough," *Village Voice* 37 (December 29, 1992), 21; Jeffrey Goldberg, "The Exaggerators," *New Republic* 208 (February 8, 1993): 13.
9. Butman quoted in Jonathan Mark, "Harmony Between Blacks, Jews Takes Center Stage at the Apollo," *Jewish Week,* December 25–31, 1992. For other dissents, see Alessandra Stanley, "After a Night of Unity at the Apollo, Optimism Wavers," *New York Times,* December 19, 1992, and Estelle Gilson, "Liberators and Survivors: Showtime at the Apollo," *Congress Monthly* 60 (March–April 1993): 8–10.
10. Dinkins quoted in David Seifman, "Dinkins Calls Yankel Murderers 'Bigots,'" *New York Post,* November 11, 1992; Dinkins quoted in Ellen Tumposky and Jere Hester, "Dave's Reel-Life Lesson," *Daily News,* December 18, 1992. For a statement by Harlem Congressman Charles Rangel in this same vein, see Norma Harris, "Documentary to Focus on Liberation of Jews by Black WWII Soldiers," *Amsterdam News,* October 12, 1992.
11. Clement A. Price, "Black Soldiers in Two World Wars: 'Men of Bronze' (1980) and 'Liberators' (1992)," *Historical Journal of Film, Radio and Television* 14, no. 4 (1994): 468–69.
12. Richard Cohen, "*Liberators:* It's Not Only About the Holocaust," *Washington Post,* March 30, 1993.
13. *Volunteer Voice* 2 (March 1993): 1, 6–7. *Volunteer Voice* is the newsletter of WNET, New York's public television station.
14. Newfield, "New Film Could Help Heal Wounds of Race Hate."
15. Doherty, "Strange Case of *Liberators,*" 22; Dubner, "Massaging History," 51.
16. Christopher Ruddy, "PBS Documentary Lies About Liberation of Concentration Camps," *New York Guardian* 2 (December 1992), 1, 16–17; Ruddy, "'Liberators' Took Liberties With the Facts," *Newsday,* December 15, 1992.
17. "A Night at the Movies," *New York Post,* December 21, 1992; "'The Liberators': Trendy Politics, Dubious History," *New York Post,* February 3, 1993; Eric Breindel, "Concocting History," *New York Post,* February 6, 1993; "Hats Off to Channel 13," (editorial), *New York Post,* February 12, 1993.

18. "Vets Ask, Is 'Liberators' Fact or Fiction?," *Forward*, January 22, 1993; Jeffrey Goldberg, "'Liberators' Controversy Fueled by New Charges," *Forward*, February 5, 1993; "Blacks, Jews and 'Liberators,'" *Forward*, February 5, 1993; Jeffrey Goldberg, "The Exaggerators," 13–14.
19. Kenneth S. Stern, *"Liberators": A Background Report* (New York: American Jewish Committee, 1993), 1, 12–14.
20. WNET report quoted in Doherty, "Strange Case of *Liberators*," 3; Calvin Reid, "*Liberators* Found Inaccurate: Harcourt Will Not Recall Book," *Publishers Weekly* 240 (September 13, 1993): 14; Wilbert A. Tatum, "*Liberators: Fighting on Two Fronts in World War II*," *Amsterdam News*, October 16, 1993; "*The Liberators*, the American Jewish Committee, and a Challenge to Channel 13," *New York Amsterdam News*, September 18, 1993; "*The Liberators:* ADL, AJC, PBS, and Channel 13's Attempt to Rewrite the History of W.W. II," *New York Amsterdam News*, September 25, 1993.
21. Harcourt Brace statement quoted in Daniel J. Leab, "Clement Price, 'Liberators' and Truth in History: A Comment," *Historical Journal of Film Radio and Television*, 14, no. 4 (1994): 477. In his review of *Liberators* (*Journal of American History* 80 [December 1993]: 1192), historian Lee Finkle described it as historically "flawed."
22. Rosenblum claimed that McConnell was an untrustworthy witness because he was "severely brain-damaged" as a result of being hit in the head with shrapnel during the war. She excused her failure to consult military records by claiming that military historians were prejudiced against blacks. Ruddy, "PBS Documentary Lies," 16.
23. For comments by Tishman on Crown Heights, see "A New Year's Resolution: Ending Racism and anti-Semitism," *Amsterdam News*, January 2, 1993; Jonathan Mark, "Role of American Black Soldiers as Camp 'Liberators' Questioned," *Jewish Week*, February 12–18, 1993; and Goldberg, "The Exaggerators," 14.
24. Pogrebin, "Truth or Consequences," 56–57, 73.
25. Spiegelman quoted in "Editors' Note," *New Yorker* 68 (February 15, 1993): 6; Bette Ann Moskowitz, "A Valentine Nobody Could Love," *New York Times*, February 13, 1993.
26. Brown quoted in Manuel Perez Rivas, "Unhappy Prelude to a Kiss," *Newsday*, February 6, 1993; Cynthia Ozick, "Literary Jews and Blacks," in *Blacks and Jews: Alliances and Arguments*, ed. Paul Berman (New York: Delacorte, 1994), 68–69; see also Berman's essay "On Spiegelman's Valentine and Having a Headache," which is the preface to this book.
27. Abbott Katz, "This Kiss Ain't Just a Kiss," *Newsday*, February 11, 1993; Carroll Carey Howard, "Disrespect of the Black Woman," *City Sun*, February 17, 1993; Daughtry quoted in Perez-Rivas, "Unhappy Prelude to a Kiss."
28. *Jewish Press*, February 12, 1993; Spielman quoted in Perez-Rivas, "Unhappy Prelude to a Kiss."

29. Spiegelman and Flint quoted in Toby Axelrod, "Valentine Controversy," *Jewish Week*, February 12–16, 1993.
30. Stern, *"Liberators,"* 14; *New York Times*, October 2, 2000.
31. Robert S. Rifkind, "Statement by the President of the American Jewish Committee," *CommonQuest* 1 (Spring 1996): inside front cover.
32. Russell Adams, "As the Twig is Bent," *CommonQuest* 1 (Spring 1996): 7; Jonathan Rieder, "Beyond Frenzy and Accusation," *CommonQuest* 1 (Spring 1996): 2, 6.
33. *New York Times*, October 20, 1993.
34. Smith quoted in Chris Smith, "Crown Heights Witness," *New York* 27 (August 29, 1994): 36–37.
35. Cornel West, foreword to *Fires in the Mirror: Crown Heights Brooklyn and Other Identities*, by Anna Deavere Smith (New York: Anchor Books, 1993), xvii–xviii, xxii; Melanie Kirkpatrick, "A Summer Day When Emotions Boiled Over," *Wall Street Journal*, May 27, 1992; Frank Rich, "Diversities of America In One-Person Shows," *New York Times*, May 15, 1992.
36. John J. O'Connor, "One-Woman Show on Black vs. Jew," *New York Times*, April 28, 1993.
37. Smith quoted in Mervyn Rothstein, "Racial Turmoil in America: Tales from a Woman Who Listened," *New York Times*, July 5, 1992.
38. Ward Morehouse III, "City Youths Reach for 'Heights'," *New York Post*, August 21, 1998; Grunwald quoted in *New York Times*, December 10, 1998.
39. Julia Goldman, "'Crown Heights' Fires Rekindled? Anger Over Factually Inaccurate Play at Fulani-Related Theater," *Jewish Week*, January 30, 2004.
40. Zackary Sholem Berger, "New Play About Crown Heights Blames Jews for Deadly Riots," *Forward*, January 30, 2004.
41. Adam Dickter, "She Records Her Angry Feelings in Song," *Jewish Week*, August 20–26, 1993.
42. Snitow and Scott quoted in Samuel G. Freedman, "Blacks and Jews and a Friendship That Faltered," *New York Times*, July 20, 1997.
43. For two reviews of "Brooklyn Babylon," see Dave Kehr, "Hip-Hop Romeo, Hasidic Juliet," *New York Times*, August 17, 2001; and Daniel Belasco, "One Love: Filmmaker Mark Levin Envisions a Magical Black-Jewish Romance in Crown Heights," *Forward*, August 10, 2001.
44. Fred Tasker, "Movie Tells How Peace Emerged From Riots," *Miami Herald*, February 14, 2004; Alessandra Stanley, "Finding Crown Heights Peace: Hip-Hop and Hope," *New York Times*, February 16, 2004.
45. Nacha Cattan, "Reviving a Defunct Dialogue About Crown Heights," *Forward*, February 13, 2004.
46. Henry Goldschmidt, "Peoples Apart: Race, Religion, and Other Jewish Differences in Crown Heights" (Ph.D. diss., University of California at Santa Cruz, 2000), 192, 201–3.

47. Maynard quoted in Annette Walker, "B'klyn Institutions Initiate Crown Hts. Educational Project," *New York Amsterdam News,* January 9, 1993; Vinette K. Pryce, "Art Brings Blacks and Jews Together in Crown Heights," *New York Amsterdam News,* February 8, 1992; *New York Times,* January 3, 1993.
48. Ira Berkow, "Question: Can We All Run Together?" *New York Times,* January 25, 1993; Herb Boyd, "Crown Heights Blacks, Jews Mix It Up On the B-ball Court," *Amsterdam News,* November 30, 1991.
49. Steve Lipman, "No Sticks or Stones, Just Words of Understanding," *Jewish Week,* September 20–26, 1991; Lipman, "Brooklyn Teens Find a 'CURE' to Ease Black-Jewish Tension," *Jewish Week,* December 18–24, 1992; Lipman, "David Lazerson: Rap and Respect," *Jewish Week,* August 19–25, 1994. The movie *Crown Heights* was based on Lazerson's memoir *Sharing Turf: Race Relations After the Crown Heights Riots* (Brooklyn: Mendelsohn Press, 2004).
50. Green quoted in Andrew L. Yarrow, "Blacks and Jews Take It to the Hoop," *New York Times,* October 13, 1991; Lazerson quoted in Mordechai Staiman, "Jews and Blacks Meet Again: 'Everybody's a Winner at This Ball Game,'" *Algemeiner Journal,* October 18, 1991.
51. Jacobs quoted in Stewart Ain, "Hatzolah Volunteers to Assist New Black Ambulance Corps," *Jewish Week,* September 6–12, 1991.
52. *New York Times,* August 28, 1991; Ari L. Goldman, "Religion Notes," *New York Times,* April 18, 1992; *Amsterdam News,* May 22, 1993.
53. Goldschmidt, "Peoples Apart," 203–8.
54. Letty Cottin Pogrebin, "The Twain Shall Meet: Blacks and Orthodox Jews, Mothers All, Find They Share a Lot," *New York Times,* March 16, 1997; Elicia Brown, "Homegirls in the Heights: For Black and Chasidic Mothers on Either Side of Eastern Parkway, an Island of Hope," *Jewish Week,* August 10, 2001; David Lazerson, "Beyond Crown Heights: Strategies for Overcoming Anti-Semitism and Racism in New York," *Tikkun* 8 (January–February 1993): 60.
55. Jennifer Steinhauer, "10 Years Later, a First Meeting of 2 Symbols of Crown Hts.," *New York Times,* August 21, 2001. A mention in a *New York Post* article of August 12, 2001, of Carmel Cato's desire to meet the Rosenbaum family was the spark that led to the meeting. See Leonard Greene, "Healing Old Wounds: Crown Hts. Tried to Bridge Divide 10 Yrs. After Riots," *New York Post,* August 12, 2001. This was not the first time Cato had met with Jews. In April 1998 he met with four representatives of the American Jewish Congress, the American Jewish Committee, and the Jewish Community Relations Council of New York at a restaurant in Queens. This well-publicized meeting was criticized by the Rosenbaum family and others for not including any Jews from Crown Heights and for including Al Sharpton, who accompanied Carmel Cato. See Adam Dickter, "Jewish Delegation to Visit Catos: Remembering Crown Heights Accident Victim a 'Significant Ges-

ture,' Says Sharpton; Some Fear Wrong Message Will Be Sent," *Jewish Week*, April 17, 1998; *Forward* editorial "Remembering Gavin Cato," April 24, 1998. Members of the delegation defended the meeting. See Dickter, "Aftermath of the Cato Visit: Jewish Leader Who Arranged for Crown Heights Condolence Call Defends Meeting," *Jewish Week*, May 1, 1998.

56. *Forward*, August 4, 2001. Fay and Max Rosenbaum would meet for the first time with Carmel Cato at a Manhattan restaurant in August 2003 The couple was in New York to observe the sentencing of Lemrick Nelson. "We are parents and we grieve," Cato said after the meeting. "We know the pain no one else can share. I'm very grateful. This is one meeting I was looking forward to for a very long time." Herbert Lowe and Anthony M. DeStefano, "Parents United in Their Sorrow: First Meeting After Crown Heights Riot," *Newsday*, August 20, 2003.
57. Kirsten Danis, Ed Robinson, and Dan Mangan, "Crown Hts. Peacemakers: 10 Yrs. After, Victims' Kin to Meet," *New York Post*, August 20, 2003.
58. *Forward*, August 24, 2001. For another statement on the difference between the deaths of Rosenbaum and Cato, see the editorial "Behind the Healing . . ." in the *New York Post*, August 21, 2001.
59. *Jewish Press* editorial "Crown Heights and the Revising of History," August 24, 2001.
60. Butman and Hecht quoted in Robin Pogrebin, "Rabbis Resisting a Project's Cure for Crown Heights," *New York Observer*, December 28, 1992–January 4, 1993; Goldschmidt, "Peoples Apart," 193.
61. Butman quoted in Jonathan Mark, "Crown Heights Spokesman Facing Controversy on Two Fronts," *Jewish Week*, November 15–21, 1991. This incident was reported in the black press; see *Amsterdam News*, November 2, 1991.
62. Michael Meyers to Rabbi Shmuel M. Butman, October 21, 1991, Crown Heights file, Jewish Community Relations Council Papers; Marc D. Stern to Rabbi Joseph Spielman, November 18, 1991; Butman to Meyers, December 3, 1991, Robert A. Bush Papers, Brooklyn, New York; Mark, "Crown Heights Spokesman."
63. Steve Lipman, "Tragedy Without the Turmoil," *Jewish Week*, September 1, 2000. See also the editorial "No Riots" in the same issue.
64. Todd Venezia and William J. Gorta, "Crown Hts. Heroes: Save Hasidic Driver Who Hit Black Child," *New York Post*, August 21, 2002. There was no mention of the Gittens or Curtis accidents in the *New York Times*.
65. Richard T. Foltin, "National Affairs," in *American Jewish Year Book 1997*, ed. David Singer and Ruth R. Seldin (New York: American Jewish Committee, 1998), 97:155; Philip Kasinitz and Bruce Haynes, "The Fire at Freddy's," *CommonQuest* 1 (Fall 1996): 25–34.
66. William McGowan, *Coloring the News: How Crusading for Diversity has Cor-*

rupted American Journalism (San Francisco, Calif.: Encounter Books, 2001), 64–67.

67. Mendy Cohen, "Mayor Calls for Grand Jury Investigation of Harlem Massacre: Jewish Action Alliance Calls for Federal Probe," *Jewish Press*, December 15, 1995.
68. Wilbert A. Tatum, "After the Fire and the Deaths—Charges of Black Anti-Semitism," *Amsterdam News*, December 16, 1995.
69. *New York Times*, November 5, 1997.
70. Elizabeth Kadetsky, "Racial Politics in New York," *Nation* 255 (November 30, 1992): 658; Rick Brand, "Jewish Vote Likely to Be Vital," *Newsday*, October 7, 1998; Todd S. Purdum, "D'Amato Is Victor Over Abrams in New York's Bitter Senate Race," *New York Times*, November 4, 1991.
71. John Shultz, "Help From the Past," *Newsday*, November 2, 1998. *Algemeiner Journal*, November 6, 1998.
72. *Algemeiner Journal*, October 23, 1998.
73. Adam Nagourney, "Schumer Uses D'Amato's Tactics to Win Senate Election Handily," *New York Times*, November 4, 1998. See also James Dao, "D'Amato Fails, Finally, to Confound Rivals," *New York Times*, November 4, 1998.
74. *Forward*, August 7, 1999; Peter Noel, "Hillary's Crown Heights Problem," *Village Voice* 44 (August 24, 1999), 43–45.
75. Adam Nagourney, "Big Victory for First Lady in Contest with Lazio," *New York Times*, November 8, 2000. Clinton won 75 percent of the vote in Brooklyn.
76. Adam Dickter, "Poll: Little Change Since Crown Heights: On 10th Anniversary of Riots, Study Finds Hazy View of Relations Between Blacks and Jews," *Jewish Week*, August 17, 2001.
77. Uriel Heilman, "Black-Jewish Relations in New York City," *Jerusalem Post*, May 25, 2003.
78. Adam Dickter, "Is Crown Heights Over? 'We Have to Move On,' Neighborhood's Jews Say After Last Week's Sentencing," *Jewish Week*, August 9, 2003.
79. See, for example, Stewart Ain, "Warning of More Racial Violence Sounded," *Jewish Week*, November 15–21, 1991.
80. Craig Horowitz, "The New Anti-Semitism," *New York* 26 (January 11, 1993), 23.
81. Ben Halpern, *Blacks and Jews: The Classic American Minorities* (New York: Herder and Herder, 1971), 16–17.

Index